P9-BYZ-175

You Own
the Power

ALSO BY ROSEMARY ALTEA

The Eagle and the Rose
Give the Gift of Healing
Proud Spirit

You Own the Power

Stories and Exercises to Inspire
and Unleash the Force Within

ROSEMARY ALTEA

EAGLE BROOK
WILLIAM MORROW AND COMPANY, INC.
New York

Copyright © 2000 by Rosemary Altea

Published by Eagle Brook
An Imprint of William Morrow and Company, Inc.
1350 Avenue of the Americas, New York, N.Y. 10019

All rights reserved. No part of this book may be reproduced or utilized in any form or by any means, electronic or mechanical, including photocopying, recording, or by any information storage or retrieval system, without permission in writing from the Publisher. Inquiries should be addressed to Permissions Department, William Morrow and Company, Inc., 1350 Avenue of the Americas, New York, N.Y. 10019.

It is the policy of William Morrow and Company, Inc., and its imprints and affiliates, recognizing the importance of preserving what has been written, to print the books we publish on acid-free paper, and we exert our best efforts to that end.

Library of Congress Cataloging-in-Publication Data

Altea, Rosemary.
    You own the power : stories and exercises to inspire and unleash
the force within / by Rosemary Altea.—1st ed.
        p. cm.
    ISBN 0-688-15276-7 (alk. paper)
    I. Self-realization. 2. Spiritualism. I. Title.
BF1275.S44A48 2000
131—dc21   99-16820
                                        CIP

Printed in the United States of America

First Edition

1 2 3 4 5 6 7 8 9 10

BOOK DESIGN BY GIORGETTA BELL MCREE

www.williammorrow.com

Author's Note

This book and the exercises contained within are not a substitute for medical advice. If you have or suspect you have a medical problem, see your doctor or a professional health-care provider. In addition, the author is in no way responsible for the effects that come from following the exercises.

I am but one small voice . . . hoping to rock the world, just as God rocked my world.

I am but one little human being . . . trying, in faith, to show to others the light Christ showed me.

I am but a student . . . striving to bring to the world the wonderful teachings of my guide, Grey Eagle.

I am merely a mother . . . grateful beyond words for the miracle of my child, who loves me enough to mother me, too.

My gratitude is endless . . . my cup is truly overflowing.

Contents

CONTENTS

Acknowledgments

To my mother who bore me, finally I offer my thanks, thinking of her with great sadness, knowing that her negativity brought her terrible misery. By her example, I learned how not to be. Through her example, I gained my strength.

To my father who sired me, I send my love, and tears reach my eyes as I think of him in his confused and angry life. His bullying and need for control brought him only a life without hope. I saw it in his eyes. By his example, he taught me how not to be, and I will be forever grateful, for he made me face myself. His power gave me my beginnings. His strength helped me own my power.

To my brothers, Terry and Malcolm. They fought and were constantly angry with each other. A legacy from my mother, whose misery and anger touched us all. My prayers go out to them, and I thank them for helping me see, by their example, how not to be.

To my sisters, Audrey, Judy, and Madeleine, for the good times and the bad. For their companionship, for the games we

xiii

often played together, for just being there, as we all stood, separated but together, in our confusions, learning how not to be. I thank them.

From my beginnings I have met so many people who have influenced me, who have helped me be the person I am today, mother, medium, healer, speaker, author. Too many to name, I thank them all, and acknowledge their individual importance in my life.

Though I am only one small person, just a little human being, I thank God for the experiences in my life that have enabled me to stand tall and strong. To own my power.

PREFACE
Are You at Home Today?

The room was easily fifty feet long by about thirty feet wide. Empty save for those of us gathered together at one end. Empty, bare, polished wood floors, no furniture, drapeless high windows, empty, save for the lone figure sitting in the tubular steel chair, in the middle, at the far end of the room.

Everything about her was odd, strange, unfathomable, even from a distance. The way she sat, upright and unmoving. The way she had removed herself, used the space and coldness of the room as an invisible wall that she sat behind.

"You go."

"No, I don't want to go."

"Well, you go, then."

"Oh no, not me."

And it was I who said, "I'll go, I'll go," and with my heart beating wildly in my chest, I began the long walk down the room to where she sat.

It seems strange, odd perhaps, that I should begin this new

book with a story taken from my first book, *The Eagle and the Rose,* but Grey Eagle guides my pen, my thoughts, and I must follow.

I was only fifteen years old, and in many ways young for my age, although my instincts were good. My instincts have always been good.

The psychiatric hospital we were at, my school friends and I, was the one my mother had always threatened I would one day end up in. Well, here I was, so it might seem she was right, although my mother was sure I would be here as an inmate, when in fact I had come with my drama class to entertain the patients. Now we were having tea, and my friends and I had been instructed by our drama teachers to do our best to make sure everyone had plenty to eat and drink.

Offering tea and sandwiches to our audience was easy, as most were friendly and wanted to chat. One young woman cried a lot, and in later years, looking back, I realized she must have been suffering some kind of depression, which was probably why she was there.

The walk down the room seemed endless. I was afraid. Something about her made me afraid, and as I drew close, my heart was thudding so loudly my ears were pulsing, and my throat became dry.

It is hard to describe how still she sat, the cigarette burned down almost to her fingers, the ash as long as the cigarette had been. I gazed at it in amazement.

Her hair, black, streaked with gray, was cut short and as if someone had placed a pudding basin on her head, cut straight around. The dress she wore was navy blue with small white flowers on it. My memory of her is vivid. My feelings as I recall them are easily remembered. My smallness, my humanness, my inability to communicate with her, to her, for her, are stark memories in my mind.

Timidly I asked, "Can I get something for you? A cup of tea? A sandwich?" She didn't move. Not a flicker, or a blink of an eyelid to show she had heard me. The ash on the cigarette held still, intact.

"Perhaps a glass of water . . . or tea . . . or . . . ?" My voice faltered, but still I had to try.

The thumping in my chest had eased a little, the hammering of my heart was not so fierce. The fear I had first felt had gone and in its place was a mixture of feelings I did not yet understand. Except the feeling of sorrow, and I knew that feeling well.

I was about to try again when a nurse came up behind me and, tapping me on the shoulder, said gently, "It's all right, dear, don't you worry, she's not at home today."

• • •

I wish, I wish, I wish.

I wish I had been older and wiser.

I wish I had known then, as I do now, that you don't need words to communicate.

I wish I had understood and had the confidence to reach out to hold her hand, to kneel beside her, to touch her gently.

Because I did not know, I turned away, and headed slowly back to where the others were.

It is almost forty years ago, yet I remember as if it were yesterday.

"She's not at home today."

As I write the words I hear them spoken as clearly as I heard them that day. I remember the hurt, the frustration, the feeling of being powerless, disabled, inadequate. All those same feelings that those in the spirit world must feel when they try to get through to us, when we are "Not at Home."

I've often pondered this thought. How must they feel? They, our loved ones who have died and are now living in another place.

When they call out to us and we do not hear, or when they touch us, stroke our hair, our cheek, and we do not feel. Or when they stand, arms waving to attract our attention, right in front of us, and we do not see. It must seem to them, as it did to me all those years ago with the lady in the blue dress with white flowers, whose name I never knew, it must seem that "we are not at home today."

But I want to be at home. I want to be aware when someone comes knocking on my door, I want to be there to open the door, to welcome in all who want to visit. When the spirit world comes calling, I want to be home. Don't you?

Did it ever occur to you that in those moments when you wish your loved ones in spirit could communicate with you in some small way, that you have to be home, and ready to receive your visitors? Did it ever occur to you that it is you who must oil the locks, turn the key, open the door, and let them in?

As we begin our journey, it is important that we "be at home today," but it is also important that we strive to "be at home" every day.

I can show you how to oil the locks, to turn the key, to open the door. As I write, I will try to be attentive to your needs and wants. I will "be at home" for you. In turn, you have to be attentive, attentive to the needs of others, your friends, your family, neighbors and strangers alike. You have to learn to be "at home" for them. You also have to be attentive to your own needs and wants, to the needs of your soul ... to be "at home" for yourself. And through this, as the locks begin to turn, the door to open wide, as you become more attentive to the needs and wants of the spirit world, you will discover that you are "at home today" and every day, and that "home" is a very good place to be.

You Own
the Power

We have met the enemy,
and he is us.

Walt Kelly

CHAPTER I

Releasing Stress and Finding Peace

A brief flash, like a movie, rolled before my eyes, fast but very clear. This was all I had, but it was enough to tell me that someone was waiting to deliver a message.

As I watched the "film," the vision, I heard shouting and saw a young man, taken at gunpoint by two youths and forced into a car. For now, this was all I saw and heard.

Who was he? Who were they? I knew it was my job to find out.

I was in New York, giving a lecture, my audience of more than twelve hundred all wanting something special from me. My larger audience, those in the spirit world, trusting me. Trusting that I would do my best.

Michelle and Ken Martin were there that night. Their anticipation and desperation for a message was great, as their eldest son had been tragically murdered.

Neither of them had been to such an event before, and they had no idea what to expect. Having heard of me, having read my first book, Michelle had felt a desperate urgency to find me, and

1

the couple had traveled from Colorado to New York with the single hope of somehow contacting their son. Theirs was the first boy I connected with, but it took me a while to figure it out, as you will see.

"My name is David... Michael... Michael... David." I heard the voice, but I was confused. Was he saying he was Michael David, or was he David Michael, or more confusing, did I have two young men in the spirit world trying to communicate? I tried again, and this time I saw a young man about eighteen or nineteen years old.

"Ha, good for you," I said, sending my encouragement as I went into my audience. "I'm hearing the name David Michael," I said, and was stunned at the amount of hands that went up throughout the crowd. "In his late teens, early twenties, he died very tragically."

Most of the hands stayed up, so I knew I had my work cut out for me. This could be tough. So many people wanting messages, and I had to discover who it was that David or Michael, or both, wanted to speak to.

"My son's name is David, he died two years ago," called out one woman. "His brother is Michael."

"My son's name is Michael David," called out a man from the back row. "He died three months ago."

A couple to my left, clutching each other, crying, called, "Our son is David, he was killed just a few weeks ago."

Then others began to call out, and for a moment there was utter confusion as desperate parents called out for their children, hoping against hope for a message.

It took a while to sort things out, as first I had to calm everyone down. Finally, we had quiet while I tried to see where I must go.

"Okay," I said, "I need to speak to anyone who has lost a Michael or a David, in his late teens, who is the parent of that boy." I was sure that this would narrow it down, but I was mistaken, as about ten couples raised their hands. This was time to call for Grey Eagle. He'll know what to do, I thought.

"Where should I go?" I asked him, confident that he would show me, and to my surprise, he said, "You speak to all of them." They are all here, all sons, waiting to talk with their parents.

"But what if I get them mixed up?" I asked, a little confused, yet knowing even as I voiced the question that I would have help sorting things out. I was right, of course, and it was easier than I thought it would be, for as I asked the parents to step up onto the stage, I could see each of their sons quite clearly standing beside them.

"I'm David. I was killed in a car accident," said one, and as he spoke, I witnessed the accident as he described it to me, saw the car skid around a bend in the road, watched as it turned over and rolled down the bank. "It was very sudden, very quick," he said. "Tell my mom and dad, Rosemary, that I felt no pain. Please give my love to my brother Michael, and tell him I watch over him. That I'm with him always."

David's parents, nodding, held on to each other, tears raining down their faces, a little peace entering their hearts.

Then the next boy. "I'm Michael David, I was killed on a motorbike." And again, a flash, an insight, as I saw the bike spinning off to the side of the road. Saw as it hit the tree.

"I'm Michael, my dad's name is David," said another. "I died from a brain tumor." Another flash, and I saw the boy as he lay in the hospital bed before he died.

"I'm David, I want to speak to my dad," came from yet another of the boys.

On and on it went, until all the boys had given messages, messages of hope and love, and clear evidence of their survival.

My audience was riveted. So was I, and each time one of my communicators spoke, I saw a flash, a film, some kind of play-back, as if I were present at the scene of their passing and their lives here on earth. Sometimes one message overflowed into another, and I had to ask the Davids and Michaels to try not to interrupt each other. "It's difficult enough"—I laughed at them—"without you making it more confusing. Please just speak to me one at a time, if you can, and try not to butt in on each other's conversations." But it was hard for them. They were excited, and they all had so much they wanted to say.

One boy, in his early twenties, described to us what his last weeks on earth were like, and as he spoke to me, I did my best to fine-tune all of my senses. Not just my sixth sense, but my hearing, my sight, touch, taste, and smell. Who knew which of these senses would give me my clearest impressions? I needed them all.

"Terrible, it was terrible," I heard him say. "I had AIDS and was in a hospice. All my bodily functions were out of control, I was wearing diapers, and I was in a place where there were others, just like me, some even worse than me."

I watched and saw, and yes, I saw him in his hospital bed. But also I could smell that hospital smell. I could feel the despair as it touched my senses. I could see and hear and even taste what the place was like. Then he began to cry: "All I wanted was to go home, to leave the hospice, but who would possibly be able to take care of me? I knew it was hopeless, I was a mess, and would only get worse." I watched and saw his tears run down his face, into his mouth, and as he spoke, I tasted their saltiness. "Then, one day, in walked my dad. He's not my real dad, but he adopted me when I was in my early teens. Anyway, in walked my dad. He strode up to my bed, lifted me up into his arms, and said, 'I'm taking you home, son, I'm taking you home with me.'"

I saw, I watched, seeing everything, all my senses alert, I saw the boy as he had looked just before he died. Emaciated, lost, and seeing him that way, I was heartbroken, even knowing that now he was okay.

As I recounted this story, my audience was spellbound, not a dry eye anywhere, and David's father was openly sobbing, remembering back to that terrible time.

"He looked after me, and I died in his arms," continued David, "and he gave me the most precious gift of love a man could ever receive. Tell him I love him, Rosemary, tell him I'm safe, and that I will always be near to him, I'll always be there, just as he was always there for me."

On and on it went, with more and more messages, just as clear, just as strong, more hope and more love, an outpouring of love. Then it came time to speak to Michelle and Ken Martin, to speak to the boy I had seen right at the beginning. Again, I could see him clearly. Young and handsome, a certain sparkle in his eyes, his arms around both his mom and his dad as he stood firmly between them both. He told of his tragic death, of his murder, and how his passing had affected his family, especially his mother.

"She won't eat, can hardly sleep, and until she read your book, Rosemary, she had been unable to speak. For months now, nearly a year, she has been unable to speak one word."

All of this was true, and the Martins understood every word. Michelle, David's mother, had been seeing a therapist since her son's death, but was showing no signs of improvement, and everyone was worried.

Then one day, on one of her visits, not knowing what else to do, Michelle's therapist handed her a book, saying she felt Michelle might benefit from reading it. Looking at the cover, Michelle's heart leaped into her throat as she saw The Eagle and The Rose. These were the very symbols she and her husband had had engraved on David's tombstone. This was the sign Michelle had been waiting for, a sign from her son.

She began to read, first by herself, then asking her young son Daniel to read with her. Everything they read made sense, gave her hope; she began to speak again, and determined that whatever it took, she would find and speak to the author. This was the way to find her son again, of that she was sure.

As David spoke, giving clear evidence of his survival after death, Michelle stood, her husband's arms about her, and also her son's, even though she could not see, silently, painfully crying. Tears of sadness, tears of joy.

"Tell them I'm safe," said David, "that I am with God. Tell my dad I was with him in the dentist's chair." He chuckled. "And Rosemary," he added, "send them my love."

All the Davids, and all the Michaels, and all the confusion. The result was that oh so many parents left my lecture that night feeling more at peace than they had in a long time. And not just the ones who had been given a personal message, but, too, all those who had suffered a loss and who had witnessed a very special evening.

• • •

We move on now, away from New York and from that wonderful lecture. We move on to another time, another place, and another lecture, this one in Boulder, Colorado. It was a smaller event, held in a bookstore, with probably five to six hundred people, crammed, a little like sardines, into a small area of the shop. A makeshift stage had been erected, which was perfect, and my microphone and drinking water had been placed on a small table to one side.

Less than five minutes into the lecture, I noticed, as I was speaking, a young boy, about eleven years old, wearing a baseball cap. What caught my attention, or so I thought, was the intensity of his expression as he listened to what I was saying. Smiling at him, I continued my introduction, and then began to give messages to my audience from the spirit world. An hour passed, then for no apparent reason, none that I could see anyway, I went forward to the front row, took hold of the boy's hand, and invited him to step up onto the stage.

"What's your name?" I asked, giving him the microphone.

"Daniel," the boy replied, with a small grin. Instantly we had a rapport.

"Are you going to take your cap off, Daniel?" I asked mischievously. "I wouldn't mind owning a hat like that."

"Oh, no," said Daniel shyly, "I always wear this hat, it's my favorite."

"Did you come with someone tonight, Daniel, or are you by yourself?" was my next question, but as I asked this, as if in answer, I heard, behind me, a loud rustling noise.

"I'm with my parents, they're a few rows back from me. I wanted a front-row seat," Daniel said, but although I heard Daniel's reply, I was much more interested now in what or who was on the stage with us. I turned my head, and instantly saw the light. I heard a voice, not of this world, yet at the same time, very much with us. "I'm his angel," I heard my visitor whisper. "I'm his angel, and I've spoken to you, Rosemary, before."

I needed Daniel's parents. If I were to pursue this connection, I needed permission from Daniel's parents, for I felt that Daniel was too young and vulnerable to do this on his own. It would not be right.

"We're here," they called, from about the third row, as I asked if they would stand. "I have someone trying to communicate," I said. "He tells me that he is Daniel's angel, and he gives me the name David."

"That's our son," said Daniel's mother. "We lost him over a year ago."

Again I heard a rustling sound, and looking behind me, I saw the most incredible sight. An angel, filled with light, so bright I could hardly see, for the light was almost blinding. A sound, a voice, seeming to emanate from its center. "I'm his angel, I'm his angel."

I was so wrapped up in what I was seeing that for a moment my audience was forgotten. Turning again to face them, I was even more amazed, for all around the room stood angels of light. My eyes welled up with tears, I couldn't help myself, and I stood pointing, sure that the crowd before me could see what I could see. How could they not?

Another movement, this time a gentle yet firm hand on my arm; I looked and saw Grey Eagle, reminding me that I had work to do.

Pulling myself together, taking a deep breath, I remembered David, Daniel's brother, and looking now to where he stood, next to my guide, I asked David what he would like to say. A flash, more than a picture, more than a film being played over, I heard them shouting, saw a young man taken at gunpoint and forced into a car. Then I heard David's voice clearly: "I was shot. My head. Bang, bang. They came, four of them, and dragged me from the house, into the car. I knew they were going to kill me and I was terrified. Nothing I could do. My head hurt for a brief moment. Then I went home . . . my angels came for me, and carried me home."

Without realizing it, as David had begun to speak, I had taken hold of Daniel's hand. Now I put my arm around the boy as he told me that David was his brother and what I had said was right.

The evening was over, more messages had been given, and I had finished signing books. It was time for a rest and dinner, and I was ready for both. But first I had to say goodbye to Daniel. He was standing by the signing table, and as I turned and waved, he came over, bringing his parents with him. They couldn't thank me enough, and told me how wonderful it made them feel to hear their son again, speaking through me.

"Of course," said Daniel's mother, "the first time was more of a shock; it was hard to take it all in. This time we wanted David to come through just for Daniel, and he did."

"The first time?" I asked. "Has David communicated with you before then?"

"Oh, you won't remember, you speak to thousands of people, so you won't remember my husband and me. We were at your New York lecture earlier this year. You know, when all the Davids and Michaels were present. You told my husband about his teeth, and you told us how David had died. We went home full of it, and told Daniel everything that had happened. He was so upset that he had missed seeing you, but here you are in Boulder, and we knew we just had to come."

It was true, I didn't remember the Martins. I see so many people, talk to so many in the spirit world, and I have a terrible memory for faces and names.

But I did remember the evening in New York. How special and wonderful it was that so many children had been reunited with their parents. That is something I will never forget.

The Martin family joined us that night for dinner—us being my editor, Joann, and I. And Daniel was able to ask his thousand questions about where his brother was and what he was doing.

"Does he still snowboard?" young Daniel innocently asked, just before we left the restaurant. I smiled, thinking what a cute question it was. David was ready with his answer. "Tell Daniel that no, I don't snowboard anymore. I do something much more fun. Tell him I 'cloudboard'... skating from one cloud to another, right across God's skies. Tell him also, please, Rosemary, that I am his own personal angel, here to guide him for all of his life."

I heard a rustling sound, felt a small breeze float across my face. The light behind Daniel was dazzling bright, and almost blinding. Did I really see those feathered wings? I know I heard David, sending Daniel his love.

• • •

9

I can hear. And I can see, and feel and sense. "But how," asked Michelle Martin one day, "how can I? What can I do to help me connect with my son?"

It is not an easy question to answer, except to say that we all have to begin somewhere. And it really is best to begin at the beginning. Slowly and carefully, and with patience and discipline. But the human being is generally impatient, undisciplined, and often careless, especially with regard to the soul.

The idea of connecting with our soul, with our spiritual force, sounds too hard, too difficult a task. Very few of us want to spend the time and expend the energy that it takes. But what if we could take baby steps? What if we could begin with easy steps and progress slowly to the more demanding ones? What then? Sounds boring, frustrating. What about a miracle, an easier way? There isn't one, and you know there isn't, there simply isn't.

But what is the power?

What is the power we talk of owning?

1) Your own inner self.
2) Knowing the rules.
3) Having faith.
4) Believing in the impossible.
5) Magic.
6) Accepting, acknowledging our primitive or instinctive feelings.
7) A force that makes all things possible.

When we normally think of power, or of powerful people, we think of a force that is available only to a certain few or under certain circumstances. Most of us see ourselves as powerless to affect anything other than those situations that are part of our own small world, and we often feel powerless even in that realm. It is also the case that the very word "power" is often connected to ideas of aggression, control, rule. The power of the president, the principal, the one "in charge," the power of the king to make his subjects subservient. In the presence of powerful people we can feel intimidated, undermined. A council may rule that we are evicted from our homes. We are powerless to stop the eviction. Does this mean then that we have no power? No, it does not.

A king may have the power to force us to kneel before him. Does this make us powerless? No, it does not.

Life deals us a bad hand. Should we presume that we are powerless to change it? No, we should not.

Michelle and the countless others who have been forced to face their cruel reality have more reason, it seems, than most of us, to try, to work at life, and to enhance their spiritual connections, to be "at home" to the spirit world. The road is difficult, but they see their potential rewards as great . . . and they are.

Some people come to a book containing exercises and instructions with the expectation of finding instant knowledge, or at least an easy way to discover it. "If I follow exercises one, two, and four, this will be my expected result." This is how many view the learning process, and after all, this is the way we are often taught in school. The "no pain, no gain" philosophy is not really taken too seriously, and as with most teaching manuals, some kind of time frame is expected. You know that question— "How long does it take?"—requires an answer.

Those who come to me as their teacher, expecting the norm, the usual teacher/student relationship, the standard pat answers, and the ever-present, instant miracles of enlightenment that many would expect to see scattered throughout this book, those of you looking for the norm, for the pattern you may have followed throughout your lives, will surely be disappointed with my work, with my writings, and with my lessons. But though I am truly saddened by your failed expectations of me, I can only be myself.

This is a book that is more than just a manual, more than the many true accounts of mine and others' experiences. It is meant to be a book of enlightenment, but the kind of enlightenment that you must earn, struggle for, work for, strive toward. This is a book that is strewn throughout with many miracles, miracles that are yours, for any one of you who wishes to find them. This is a book that is somewhat akin to one of those picture puzzles— you know the kind, you look and see a house and trees and a garden, and really nothing more. Then you read the caption underneath that asks, How many birds, how many animals can you find in this picture? You look again, seeing only the house, the trees and garden, but because the caption tells you there is more to see, you look harder. See the bird hidden in the swirl of the gable end, the squirrel in the lines of the branch of that tree on the left, and the spider hidden in the folds of the rose petals. The more you look, the more you see that you did not see before. And if you get tired of looking, you can, of course, look in the back of the book for the answers.

This is not a book of instant anything, but a work designed to teach, to enlighten, in a way that you will remember. And if you didn't want that much in the way of enlightenment, still you may find excitement and emotional growth through the many stories that are told. A work of hidden wealth and beauty, and that which is hidden, if you look hard enough, if you seek it out, will unleash that which is hidden in you. Your power.

None of the exercises is wrapped in mystery, and they will sometimes seem too simple, too easy to be considered in any way magical. Yet they work. Tried and tested over many, many years, I have watched my students blossom with each small and uncomplicated step. More than magical, each exercise is a tiny miracle of light, helping us find our way.

Of course, there is no expected time frame of learning. Each individual decides for his or her own self how much effort to put in, how much hard work, how much time and energy. As your teacher I would encourage each of you to go at your own speed, not mine or anyone else's. When you are ready, you will find the lesson that is right for you. I encourage you to trust your

own process, your own instincts, and to use what little I have
written as a guide only to your learning process.

Each of us is a work-in-progress. No matter how slowly, no
matter how much we stumble, we do indeed progress, if that is
what we want.

When I think of the exercises I have used here, I am reminded
of Arthur Conan Doyle, who wrote, "You know my method. It
is founded upon the observance of trifles."

Some of you may consider my methods of teaching, my suggested exercises, mere trifles compared with the wonders and
magic of the universe. But like Arthur Conan Doyle—and we
know his method worked—the less complex I can make your
progress, the less confused you will be, and the more likely it is
that you will stay on your path toward discovery. I believe we
should not complicate, or make more complex, a subject that is
already complicated enough.

My agent and good friend when first reading the manuscript
was disappointed, as much of what she read, she said, seemed
trifling. She asked of one exercise in particular, an exercise in
Chapter Three, where I suggest making lists of our positive and
negative natures, "Surely this is just psychology? What is the
point?" I could answer in the words of Lewis Carroll: "Begin at
the beginning . . . and go on till you come to the end: then
stop." For I know that if she simply worked on the exercise,
looked at herself in a way she had not done before, if she took
on trust what I suggest all my students do in the beginning,
which is to steadily work their way through the exercise, then
she would not need to ask what the point is. She would discover the point and, in doing so, would discover a part of herself
that is as yet hidden.

We want the instant miracle, the instant answer. But when
dealing with our spiritual growth, we must take no shortcuts.
Indeed, there are no shortcuts to take. So I have tried to keep
the exercises as simple and easy to understand as possible.

It is a simple truth that man is energy. It is a simple truth that the power of the mind, the power of thought, is the most powerful energy that man possesses. It is a simple truth that man can learn to use his energy, to control his power, and to become more powerful, the more he uses his energy. Simply put, so that we all can understand, all of us, from the educated to the uneducated, simplicity is a key to knowledge.

We know what willpower is, but by some misguided conception, many of us believe we have to be a certain type of person, strong, determined, extroverted, to be able to be willful, to exercise willpower. Not so. We all have it and just don't know how to use it.

We all have the power to direct our thoughts, meaning that we all are capable of willpower, willing our power by a process of thought energy, but we either don't believe ourselves to be strong enough or don't believe ourselves to be good enough.

We own the power of thought, of thought energy.

We own the power of the universe, and the universe within.

We own the power of the earth, the sea and stones, of mountains.

We own the power of the soul, for the soul chooses.

We own the power of dreams, of our sleep state.

We own the power of experience.

We own the power of our knowing, our instinctive self. The knowledge we were born with, within us.

We own the power of our inner power, our faith, our belief, our spirit.

We own the power of collective consciousness, collective thought energy.

We own the power of will, of our willpower.

How do we access it? We believe. We trust. We wish. We make possible. We dare to be good enough. We dare to will it to be so. For if you think it, then it becomes so. You own the power.

How do we make it grow? We ask for the right things. We ask nurture for our souls. We ask for love. For gentleness. For strength. For energy. We ask only for those things that our soul needs. That our spirit needs. For if we ask these things, then we are given what we need, all things become as they should be. You own the power.

A simple person will find it easy to see God, is always at home to him, for his mind is uncluttered by the whys and hows of life. I have seen this simple truth a thousand times.

Connecting with our soul, finding out what kind of soul we are, learning to connect in some way with those souls who are in the spirit world. Why would we want to? What's in it for us? Can we really be bothered? We have to be. We just have to be. Those of us who want a better and more tolerant world, with kinder, gentler, more understanding people in it, we just have to care enough to try. So, in the words of Lewis Carroll, "Let's begin at the beginning, and don't stop until we come to the end."

• • •

There are countless reasons why we begin the journey, and it is, for many of us, the result of a personal tragedy, or a life-changing and traumatic event that leads us to pose the question "What is it all about?" The "it," of course, is life. Then there is that more personal question: "What is my life all about?" That's when the search begins, and we take our first steps toward spiritual enlightenment.

I have been working as a spiritual medium and healer for more than nineteen years, and run a healing organization in England. Over the last two decades I have had hundreds of students pass through my hands, and without exception, their initial reason for seeking me out as their teacher was a direct result of a life-changing trauma—either an emotional or a physical injury severe enough to arrest, or change, what used to be "normal" thinking. The loss of a loved one. The loss of a child. The breakdown of a marriage. The termination of a job. A serious accident, eviction, major health problems, and so on. These are a few of life's tragedies that will stop us in our tracks and force us to ask the question "What is life all about?" Just as it did for the Martin family.

A friend of mine was recently diagnosed with cancer, and given a fifty-fifty chance of recovery. Not great odds, but in the scheme of things, not bad odds either. An operation was advised, to be performed as soon as possible, within three weeks.

She came to me immediately, seeking my help, not just as a healer, but also as a friend and counselor. Scared, uncertain, her life rocked to its very foundations, she asked, "What is it all about? In God's name, tell me. What is life all about?"

She was a doctor, and had for many many years been dealing with life and death and dying. That, you might think, should have given her more insight, more awareness and knowledge of what life is all about. But it had never touched her personally, and so when it came to herself, when she was faced with her own vulnerability, she was unprepared and just as confused and afraid as the rest of us would be.

So what could I do? As a friend, a healer, the all-knowing and all-seeing, the one with all the right answers. What could I do?

Every time someone asks for my help, which can be several times in a day, certainly in a week, I feel that I am being asked for a miracle. Sometimes a small one, often a bigger one. Like the magician who is expected to pull the rabbit out of the hat, I am expected to know, to have the right answers. This is when I feel my vulnerability as a human being.

As a friend, as a healer, and definitely not all-knowing and all-seeing, I often feel so inadequate, so small and frail. It is at these times that I look to God, to Christ, to Grey Eagle. It is at these times that I might feel my guide's hand, gentle, reassuring, laid on my shoulder, and it is at these times that I take a deep breath, remembering that I may be just one little person, but I have a good team working with me. I'm not alone.

So when my doctor friend came seeking my help, I did not say smoothly, "We're here to learn and grow, or we're here for life's lessons, etc." Those answers sound so glib and out of place, given the circumstances. Anyway, she knows that. Her real question, one she could not force herself to ask out loud, was "Why me, why is this happening to me?" And the answer to that question, she already also knew, was "Why not to you?" After all, what makes any one of us so special, so different, that we should be exempt from pain, from trauma?

So what did I do?

First of all I listened, as she talked to me, told me of her fears, her hopes and aspirations for a future she might not have. When she cried I gave her tissues and the comfort of my arms around her. So far, I had done no more or less than any friend would do.

As a healer, I suggested that she have healing, on a regular daily basis. She had already experienced healing, was familiar with the process, and had read and done most of the exercises in *Give the Gift of Healing*. So far the healing process was straightforward. So far, as a healer I had done no more or less than any other healer might do.

Could I do more? Should I do more? I had exercised my role as a friend. I had exercised my role as a healer. But what of my role as a teacher? Should I, could I, exercise or escape my role as a teacher, a spiritual teacher? And what, after all, is that role? I smile, knowing that there is no escape, nor, if an escape route was presented to me, would I take it. My task is clear. For my friend I must be friend, healer, and teacher. For the purpose of this book I must be the same: friend, healer, and teacher. And for all who come seeking my help, I must be the same. Friend, healer, and teacher.

The role of a spiritual teacher is not just to bring light and enlightenment, not just to talk about or to demonstrate what she knows, but to bring empowerment to her students—knowledge of the personal power that each of us was born with. So what more did I do?

I began by placing in my friend's hands certain tools, various exercises, with which she could begin to mold her attitude, change her perspective on life, be more positive, give healing to herself. In doing this, I gave her back the control over her life that her disease had momentarily robbed her of. Encouraged to believe in herself, in her own capabilities, and working on her exercises, she found the strength she needed. Her operation was successful, the cancer eliminated. It could easily have gone the other way. I did not give her the big miracle. I did not cure her cancer. Only God makes these decisions. But I did, in my own small way, encourage her to take control of her life, of her emotions, of the way in which she now approaches life. I showed her, as her spiritual teacher, that she, and she alone, owns her own power. And I taught her how to use that power.

I taught her slowly and carefully, always mindful of my great responsibility to ensure, as much as I could, that she would grow in the right way. Mindful, too, that she accept responsibility for herself and her own welfare.

If you want to be a carpenter, to use high-powered or potentially dangerous equipment, first you must learn all the safety precautions. No responsible person would ignore the need for a safety helmet when working on a construction site. Of course we know that some do. They break the rules. The consequences are their responsibility, and theirs alone.

We send our kids to school. We pray that they have good teachers. We expect our children to obey the rules that the school has laid down, and we understand that these rules have been made for the good of our children and for the good of all. Break the rules, take the consequences. And we all know that some of the consequences are harsh.

Life is full of rules and consequences. Our society would not be ordered if there were no rules, nor would there be such chaos if more people obeyed the rules. Everybody suffers the consequences of the lawbreaker.

As a mother, my worst nightmare, my greatest hurdle happened when my daughter reached adolescence. We had, I think, done all the right things, talked openly about procreation, the physical and spiritual needs of the human being, and the emotional needs, too. We were well prepared, and I had always told my child that when the time came that she might think enough of someone to become more involved, more serious, that she could come to me and talk it over. I was well prepared; only, when the time came, I really messed up. Several times my daughter tried to talk to me. Each time I found an excuse to fob her off. Finally she cornered me, and yes, I did say she cornered me, because I had done a lot of weaving and dodging. But why? I knew and liked her boyfriend. They had been going out together for over two years. She was way old enough to do whatever she liked, she was way beyond adolescence and certainly didn't need my permission to do anything, so what was wrong with me? So, well and truly cornered, I blew my top.

"You're not old enough, how could you possibly think you are ready for this, this cannot be, I won't allow it," and so on and so on. You can see how well prepared I really was.

My daughter was shocked by my mean and unfair attitude. "What happened to 'come and talk to me'?" she screamed at me, bursting into tears.

She was right. And I was wrong. I was being unfair. My child had put her trust in me, and I had failed her, big time. Big time. Why?

All that talk about "one day," all the care and concern and

consideration that I as a loving mother had taken to educate my daughter, was momentarily laid aside. My emotions, my protective instincts, my reluctance to let go of my little girl, to accept her womanhood—all these things got in the way. This was real life and I was scared. Scared for her. Scared that all the talking, all the preparation, the care that I had taken to ensure that she made all the right decisions, I was scared that she might, when her emotions were as cluttered as mine had been when she tried to talk to me, that she might forget what I had tried to teach her, and she would get hurt.

This was the "one day." I must let her go. Trust in her, and also in myself. She was on her own, to choose to take all the right actions for her safety and well-being or not. A new, wonderful, and oftentimes confusing life was ahead of her. Break the rules, take the consequences. I could do no more than pray I had been a good enough teacher.

As we travel together on this journey, it is easy to be overwhelmed by the desire to know everything, try everything, all at once. We are excited, passionate, eager, rather like an adolescent approaching sex. It's new and wonderful, but requires us to be discriminating and to take precautions. So we have rules, or guidelines, for our own sake. We want to own our own power, to know what that means, and what it feels like. Also, we want to get the best from our experiences, and so it is important that we take the journey slowly, one step at a time.

OWNING YOUR POWER

The first step to "owning your power" is to learn the art of relaxation and meditation, and I thought it would be fun to begin with a story about one of my students.

For Lynn Bolton, the relaxation exercise I suggest you use was most difficult, as you will see. I told the very traumatic and heartrending story of the Boltons, a wonderful English family, in *Proud Spirit.* The Boltons had lost their son, Nigel, very tragically, in a moped accident when he was just seventeen years old.

I met the Boltons, Peter, Lynn, Nigel, and Stephen, a year or so after Nigel was killed, and after so many years of knowing them, I count this family among my closest friends.

The Boltons are ordinary people and had never been particularly interested in things spiritual, had never seriously questioned God, the universe, or their place in it. Their lives had been centered on their children, their work, their families. And if anyone had asked them the question "Do you believe that there are people who can talk to the dead?," they would have dismissed the idea as nonsense. Lynn and Peter are definitely the no-nonsense kind, and very down-to-earth.

Peter had been brought up on the fairgrounds. His was a tough childhood, and he was thirteen years old before his parents stopped traveling the country and settled down in Thorne, a small mining town in the north of England. Lynn, an only child, had spent her life in this same town, had trained as a nurse, and she and Peter had married in their early twenties.

Their spiritual journey began when Nigel was killed. That was when they seriously began to question the point of their existence, and the existence of God. That was when they asked the question "What is life all about?"

It was shortly before I met them that my students and I had begun our first healing clinic, and not long after a lecture they had attended, the Bolton family paid our center their first visit. In need of healing, wanting to learn more about the spirit world, and their son's place in it, they eventually became my students.

At each class they were given exercises, and their training was, they found, not easy, and over the years there were many times they almost gave up, doubtful of their ability to learn. The hardest part of their learning, as with all my students, was learning about themselves, their own self-discovery. But they learned that the key to all things, to the universe, to God, and to the spirit world, is first to know yourself. To really be able to communicate with yourself, and to learn to trust your "instincts" before you can "instinctively" attune to that power, that energy, which is of God and the universe.

I can remember, quite distinctly, Lynn Bolton's reaction when she first tried Exercise I, the art of relaxation. You will see as you read through it that this exercise requires you to give loving and gentle thoughts to your physical body, and this can be hard, as there are not too many of us, I think, who are totally pleased with the way God made us. Too fat, too thin, too short or tall, we all have some complaint about how we look. With Lynn it was her legs. She hated them, always had. The shape of them, if she thought too hard, repulsed her. When she was younger she had longed to be slimmer, shapelier ... in her eyes, more perfect.

Now she was in a room with her fellow students, being asked not only to examine her physical body, but to concentrate on every inch of herself, in a caring and nonjudgmental way. Lynn had been a district nurse for many years, and was a totally professional medical caregiver. If she had had to examine one of her patients like this, someone who was perhaps crippled or deformed or ugly to look at, she would find it easy, indeed has, again and

22

again in her profession, reached out with gentleness to bathe an ulcerated leg, massage a broken body, a body riddled with cancer or some other vile disease. Her ability, driven by her compassion, to see the physical body as a wonderful creation is such that she can reach out with a loving hand and, with no thought, give love. As long as it is to someone other than herself.

So why, when looking at herself, should she feel only disgust? At the beginning of the exercise, starting with her toes, then moving to her feet, eventually she would come to her legs. As soon as she looked at her ankles, she would immediately steel herself, have to force herself to say nice things. By the time she reached her calves, her poise would be gone, her words would be sticking in her throat; anger and frustration, aimed at herself, would take its place. She truly felt hatred for her legs, and was unable to get past the feelings of disgust she had held on to for so many years. Weeks went by. Weeks of trying, bursting into tears, feeling stupid, inadequate.

Why was her judgment of herself so harsh, so uncompromising, so without love? And why is it that way with so many of us—not that we might feel disgust, but certainly dissatisfaction?

Perhaps we have never been taught to give to ourselves. Perhaps we have been taught that to love ourselves is audacious. But I truly believe that if we learn to like ourselves, it is because we have dared to become better human beings. To learn to give to ourselves is to understand the need of the self for self-respect. And to learn to love ourselves is to come to the awakening, the realization of the fact that we, each individual, is of God, a part of God and of His light. And how can we not love God? And how can we not give to God? And how can we not like God, and the light that is God? All of us have God within, and if we deny ourselves love, we deny our God within us.

When Lynn heard me say these things, she was confused. She hated her legs, hated her body, and had never ever considered that they had anything to do with her love of God. God was,

23

after all, separate, the Almighty, residing in heaven, not of earth. The idea of Him residing within her was new, and she was confused. If she accepted the idea that God was within, then she must accept herself, and all that she was, just as she was. To do otherwise, she realized, would be to deny some part of God. This lesson was tough. It was so easy, she thought, to understand God in others, but "No, oh no, not in me. I'm not worthy enough, good enough, pretty enough, or . . . well, enough of anything. I'm just me."

"If you believe in God, in His power, His presence, His truth and wisdom, His ability to encompass all things, and I know you do," I said to her one evening during class, "then to believe that He loves you, holds you dear, that you are precious to Him, is simply one tiny step toward understanding that you must love, cherish, and be precious to yourself. Lynn," I added, "God doesn't care if you're fat, thin, ugly, or handsome. He cares only that your life has some meaning, a purpose, and that you cherish your soul."

It took a while. There is no point in saying differently. Habits of a lifetime can be hard to break. But eventually Lynn was able to do her exercise without feeling inadequate, and after a while she came to accept and love herself as one of God's children.

It was at a workshop in New York, some years later, and I had brought over some of my team of healers from England to help. They were so excited and loving every moment of their experience, until, that is, I asked them up onto the stage with me. I had been explaining the relaxation exercise to my audience, and had told them the story I have just told you. Asking each of my team for their comments, it was so good to hear Lynn say, in a small yet confident voice, "I like myself . . . even," she added as she looked directly at the audience, and blushing a little, "even my legs."

Lynn and Peter Bolton began their journey of self-healing and spiritual awakening as a result of losing their son. They found their journey a hard yet fulfilling one, full of surprises, mostly good ones. They began, uncertain of their future, but wanting something more from life than they had yet experienced. Like the Boltons, taking one tentative step after another, as you read on, you will begin a journey. Sometimes hard, full of surprises, and yet, I am sure, if you persevere, this will be a most fulfilling experience. So hold my hand, and let's begin.

EXERCISE 1 . . .
RELAXING WITH ROSEMARY

If you have already learned the art of relaxation and meditation, this first exercise will be easy, but don't be tempted to skip it. It takes time for most of us to learn to visualize, although when we were children we did it all the time. Ask a child to "imagine," and the child is instantly able to create, through visualizing in the mind, a scene, a situation, an experience. Often a child's imagination knows no bounds. We adults, however, can have a much more difficult time, and find ourselves restricted by what we think we know to be real. In other words, we use tunnel vision.

Stephen King makes a perfect observation when he writes about "the perception of a child who has not yet learned to protect itself by developing the tunnel vision that keeps out ninety percent of the universe."

We tell ourselves that we must use our common sense, and, of course, we should, there is nothing wrong with that. But we don't want to be afflicted with tunnel vision, vision that narrows and restricts.

Now we are entering another dimension, widening our vision, exploring facets of ourselves we may never have explored before. Our goal is to encounter other realities, to take off the blinders, which can take us to a higher level of understanding we never before dreamed possible. As we journey, we will try to combine

25

our common sense with our sixth sense. As children, our sixth sense was much more finely tuned. Our instincts about people and situations were rarely wrong. Now, as adults, we must try to create a balance. Our common sense comes from the common ground that we have walked . . . the earth. Our sixth sense, our spirit sense, comes from that which is the soul, which is of God, and of the universe.

Taking off the blinders is hard to do, and when I ask, throughout the exercises, for you to visualize, many of you may have a hard time at first, as do many of my students. It takes time to rediscover the art of visualization, but don't be disheartened— the exercises we will be using will help you.

To begin. First ask the question "What is my goal?" Keep a record. Make a note of any improvements in your state of mind, no matter how small, and decide how often you want to work on your exercises. Once a day? Once or twice a week? Be realistic about how much time you can give each week. Make your decision. Then stick to it as much as possible. Wear something that makes you feel good, a warm, soft color. Perhaps a scarf or sweater. You might like to choose some soft and gentle meditation music. This is the time you might choose to use my meditation tape *Give the Gift of Healing.* Find your place, somewhere where you will be undisturbed. A place of peace and tranquillity. No phones, no interruptions.

Next, try to connect with your higher power. This can be done simply through prayer. Let your thoughts flow, let yourself go.

Just following these basic steps will put you in the right frame of mind to begin your relaxation exercise. To get the best results, I believe you will need to set aside at least fifteen minutes each day. First, find a comfortable place to sit. Do not lie down. The aim of this exercise is not to relax to the point of sleep, but to relax to the point of awareness of your inner self.

Sitting comfortably, with your legs uncrossed, keep your back straight and place your feet firmly on the ground, your hands, palms up, on your lap.

Close your eyes and begin by breathing deeply but gently in through your nose, out through your mouth, and slowly relax the muscles in your body. Starting with your feet, begin talking to your body, gently, softly, first to your toes. Slowly become aware, minutely aware, of every small part of you. Wriggle your toes, and in soft, soothing tones, tell them, nice toes, tired toes, relax toes, relax, and when you feel your toes relaxing a little, then move to the soles of your feet. Working slowly, talking softly, let your body respond to your voice. Nice feet, pretty feet, relax, relax. Moving to your heels, then slowly up to your ankles, keep talking, softly, gently, relax pretty feet, poor hardworking feet, relax.

Remember, you may feel, as I do, that feet are not especially pretty things, but move your mind away from physical impressions. God gave us, those of us fortunate enough to have them, our feet. They do a good job for us. Let us show them our appreciation.

Slowly, little by little, allow your mind to move upward. Concentrate on your body, inch by inch, slowly, slowly, visualize yourself massaging each area. Working slowly, move to your legs, your knees, your thighs, pausing when you reach areas that you "feel" need gentle mental massage. Still breathing gently, with each new breath allow yourself total awareness of the vehicle that you use and abuse each and every day of your life—your body. Keep working until you feel totally rested and relaxed.

Beauty, they say, is in the eye of the beholder. When Lynn Bolton first began this exercise she was unable to behold her body as anything other than ugly. Consequently she found it difficult to relax, to give to herself. As her teacher, I pointed out some simple facts to her—well, facts as I saw them anyway. God is the creator of our being. That includes our physical body, which

I do not believe He sees as ugly, but is in fact beautiful. The human body is a vehicle that houses the soul, and as such, no matter what shape it takes, we should really learn to appreciate it more. To see our bodies as beautiful is not vanity. To learn to cherish that which not only houses the soul, but enables the soul access to the planet on which we live, is a joyful thing. This vehicle of ours gives us the greatest access to that which we came here for, it gives us access to our lessons on this earth, and to growth. If we learn to think this way, it doesn't feel so ridiculous an exercise to express our love, our caring, and our gratitude to the body we so often take for granted. The house, the vehicle, the church, in which our soul resides.

Hearing these simple truths, Lynn was finally able to view her body without anger or vanity, as a wonderful and poised asset.

So now, back to our exercise.

Slowly still, and very slowly, tell your body how special and wonderful you think it is, and how much you love and want to care for it. On reaching the area around the solar plexus, the middle stomach area, just above the navel, take more deep breaths, and visualize, if you can, the universal healing color blue surrounding that area. Again, slowly, using gentle mental massage, visualize and become aware of your chest, your lungs, your arms and hands. Wriggle your fingers, talk to each area of your body lovingly, bring your thoughts to your neck, your cheeks, your lips. Become aware of the top of your head, the back of your head. Using gentle mental massage, center your thoughts on your temples, and visualize all the tensions of life and all of the impurities of your body washed away. Breathe in deeply but gently and again visualize the color blue, this time in the form of a soft blue blanket of down, wrapped around you, giving you a feeling of warmth and comfort and security. Keep working on it every day, and pretty soon you will feel so much healthier and happier. It really works.

This exercise is self-indulgent, absolutely self-indulgent, so enjoy it, make the most of it, revel in an experience that is just for you. If you are patient and practice regularly, not only will you become more aware and in tune with your mind and body, you will also achieve a state of real peace, an inner peace, from which all things are possible.

MEDITATION

Meditation is a different experience for everyone, so before we go forward, I thought you might like to hear some comments from a handful of my students about their own experiences with meditation.

PAT MASON: It was quite a revelation to discover how poor my concentration was and how easily my thoughts could play "truant" without my realizing it. After many years I still have difficulty, though even if my meditation is less than successful, the time I spend seeking the calm is always valuable.

NIGEL HUTCHINSON: I did not find it difficult to meditate. My difficulties were, first, where to do it. I needed a place away from the mainstream of family life, where I would be undisturbed. And, second, when, what time of day should I meditate? In spite of doing the hundred and one things that are necessary for my well-being, like eating, drinking, washing, shaving, dressing, and appearing at events that are part of my daily life, I fear that sometimes I am guilty of not sparing the time for myself that I deserve. Meditation is something I find hard to fit into my life, even though it takes such a short time, but it is definitely something I deserve to do.

This suggests to me that I should become more structured in the timing of my meditation, at least until I become more adept at the skill.

JEANNE HINSLEY: When I first began meditating I was both excited and apprehensive, wondering if I was doing it right. I first began, using a candle. To sit and watch the candle flame, the warmth and feelings of security as I saw the colors, was magical. Sometimes, when I am affected by the ordinary day-to-day events in my work or family life, it is hard to settle down to meditate. At these times a change of medium, from a candle to a flower or butterfly, brings me inspiration.

GEORGIE JACKSON: The difficulties I first encountered with meditation were first with the candle. I could not keep the image of the flame still. It would dance about, reduce in size, or disappear altogether, which would leave me feeling very frustrated. But my greatest difficulty was with my own expectations. I expected that I would be able to meditate easily. When I could not, I became very agitated, almost angry with myself. Things only got better when I stopped expecting anything of myself. I became more relaxed, less agitated, and meditation became easier.

LYNN BOLTON: I have always found meditation difficult, especially candle meditation. The flame would constantly disappear as soon as I closed my eyes. I felt tense, frustrated, and agitated by my lack of self-discipline. Then I tried flower meditation, and I immediately found I could do this with ease. I could visualize, smell, and almost touch each flower petal. My feelings of frustration left me, and I felt instead a feeling of warmth and comfort. I felt peaceful, calm, and relaxed.

ALAN GEE: Meditation was difficult in the beginning, and it was many weeks before I could relax and concentrate enough to meditate either at home or in class. I felt frustrated at my lack of ability to settle down, but I persevered and eventually was able to meditate calmly and peacefully. I was surprised at the results. I felt warm and at peace with myself. My barriers had begun to slip. Meditation is for me a wonderful experience.

As you can see, of the six examples shown, only one, Nigel, is able to say that he finds meditating easy, which is not surprising, as most people find meditating a struggle to some degree. Many give up, fearing that they are attempting the impossible. However, look at what Pat Mason writes: "Even if my meditation is less than successful, the time I spend seeking the calm is always valuable."

These are the words I would like you to remember, for whenever you attempt any of the exercises in this book, the art is not in winning or losing, succeeding or failing, the art is in the trying, simply in the trying. Like the man who climbs the mountain, his goal ultimately is to reach the top, but his goal is also to learn as much about the mountain as he can, to stop along the way and find excitement in discovering the small things.

Now I must tell you, and this might sound like the greatest excuse in the world, but I have often found it impossible to meditate in the usual way. I love the relaxation exercise, and thoroughly enjoy every moment of it, but each time I relax and close my eyes, because I am always "at home," there is always something to see, to hear, to feel, which distracts me from my initial purpose. For instance, Grey Eagle might take the opportunity of my quiet time to take me somewhere or show me some new thing. Always curious, I'm always ready to learn, to go off, to explore. Yet the first rule of meditation, for me, for my students, is to remain in control, that you do not "go off," do not explore the realms of your imagination, until you are able to distinguish imaginings from reality. That takes time and experience, and until you can trust that you know the difference, don't go too far, too fast. Stick with the program. Safe is best. The last thing we want to happen is for an overripe, overeager imagination to lead us into confusion.

My trust in Grey Eagle has come from a lifetime of learning and growing. I hold his hand, we fly, and I have no fear. This is who I am. You have yet to learn who you are, so go slowly, be patient, your time to explore more will come. As your teacher, I want the best for you, so before you fly, learn to walk.

To ponder, to reflect, to be in deep thought, this is what the word "meditation" means. Reflecting on "being at one, seeing, feeling, sensing," nothing other than that which we are meditating upon. A candle, a flower, or butterfly, whatever it is we use. The purpose of meditation generally is to fill the mind with the object of one's choice. The art is in being able to "tune in," to be totally in tune with the medium you have chosen, to see, feel, and sense nothing else. But why do it? What is the purpose? Perhaps to relax, as when the mind rests, is renewed, it is given the opportunity to release any and all stressful thoughts, to "let go." My students, as you might gather from some of their comments, sometimes believe my insistence on their trying this exercise is my own particular brand of torture. Now, I'm a tough teacher, but not that tough. My reasons for including meditation as one of our exercises, even though I am a self-confessed failure at it, is that I do believe by trial, error, and effort we can develop a self-discipline which is very necessary in achieving spiritual attunement.

So don't beat yourself up if you can't achieve a total state of meditation. Just remember, the goal is not to succeed, simply to try.

Meditation helps bring a feeling of calm and peace, helps create an inner stillness and quiet that is so alien in today's materialistic, fast-paced society.

We waste so much time in idle and unconstructive thought, "daydreaming," thinking on past regrets, imagining future problems, and when we go for a walk or a drive in the country, how much do we really see? Busying our minds with plans, sifting ideas, puzzling over options and opportunities, we can be so unaware of the world around us, the beauty of nature, of the trees and flowers, of how green the grass grows. Unaware of our own selves, of our breathing, or of breathing in the air around us, we miss, totally and completely, our *true present*, the *now*. Minutes and hours tick by, and before we know it we have lost time, precious time, and within that time we ourselves have often become lost.

So what can we do about this? When we become lost, how do we find ourselves?

Learning the art of acknowledging our true present is difficult for most of us, but not impossible, and we can begin by learning the art of meditation. A disciplined act of the mind, body, and spiritual self, meditation has, through the ages, been the key to fulfilling our need of inner peace and self-discovery. A discovery that brings us real tranquillity.

Through the ages, people of all races and creeds the world over have searched for themselves through quiet contemplation and meditation of one sort or another, becoming aware of a heightening of their conscious thought processes and a heightening of their sensitivities.

Finding our true self, we acknowledge contact with our *knowing selves,* that instinctive and wise sense we are all born with. We begin to trust our instincts, to discover that we need to give to ourselves. This is a message of loving and giving, a message of profound beauty. A message that we truly do *own the power.*

I believe that within every human being there is a soul, our very essence, which has its origins in God. Within and surrounding this soul lies a divine light, the very essence of which is pure spirit, the aura, or energy of the soul.

Often unacknowledged and neglected, but still a light, however small, this beautiful light can, with gentle guidance and loving persuasion, grow into a strong and positive energy, which will lead us, steer and encourage us, out of dark confusion and into the sun, which will be our understanding.

There is a story, supposedly true, about a Buddhist priest who could be seen each day in the temple, meditating upon a peach stone. He sat cross-legged, on the floor, the peach stone, also on the floor, in front of him.

The temple was a busy one, and many monks and priests and visitors would come each day to pray. Always, no matter what time of the day or night, the Buddhist priest could be seen in the same place, never moving, never eating, never sleeping, meditating on the peach stone.

Days went by, then months, then years and years and years.

The Buddhist priest became a very old man, his hair now grown almost to the ground, his beard white, long, and flowing; he had become a legend.

The temple was still a busy one, and the many monks and priests and visitors would often contemplate and talk among themselves, wondering why the Buddhist priest had sat for so long and meditated upon the peach stone, but none could find an answer.

Then one day, when so many days and months and years had passed, the many monks and priests and visitors came to view the Buddhist priest, only to find him gone. One day he had simply disappeared. And all that was left of him was the peach stone.

Some, the wise ones, say that the Buddhist priest meditated for so long upon the peach stone that he became the peach stone. Some, the wise ones, say that this is the goal of meditation, that this is the true art. To become one with whatever you require to be at one with.

The story goes, and it is supposedly true, that somewhere in India, in a temple with no name that I know, a temple that is busy with monks and priests and visitors who go to pray, in a room in the temple, on the floor of the temple, after hundreds of years have gone by, you can still, if you know where to look, see the peach stone, or the Buddhist priest, or the peach stone . . . or are they one and the same?

There are many types of meditation, and many ways to meditate. You may already know, and already be happy with, "your" way. If not, try investigating some of the many books or magazines on meditation that are readily available. My patients and students use my meditation audiotape *Give the Gift of Healing*, which can be an excellent aid in learning the art of meditation, as well as an aid to healing.

Whichever way you use, to get the best results you need to put aside time, at least three times a week, but preferably every day. Just fifteen minutes is all that it takes to begin with, and some of you may want to extend the time as you progress. Remember that with any exercise you choose, meditation should be an enjoyable as well as an enlightening experience.

Here I am going to suggest two types of meditation, very simple easy exercises, helpful to those of you who are pure beginners. Both candle meditation and flower meditation are based on visualization techniques that are described often throughout the book. Many people, however, find the use of a meditation tape easier, and if this is your choice, it is not necessary to meditate in any other way, although practicing different styles of meditation can be fun.

LIGHTING THE WAY THROUGH THE CANDLE

Unlike the Buddhist priest, our aim is not to disappear into the candle, simply to experience being at one with it. Blocking all other thoughts and emotions out of our mind. Giving our mind a rest, so to speak. So let us begin.

First perform your ritual relaxation technique, Exercise I, which is a must prior to all forms of meditation.

Now, placing a lighted candle on a table in front of you, concentrate on the flame, and fill your sight and mind with the light, color, and shape of the flame.

When I was a child I remember my sister and I staring at a lightbulb until it made our eyes hurt. Then we would close our eyes, and the image of the lighted bulb would be right there in our mind's eye. We would keep our eyes closed until the image faded, then we would do it again and again.

In the same way, this is what you must try to achieve now.

Close your eyes and try to retain the image of the flame in your mind's eye. Hold on to the image of the flame for as long as you can. When you feel the image fading, open your eyes, concentrate again on the candle flame for a few seconds, then close your eyes and once again retain, if you can, the image of the flame in your mind's eye.

The idea here is to fill your mind full of light, so full of the candle flame that there is no room for another single thought. The mind can rest, we can get rid of all those niggling thoughts, like, what we should have for dinner? How late am I for work? What are the kids up to? We get rid of all emotion and can truly relax.

Keep working with the exercise until you find it possible to hold the image of the candle flame in your mind's eye for ten minutes without opening your eyes.

Lots of people find this hard to do at first, but try not to concern yourself if you are one of them. As long as you attempt the exercise and persevere with it, you will be achieving. The art of self-discipline is hard, but it is the key to success. Meditation of any kind requires discipline, but as you acquire it, it will produce immense benefits in your daily life.

As you work on your exercise each day, you may find that the candle flame will change shape and color and will possibly move out of your vision. Stay in control, hold it in the center of your vision for as long as you can, and if you lose sight of the flame, simply stop and then begin again.

Some of you, after a while, may be able to visualize the flame without the use of a candle. Some of you may find the exercise easy to do with your eyes open, although closing your eyes is better, as it avoids any external distractions.

When you feel sufficiently confident and at ease with your ability to master the candle flame, take a small step forward. See if you can explore, in more detail, the shape, color, and depth of the flame. Ponder it. Try to visualize yourself, if you can, becoming the flame. Dance with it, move with it, blend with it. What does it feel like? How do you react? Which of your senses becomes heightened? Does your mood change?

Ask yourself these questions and others. Make notes, write down your thoughts, describe your feelings, explain, in as much detail as you can, everything you saw and felt. Take your time and remember that there is no great urgency to get to the next stage. There is no hurry, so savor every moment, be self-indulgent. You are on a journey of discovery, you are discovering *you*. You are discovering your soul. And your journey is never-ending.

• • •

A student of mine for many, many years, Kay Warburton is a prime example of someone who learned to discover herself, and learning to meditate was definitely her key.

Kay, mother of three wonderful girls, Anna, Chloe, and Jessica—they would never forgive me if I didn't mention their names—was, as a young mother, very confused about who she was and what she wanted from life.

When I first met Kay, I saw a woman with extremely low self-esteem. Always trying to be what she thought others wanted her to be, like many of us, never allowing herself to be who she wanted to be. And in desperately trying to please others, she lost any sense of who she truly was.

In learning to meditate she acquired self-discipline, and she gained insight into her own personal needs as a human being. Many times throughout her training with me over the years she would become confused. It is one thing to discover your needs, another thing to find the strength and courage to reach out to all that life holds, and being afraid, it is easy to find excuses to hold back.

Whenever Kay had her moments of doubt, often self-doubt, she would find a quiet place and meditate. The exercise would leave her refreshed, calm, and able to reason more clearly.

Visualization was easy for Kay, for she is a born artist; it was learning self-discipline that she found tough. But she persevered and she made it. Now, many years later, a student who has often made learning difficult for herself, she is really achieving. She has discovered self-worth. She has also discovered that she has a real talent as an artist and is in her final year at university. She is a fine healer, and I have no doubt that Kay will use her artistic skills to aid others in some way.

Her learning has taken years, many years. Her perseverance with her lessons has been incredible and has definitely paid off. She finally knows who she is and what she wants to be. Kay had to begin somewhere. We all have to begin somewhere. No matter how difficult it may be to learn, learning to meditate is for many a real beginning.

VISUALIZING THE FLOWER

Now, I did say that meditation should be fun, or at least a pleasant experience, and if you are struggling with your candle and feel miserable about the exercise, then stop, and let's try something else. You might find it easier to visualize a calm blue ocean, the setting sun, or a tree in full leaf, swaying in the breeze. I have known people to choose a piece of fruit, a bird, a rock, an animal, and this next exercise is one that you can, if you wish, adapt to any tangible, animate, or inanimate object. I am going to use the example of a flower. This is fairly simple, as most of us have a favorite that we can, if we try, visualize quite strongly.

Relax, take your time, do this slowly, and feel the tremendous benefits as all the tensions leave your body in preparation for your meditation. Flower meditation is such a simple and easy exercise, pleasant and fun to do.

First, choose your flower—a rose, a peony, a honeysuckle. If you wish to use this meditation as a form of self-healing, I would suggest you choose a blue flower, small or large, any shape or size, a blue cornflower, a small bluebell, whatever feels right for you, as blue is the universal healing color. (Those of you who are using the audiotape *Give the Gift of Healing* will understand better how we use energy, color energy, in the healing process.)

If it helps, find a good picture, buy a flower, or cut one from the garden and place it in a vase close by, so that anytime you need to remind yourself of how it looks or smells, you can do so easily. Now close your eyes and visualize your chosen flower.

Let your flower float into your mind's eye. Allow it all the room it needs, until it fills that part of you that feels, perceives, thinks, and reasons.

Breathe in gently, and as you breathe, imagine the scent of your flower, floating toward you as if on a soft breeze. As you did with your candle flame, keep the image of your flower in your mind's eye. Do you see a flower bud? If so, watch it open. Visualize the sun, warm and encouraging, helping your flower to grow. Is your flower on its own, with its head held up to the light, or is it in a garden of flowers, blowing gently in the breeze? What is its texture? What is its hue? Write down those thoughts and feelings that you have immediately after you end this exercise.

Flowers are so beautiful, so pure and bright, they can uplift your emotions and penetrate your innermost thoughts.

A solitary pink rose, in all its perfection, or a field of golden daffodils, swaying and rippling in the breeze, are both evocative and beautiful. Hold your flower in your mind's eye, and discover its beauty. When you are comfortable that you have mastered the ability to retain the image, and you feel relaxed and easy, then try, if you can, to step inside the flower head.

When we were children, in a class where free expression was encouraged, our teacher would suggest that we imagine we were a tree. "Stand tall, lift out your arms, spread your fingers, pretend they are the branches, the limbs of the tree," she would say. "Now imagine a great wind has risen up and is gusting through the forest where you are standing." We would giggle at first. It seemed silly to pretend to be a tree, but pretty soon we were reaching as high as our little arms could reach, we were swaying and bending as if we were being blown about. Pretty soon we would be lost in our imaginations, feeling like a tree, thinking like trees might think.

It was always fun, always refreshing, and looking back, I realize that it enabled us to release our tensions and expel our hyper energy in a good and creative way.

Years later I arrived at my daughter's school to pick her up. I was a little early and was delighted to watch her and her class-mates in their final exercise of the day.

"Be a tree," I heard her teacher say, and watched in fascination as these small six-year-olds, putting so much into it, reached high and wide with their arms, wriggled their fingers, shook their hair, their bodies, as the teacher talked to them about the wind blowing gustily through the forest where they all stood.

Did you have such an experience when you were young? Can you remember how to imagine, to visualize, to put yourself in another place, be something else? Here is your chance to try again. Become the flower. Experience the feeling of freedom and joy which such an exercise brings. Become your chosen flower, lift your head to the sun, and allow yourself to grow.

As you work at this exercise, and it may take you a while to feel good about it, you will find that many of your inhibitions will disappear, and you will grow in confidence.

A wonderful and uplifting meditation will with time and patience help your life become more fulfilled and enriched as you become more aware of you and of your renewed senses.

It is always a good idea as you work through your exercises to write down your thoughts and feelings. This way you learn about who you are, discovering the deeper part of you, the very essence of your being, your spirit. Don't be in a hurry. Patience is the key word, and remember, there is no race, no competition. Take your time, and allow six weeks to complete each exercise.

This is a joyful experience, so don't be afraid to let yourself go and enjoy. Discover your true present—your now.

Approaching the end of the chapter, I decided to take a break and go for a walk with my dogs. Rosie—I can't think who she's named after—is a four-year-old Brittany, lively and bright-eyed. Her favorite thing to do is walk. Nino, just a puppy, only four months old at the time of writing, a chocolate-brown Labrador, thinks he's Rosie's baby, as does she, and he is happy to follow her almost anywhere. I utter the word "walk," and as any dog lover will know, my "babies" are raring to go.

It was a bright sunny day, one of the best days of winter, with crisp white snow on the ground and a feeling of spring, not too far distant, around the corner. Well, maybe a corner or three.

I wrapped up warmly, took hold of my walking stick, a sturdy branch I had discovered in the trees the winter before, and we set off down the path through the woods leading to the ponds, which were frozen and covered with snow.

As I walked, the dogs running just a little ahead of me, I began to think about the flower-meditation exercise, and I remembered Elisabeth. Elisabeth's story was told in *The Eagle and the Rose,* and as those of you who read that book might remember, there was a point in Elisabeth's life, at the time I first met her, when she was extremely distraught and depressed.

One evening, very late, she called to chat. She told me that for several months she had been having trouble sleeping. I suggested the flower meditation. "Climb into bed," I said. "Place your head on the pillow, and see if you can visualize your favorite flower."

"A rose," replied Elisabeth. "Roses are my favorite."

"Okay," I said, "a rose it is. See if you can visualize a beautiful long-stemmed rose, any color you like, first as a rosebud, then slowly, carefully, see if you can get the flower bud to open up." Explaining that part of the purpose of the meditation was to relax, to empty the mind, to find peace, I added, "Hopefully, it will help you relax enough so that sleep will come easier."

A few days later Elisabeth called again. "This flower meditation," she said. "It doesn't matter how hard I try, I can't sleep. Every time I relax and get to the point where I can see the flower bud open up, a horrid black earwig starts to crawl out of the center and it wakes me up!"

I started to laugh, and pretty soon she was laughing with me. "I should have made it clearer to you." I chuckled. "Flower meditation is a wonderful, refreshing, and enlightening experience, and you must not allow any negative thought or visual expression to interfere with that. So before you begin next time, remind yourself of your goal. Peace, tranquillity, harmony of mind, body, and spirit. This is what you can achieve if you meditate in a positive and healthy way."

It took her a while. Elizabeth was so used to having bad things happen to her that initially it was hard for her to trust in something nice that wouldn't be spoiled. But she worked at it, and she worked at her life. Her attitude changed. She became more positive, and best of all, she learned to trust in life again.

Who has seen the wind? Neither you nor I.
But when the trees bow their heads,
The wind is passing by.

CHRISTINA ROSSETTI

CHAPTER 2

Finding Our Energy—
Building It Up

It is true that we cannot see the wind except when the leaves rustle on the trees, or when fields of long grasses dance, or tall poplars bend their backs. In other words, we can see the wind when it touches something. The force of God, the force of the universe and the spirit world, is much the same. Sometimes it winds its way gently, softly, into our lives. Sometimes the force of it is so strong that it blows its way into our lives like a full gale-force tornado, knocking us off our feet and in a moment forever changing our way of being and thinking.

For me, the God force entered my life gently, softly, showing itself throughout my childhood years and into my adulthood. Occasionally I would feel a strong gust blowing, but mostly it was an ever-present cool and comforting breeze. Many people, however, feel the full impact of that God force only when tragedy strikes, and because it is an unfamiliar feeling, it can be very confusing, and for some, mind-boggling.

The wind lies sleeping, ever-present, waiting to awaken at any moment. So, too, is that ever-present God force waiting to

44

awaken us at any given moment, confusing at first, then comforting and reassuring. Sometimes blowing us off our feet, at other times like a gentle breeze blowing across our hearts.

Several months after the beginning of my true awakening, I was at home, which then was in Yorkshire, in the north of England, and I was sitting with my youngest sister, Madeleine, who had come to visit for a couple of weeks. We had been discussing my spiritual development and my experiences with Irene and Paul Denham, a couple who had at that time been so instrumental in helping me overcome my fears.

My sister was very curious about what I was doing and was asking lots of questions. Duncan, her son, who was then around six or seven years old, had come with her on the trip, and he and my daughter Samantha were safely tucked up in bed, fast asleep, having played happily together all day.

I had been telling her about energy, how each of us has our own energy, and that by tapping into it we can not only learn how to communicate with our own soul, but that with time and patience we can even connect with the universe. We both laughed when I mentioned patience, for our family is known for its lack of it. "Boy, am I lucky," I said. "It's a good thing for me that all this 'stuff' comes so naturally, because I doubt I would have the patience to really work at it."

"Well, show me what you do," my sister then said. "Show me what I can do."

I thought for a moment, then said, "Okay, let's just sit together on the floor and hold hands. I will try and transmit my energy to you. You see if you can feel anything coming from me, and while we try to connect our energies, try to retain everything you see or hear, feel or sense."

Madeleine nodded. It was just a game, just like we were kids again, and as we plopped onto the floor, we crossed our legs in the lotus position and tried not to giggle.

"Come on now," I said eventually. "If we are going to do this, then let's be serious." But it took a few minutes before we were able, either of us, to keep a straight face.

Finally we were ready. I asked God and Grey Eagle for their guidance and protection, and then I took my sister's hands in my own. We sat like this for several minutes, both of us with our heads bowed, concentrating on the energy flow. It was only when I felt a slight shift in my consciousness that I looked up and saw that my sister Madeleine was sitting upright, her eyes staring out, her face muscles completely relaxed, almost trancelike. I squeezed her hands gently and was about to say something, when, looking again at her face, it changed, right before my eyes.

At first it was like seeing a white shroud move over her head, covering her to her shoulders. It startled me and I made to move, but found myself frozen to the spot, with no choice but to watch. The shroud had now covered my sister's face so completely that nothing of her own features showed through. I tried to move again, to cast my eyes down to my hands in an effort to concentrate my energy and control the situation. It was no use, still I couldn't move. But now came the biggest shock, for when I looked again to where my sister's face should be, I found myself staring into the eyes of my father. My father, dead these past five years, but sitting now right in front of me, clear as could be, too clear in fact, too clear. Every feature—his nose, his mouth, the set of his jaw. My father had, or I should say, has, a very distinctive face. His nose had been broken so many times he had been forced to have the bones removed. His nose was flat. His mouth, large and full-lipped, his bottom lip in two halves, the result of a coal shovel being thrown into his face, splitting his lip literally in two. My father's eyes, unmistakable, strong and piercing, always seeming to see everything, saw me now. For one brief moment I was afraid. And then I heard his voice, the sound coming from my sister's face—no, my father's face, coming from my father. For a moment I was stunned and could not react. Then I began to cry, but softly. I stared at him and he smiled back at me as he gently called my name. "Rosie, Rosie, Rosie."

I do not know how long we sat there, an endless time it seemed, but after a while I bent my head, able to move now, and when I looked back up he was gone, and my sister, now "back," was immediately concerned as to why I was crying.

"What did you feel, what did you see?" I asked urgently.

"It was awful," she replied, breathless from the experience, "just awful," and she began to recount in full detail everything she had seen.

"It was like watching a movie," she said, "but I didn't like it one bit," she added as she told me the story.

"There was a boy. He looked a lot like Duncan, but it could have been Duncan's friend Mark. He's small, and fair like Duncan, and they are the same age. He was in a car with his father and sister, I think, although I couldn't see their faces, and they were riding along a very narrow, steep road, going up a mountainside. Just ahead of them was a large truck, carrying huge boulders. The truck was making slow progress up the hill, and the car which the boy was in was trailing behind, as there was no chance to overtake the truck. Without warning, the tailgate of the truck broke loose, and boulders began to spill out all over the road, bouncing off the car, and I watched as the driver swerved and careened down the side of the mountain. It was awful, awful." And with that, my sister began to cry.

Oh my God, I thought, knowing what I knew, knowing that my father had come for a reason, possibly to warn us, What should I do?

Now, in crisis, every British woman puts on the kettle, and that's just what I did. A nice cup of tea solves everything. Well, it helps put matters in perspective, anyway.

It was only when I had made the tea and we had both calmed down, and had time to think, that I recounted to Madeleine what I had seen.

"What does it mean?" my sister asked me, and in truth I had to tell her that I wasn't certain. "But one thing's for sure," I said. "When you get home and Mark comes to play with Duncan, just don't let them go out onto the road. Dad is trying to tell us something here. I'm not quite sure what it is, but it pays to take heed."

Almost a year passed. Madeleine had forgotten all about her experience, but I had not. Thus, when she called, shaken and crying, to tell me that Duncan had been in a car accident while on vacation with his father and stepsister in Greece, it was not a surprise to me. Fortunately, Duncan was unhurt, had been saved from serious injury by his stepmother, who had also been in the car. They had been driving along a narrow road, heading up a mountainside, when the boulders had come flying out of the truck ahead of them, bouncing on the car, and his stepmother instinctively grabbed Duncan and placed her body over his to protect him. Her leg was crushed and she was in hospital for several months. Duncan's stepsister also had quite serious facial injuries. She had been sitting up at the front with their father, who, like Duncan, had survived the accident without a scratch.

Did Duncan have a guardian angel? I think so. But I also think that the outcome of that accident had been determined long before it took place. My father had come to warn us, but also to reassure us that we were safe and that he was watching over us.

It's called "transfiguration," and many years ago, when there were many more physical mediums about, transfiguration was commonplace among spiritualists. So was the use of trumpets, planchettes, and of course, ectoplasm, not to mention the many other psychic tools.

The trumpet, a funnel-shaped object, wide at one end, narrow at the other, usually made from stiff cardboard or lightweight metal foil, much stiffer than ordinary kitchen foil of course, was used for directing sound—for collecting and intensifying the

48

sounds or voices from the spirit world. Although I own a trumpet, or used to anyway—goodness knows where it is now—I have never seen, or should I say, heard, a trumpet used successfully in this way, though I would never dismiss the possibility of it, for I have witnessed much stranger things. Nor have I ever seen the use of a planchette, so I cannot speak of its success rate. However, many people claim that the use of a planchette aids in automatic or inspired writing. A pen or pencil sits or is balanced on a ball, which is placed on a board. The ball moves, the pen writes. The theory is that some unseen force moves the ball, controls the pen, and supposedly, words are written from the spirit world.

Nor have I experienced ectoplasm, and some of you might be wondering now, "What kind of expert is she?" I don't blame you, and thank goodness I have never claimed to be an expert. That is the claim that others may have made about me. Although I have never actually seen ectoplasm, I do believe in its existence, for many years ago, a good friend of mine, who had been involved in spiritualism for more than forty years, told me of the day he had witnessed physical mediumship. He had seen a medium go into a trance state, and, he told me, had watched as ectoplasm had poured out of her nose and mouth. There had been so much of it that he and his daughter, who was a young teen at the time, had sat and played with it, holding it, moving it through their hands. "It felt dry, but elastic," he said, "pliable and moldable." I trusted what he said. He was not a man prone to making things up, exaggerating, or dramatizing.

Now, anyone who has seen the movie *Ghostbusters* will have heard of ectoplasm, but most people associate it with a substance that comes from the spirit world, or from a "ghost." This is not so. All of us, every living thing, contains ectoplasm, and I looked up the meaning of the word in *Webster's Ninth Collegiate Dictionary*. "Ectoplasm: The outer relatively rigid granule-free layer of the cytoplasm, usually held to be a gel, but reversibly convertible into a solid." This explanation didn't do it for me, and so I went to a young sixth-grade boy to see if, in his biology lessons, he had been taught anything about cell structure. Ectoplasm is the part of a cell that surrounds the nucleus, the center of the cell, acting as a protective layer of gel, he told his mother, who then passed on the information to me. Now I could understand. Ectoplasm is, to the cell, like the fluid that surrounds the baby in the womb. A protective substance for the human cell structure. I can picture it quite easily, and hope you can, too.

During World War II, and prior to that time, there were many "physical mediums," a term I have used quite often in this chapter, so let me attempt an explanation. A physical medium is someone who can not only communicate with the spirit world, but who will use his or her physical body, or more correctly, allow the spirit world to use his or her physical body, to display spirit activity. The spirit entity enters a medium's body and is able to use the medium's voice box, and often to use the medium's ectoplasm. At the beginning of the century and up to the late forties, physical mediumship was very commonplace in England and most séances were not complete without the display of ectoplasm or the sound, coming from the trumpet, or sight of some mysterious vision. Of course, these displays, and the needs of the people who had lost someone during the two wars, provided great opportunities for charlatans to fake, mislead, and downright cheat. It was easy to fool people, to take advantage of grief, sorrow, and pain, and eventually a hunt began. Newsmen, journalists, and scientists began looking to prove that the spirit world didn't exist. And each time they uncovered a fraud, it strengthened their case. Of course, there were many scientists who became enlightened through their investigations, but these stories were rarely printed or recorded, although if you read a biography of Sir Arthur Conan Doyle, you will see many such references. In England, during the late forties to the mid-fifties, newspapers were filled with stories of fake mediums, which made the public fearful and unsure about which mediums to trust and which not to trust.

Not only was the public fooled, in many cases veteran spiritualists, people who had for many, many years been deeply involved with the spiritualist movement, were also fooled. How could that be? Surely you would think that such experts should know better, be able to tell. But this is not always the case. Human beings can be fooled, especially loving, gentle, caring human beings. None of us is infallible.

It was, if my memory serves me well, in the early eighties, when the entire Committee of the Spiritualist Association of Great Britain, the S.A.G.B., and many of its members, voted a young man "Medium of the Year." It is a very prestigious award, a great honor, and the young man in question was to receive this honor at a very fancy dinner, with hundreds attending, given at a high-profile hotel in the center of London. It was only a day or so prior to the ceremony that the young man in question had his name and face plastered on the front page of every major newspaper. A journalist, investigating, had inveigled an invitation to a closed séance, where it was said that the "medium of the year" was able to produce gifts, flowers, which he said came directly from the spirit world. The journalist, during the séance, discovered these so-called gifts hidden in the back of a large, portable radio cassette player that had been placed close to the medium's feet. Needless to say, the dinner, the ceremony, were canceled. The S.A.G.B., known and respected throughout the world, was fooled, badly fooled, by one of their own.

But that does not mean that physical mediums don't exist. Just because we find a few rotten apples in a barrel does not mean that all the apples are rotten. It does mean, however, that one might suppose the other apples are tainted. This is one reason why there are few displays of physical mediumship, as the very idea of interacting with the spirit world has become suspect. Another reason why there are few physical mediums these days is that physical mediumship can be dangerous. In the Western world, there are not too many physical mediums anymore who allow themselves to be used in this way, by the spirit world, especially as there are other ways to communicate which are just as good.

The use of ectoplasm, communication with the spirit world, using the trumpet or planchette, or simply sensing, seeing, hearing, beyond our common senses, requires energy, a certain kind of energy, an energy we all have, but so few of us know how to use. Our bodies, our mind, our spirit . . . all this is pure energy. Yes, it is possible for some people to build their level of energy to such a level of force that they can change their molecular structure to the point that the cell "changes," and the ectoplasm around the cell begins to flow out of the body. This ectoplasm can then be used by those in the spirit world to make the invisible become visible. A spirit form, unseen by most of us, can, by stepping into a mass of ectoplasm and becoming covered by it, be seen. Rather like the magician who holds up the invisible vase and throws a cover over it. The form of the vase will be seen.

Ectoplasm can be used in other ways, too. The spirit world can mold the mass into the shape of a trumpet and use it to direct sound from the spirit world into the room. And I could go on giving examples, but I know that many of you must already think that what I am saying sounds way too far-fetched. So I will give you just one more example. Not of ectoplasm, but of the fact that with the use of pure energy we can, and indeed have, seen the greatest and most deadly example of this fact, in the atom bomb. Einstein's theory of relativity has been supported by discoveries that matter can be transformed into energy, and likewise, cell structures can be, and have been, changed dramatically. No one can dispute this fact. And in understanding this, it is only a matter of taking the smallest step in understanding how powerful our own energy is.

We use it every day. Without knowing it, we affect our own lives and the lives of those around us by the use and often misuse of our energy. Each individual is a powerhouse, with his own energy field. In the same way as we use energy to heat and light our homes, our offices, our places of work, our own personal energy is powerful . . . too much or too little energy can cause disruption. It must be controlled and used wisely to yield us the best results.

For ourselves, for our own spiritual growth, we must first ask, then, what results we are looking for. If we are going to explore and use our energy, what are our reasons, and what would we like the end result to be?

It is not always possible to be specific, but generally, we know we want to become more sensitive, more knowledgeable, more caring about ourselves as well as others, and this is a good start. Most of us also know that we don't want to become physical mediums, we don't want to mess with our physical body, except to improve its balance to create a healthy structure. The exercises I suggest can only improve and enhance harmony within the spirit, mind, and body, give us strength, and show us our power.

Einstein explained all matter as a function of energy. His theory reflects the idea that matter, if it is vibrated at a high speed, can be broken up into energy. Therefore, solids must be energy that vibrates at a lower speed. Imagine, we who are matter, solid energy, placed in a container, the physical body, if we could discover how to speed up our energy force and actually change our molecular structure in the same way that physical mediums do. The possibilities are endless. We could change the structure of damaged cells, cancer cells, deformed cells. And in fact this is what healing is about—using energy, positive and powerful energy, to create a healthy person. If you want to know more about healing and other exercises, read my book and listen to my meditation tape *Give the Gift of Healing*. For now, let's try using energy in a different but just as beneficial way. First, we have to learn to discover our energy, and see how that feels; and we must do this gently and carefully, for our energy is powerful, so we must discover it a little at a time.

If we go back for a moment to the story I told at the beginning of this chapter about my sister Madeleine and me, it is important to remember that for some reason, unknown to me or anyone else it seems, I was born with a particularly acute psychic energy flow. We are all powerhouses, but it seems that for me, as a powerhouse, I have an extraordinarily high voltage, as do all gifted mediums or psychics. When my sister placed her hands in mine, it was like plugging into an unusually strong electrical force, which enabled us both to have the experience we did. This is highly unusual, and it is most unlikely that any of you, if you follow the exercises closely, will experience anything remotely similar. The exercises that follow are designed to lead you carefully and gently to a place where you will discover who you are, what you are, and what you can be. A highly tuned, sensitive, and perfectly balanced spiritual being.

So, again, each of us is a powerhouse, full of energy, which we can learn to build and to use in a beneficial and constructive way. Don't be afraid to explore, enjoy the experience of the following exercises, and be patient.

As a mother, I was amazed so many times when my daughter was a toddler by her resilience and determination to achieve. Her every new learning experience was a thrill for both of us, and my patience in helping her astounded me.

During the hours spent helping her to walk, to talk, to read and write, my patience seemed endless. But please, do not get the impression that I am a perfect mother, far from it. I was impatient about many things, and often found young motherhood a frustrating role. Inexperienced, with no one to ask, independent, yet wanting so badly to do everything right, I did many things wrong. But the things I enjoyed, the teaching-and-learning-together process, well, my patience sprang from my pleasure and from the joy I received in teaching my child.

As I seem constantly to be using the word "patience," I decided to go to the dictionary for a clear definition of the word.

"Patience: the quality of enduring with calmness; perseverance; forbearance."

A tall order. Staying calm, persevering, and forbearing. But without these qualities we will learn so much less. That we all know.

Patience, the quality of enduring with calmness. But how do we acquire this quality? There is only one way I suppose, and yes, you guessed it, with patience!

A mother teaching her child needs "patience."

A gardener tending his seedlings needs "patience."

A surgeon performing an operation needs "patience."

A baker waiting for his dough to rise needs "patience."

A student learning a lesson needs "patience."

Having patience with others, with our children, our friends, and family, can be easy, particularly if we are imparting knowledge and they are receptive. Acquiring patience for our own selves can be much more difficult, as the one person most of us are hardest on in our lives is ourselves. As you progress through the book, and your awareness of your own self grows, so will your patience with yourself grow. Just wait, be patient, and see for yourself.

As with all things, when our need is great enough, we find what it takes to satisfy that need. This second chapter can, if you persevere, bring you new and exciting discoveries of your own personal energy and will show you how to use that energy constructively, in a positive way, helping you fulfill your need to learn and grow spiritually.

LOOKING AT OUR
ENERGY CENTERS

First, we begin with the relaxation exercise, and only when we totally relax will we begin to recognize how much more there is to our earthly body than meets the eye. In the stillness we create through meditation, our senses become more acute, and the ordinary vibrations, pure energy, which run through our body, not only can be felt as never before, but can be used more creatively in a positive and constructive way.

We begin an awareness of our energy first by understanding that within the body we have seven main energy centers, known as chakras, and we also have many, many smaller energy points. The word "chakra" is a Hindu word that means spinning wheel, and we liken our energy centers to just this: tiny round areas within the body that, when used, will turn or spin like small wheels, opening and closing, pulling in and giving out energy.

In this chapter we will be attempting to develop the use of one of the main chakras, which is seated in the area of the solar plexus. Also, we will attempt to discover and to develop the use of two of the smaller energy points, which are seated within the palm centers.

Not only is the chakra, or energy center, seated close to the solar plexus, one of the seven main energy points of the body, it is also the one that is most commonly used and recognized by all of us, even though we may have been unaware of it or of its power.

When we are nervous or excited we often feel a churning or fluttering in the stomach. Sometimes a feeling of sickness or butterflies. If we are anxious we often take a deep breath or breathe in, pulling in our stomach, pulling in energy through our solar plexus, as this can and does help to relax us.

In this next exercise we are not only going to try to become more aware of the energy in this area of our body, I am going to show you how you can use this energy to enhance your lives.

EXERCISE 1 ...
THE SOLAR PLEXUS

We begin by creating a state of relaxation and meditation, using the techniques you learned in Chapter One. Take your time, go slowly, until you have achieved a feeling of inner calm and peace.

Now, placing your hand, right or left, palm down, on your stomach, over that sensitive area of the solar plexus, close your eyes and focus your mind, your energy, on the area around the solar plexus, and breathe in gently.

Each of us has an aura, an energy field that surrounds us. Each of us is filled with energy. What does it look like, this energy we all have, but do not seem able to see, what is its form or shape? Does it move or lie still? Is it large or small, dull or bright, positive or negative?

One of the easiest ways to visualize energy that we don't see is to give it shape, form, texture. A hard thing to do, since it's so abstract. So then, let us give it form, let us give it texture, let us visualize it as something concrete. A large steam cloud, colored blue, a soft baby blue. The steam cloud moves, changes shape, floats almost, as it surrounds our physical body. When touched by light, especially sunlight, it shimmers, glows, and other colors come into view. Greens, yellows, purples, like bubbles in sunlight, reflecting rainbows. Another way to visualize, a much easier way for many of us, is simply to choose a flower, a flower that grows from a bulb or tuber. Imagine that your body is the bulb, and your energy is the flower that springs from the bulb. Most people, when using this technique, find the daffodil the easiest flower to visualize, perhaps because it's natural to conceive of energy as light, sunlight. And there is very little that is more apt in our envisioning energy than the perfect bright and sunny image of the daffodil.

Those of you who wish your energy to be almost regal, strong and impressive, would find the gladiolus a perfect flower to use. It comes in many colors, so you won't feel restricted in your choice. A woodland bluebell could feel perfect for some, small but very strong, a wonderful rich color, and spreading itself like a magic carpet. If this is you, or who you would like to be, then try it out. And what about the crocus—again, so many different colors, usually growing in clusters, in a mass of vibrant color? One of my favorites is the hyacinth, its scented blooms and amazing colors bringing power and life to any dull place. Don't be hasty in your choice of flower, for what you choose will be your first indication of the type of soul you are.

As you try out the exercise, choosing your flower carefully, visualize the bulb, then yourself as the bulb, emitting all the glory and splendor and fragrance of the most perfect, energy-filled flower head. You are the host, your body is the host to the energy within you, which is so powerful, it flows out of your body, to surround you with light and color.

Allow yourself to "feel," to "sense" this mass of energy that surrounds you. At first visualize this energy as blue, even though your flower might be a different color.

Still with your eyes closed, again breathe in, slowly, gently, and as you breathe in, pull or draw your energy in through your solar plexus. Remember, this area contains one of the main chakras, like a small spinning wheel. Visualize this wheel turning, rotating slowly. And as it turns, visualize the wheel opening and then closing, drawing in your steam cloud or your flower head, pulling in the energy. The spinning wheel opens wider, like a vortex, all the while drawing in energy.

Now relax, breathe in again gently, drawing in the energy that surrounds you. "Feel" that energy as it courses its way through your body. Be a sponge, be aware of the sensation of energy as it travels up into your lungs. Mentally tune into your body, allow your energy to travel up again, across your shoulders, down into your arms, into your hands. "Feel" it reach your fingertips, stretch your fingers, then relax. Wait a few moments, then begin the process again.

Slowly and carefully, build up your skill in this exercise until you have reached a point where there is not one part of you—mind, body, and spirit—that has not been touched by this blue energy. The results should be that you feel full and warm and utterly contented.

You may find that this takes only a few days to achieve, or it could take you a few weeks. What is important to remember is that time is what you have most of, and that these exercises cannot be hurried.

After a while you will be aware of energy. You will feel it, you will sense its power, and you can use it constructively in several important ways. First, the energy we are building up is a perfect tool for self-healing, which is why I have suggested, for now anyway, that we use the color blue, since blue is the universal healing color.

The second way we can use energy beneficially involves thought. Our thoughts are everything, as you will see, and we can learn to be constructive with our energy by using our thought process, as each thought we have is a tiny pulse of energy. Collective thought equals more energy, a mass of energy, and every time we have a thought about someone, that thought, that tiny pulse of energy, goes out into the universe, and our energy travels to whichever place we send it. For example, if we are having thoughts of our children who are miles away from us, those thoughts, living energy, will speed through time and space, and in some conscious or unconscious way, our children will absorb the energy of those thoughts and will benefit from the living energy they have received. Many of you, I am sure, will have had the experience of suddenly thinking of someone, seemingly for no particular reason, and this can often be directly connected to the fact that they have been thinking of you.

What we think, and the way we think, is very important. If we send out good thoughts, good energy, then our energy will touch the person we are thinking of in a good way. However, the reverse is also true. I was recently talking to a cancer patient, a lovely woman friend of mine in her late forties who is in the process of treatment. Asking her how she was doing, she replied that she was doing great except for one thing. "It's my husband. I feel so angry with him. I want to shout at him all the time, I feel so angry."

"Why?" I asked her. "Why do you feel angry?"

"For all the mean things he's done to me over the years," she replied without hesitation.

I paused a moment, then said, "Don't you mean all the mean things you allowed him to do? Didn't you stay in the marriage? Didn't you put up with it, allow him to get away with it?" She looked at me a moment, then, "You're right," she said, "but I still can't stop being angry with him, having angry thoughts about him."

We had talked about this before, about my friend's marriage, and her feelings concerning her husband. I knew that despite everything, she loved him and she loved their life together, and becoming sick had only made her realize that more. My friend also knew how important it was for her health and well-being to have a positive and constructive attitude. Not to allow any more disruption and negativity into her life than was absolutely necessary.

"You wouldn't deliberately harm yourself, make your situation worse, would you?" I asked. Vehemently, she shook her head. Why, the very idea was alien to her way of thinking. "Of course not," she said, "I really do want to get well."

"Every time you have an angry thought, or a negative thought about your husband, that thought, that tiny pulse of energy goes out from you, goes right to him, and becomes, for a moment, absorbed by him. He is touched and affected by it, whether he knows it or not. The more angry thoughts you direct his way, the more negative energy he will receive, and the more harm you will do to him. However, because it is your energy, eventually that energy, that negative energy you have been producing, must return to you. That is the law of the universe. What is given out must return to its source. So, like the boomerang effect, all that negative energy will come bouncing back to you. But with much greater force, the energy building, growing, as it moves, rather like a snowball, which grows bigger and bigger as it rolls and gathers more snow. Consequently, unwittingly, you are damaging yourself, producing, sending out, then receiving back tremendous negative energy. Now," I then asked, "how do you think this will ultimately affect you physically?"

"Okay." She nodded, looking a little sheepish. "I've got you, and I'll stop. Right now."

Our thoughts, a major source of power and energy within our powerhouse, our physical body, need to be, to some extent, controlled. If we want our power to be creative, and if we want to advance our spiritual journey, then we must use our energy in the right way.

When we relax and begin to use the chakra point seated in the area of the solar plexus, we need to visualize our lungs, our hearts, our minds, our very being filled with the most powerful and beautiful blue energy. Breathing in gently through the solar plexus, and using our positive thoughts, let us visually create more energy. Think of good health, of well-being, of being whole, and also think of peace. Try using a mental picture of your vapor cloud or flower to visualize inner peace, tranquillity, and harmony. Use that wonderful blue healing energy. Use your thoughts to create a state of harmony within yourself, deep down. Discover and create inner peace.

As you work on this exercise, be gentle with yourself and

persevere, for it is truly worth working at, and you will learn so much from it if you take your time.

EXERCISE 2 . . .
PALM CENTERS

This is a fun exercise and can be done at any time and in almost any place. Its purpose is to show you the possibilities and uses of your own energy, your own power.

For this exercise you do not need to be relaxed or to meditate. Just find an easy chair and make yourself comfortable.

Aside from the seven main chakras, we have dozens of energy points, tiny pinpricks of light, which allow an uninterrupted flow of energy throughout the body. In the center of each palm lies one of these tiny energy points, similar to the seven main energy points, but much smaller. With practice, we can use these energy points to draw in external energy and to create more of our own energy.

First, though, we must find these energy points. With the middle finger of the right hand, trace a small circle within the palm center of the left hand. Do this slowly, and try to be aware of the sensations that you feel as you work. After a few minutes change hands and slowly repeat the process, tracing a small circle with the middle finger in the palm center of the right hand. You might feel a tingling or throbbing sensation deep inside the center of your palm, or possibly a slight itching sensation.

See if you can make yourself as sensitive as possible to the feelings and sensations you experience, as this will help you pinpoint the exact location of the energy centers in the palm of your hand.

Only when you "feel" that you have located, discovered your energy points, should you go to the next step, and this shouldn't take long. Once you are sure you feel your energy centers, place your hands, palms together, fingers straight, and slowly at first, then more quickly, rub your hands together. Keep rubbing, as hard and fast as you can, and at the same time focus your thoughts, your energy, toward your palm centers, trying as you work to be aware of these energy points.

When you feel you can't rub your hands together any longer or your arms will drop off, then stop and place your hands, palms facing upward, on your knees, and continue to concentrate on the palm centers. Your hands will tingle, your fingers will tingle with the heat and friction you created, but try to ignore everything but the sensations you feel within your palm centers.

Visualize that within the very center of your palm lies a small wheel. Feel it throbbing, turning, spinning, slowly at first and then more quickly. And as you did with your solar plexus, visualize the wheel opening and closing as it turns and spins, pulling in, opening out, opening wider. Like a vortex drawing in energy.

Now try again. Rub your hands together and repeat the exercise. Do this until you can really feel that throbbing, tingling, or itching sensation, and don't be eager to move on until you feel satisfied that you feel some pulse of energy within your hands that you were perhaps not aware of before.

Then begin again. Rub your hands together until you become aware of your energy points. Try to visualize the energy you are creating, perhaps in different colors. Blue, or pink, or maybe green, and if it helps, give it shape or form, just as we did in the last exercise. Visualize the perfect rose, or fragile tulip head. Or visualize a steam cloud, filled with the colors of the rainbow. Many people find it hard to visualize, but don't be despondent if you are one of them. Just keep on practicing until you can. Remember, nothing is impossible where the imagination is concerned. Even so, I remember a good friend of mine, a man who had been a practicing healer for more than thirty years, telling me that he had never once been able to visualize anything. But he could "feel," and he relied on and learned to trust his feelings. He was one of the best healers I ever knew.

Moving now to the next step. Rub your hands together for as long as you can, then instead of laying your hands on your knees, hold your hands about six inches apart, but keep your palms facing each other. Now slowly bring your palms together, then slowly pull them away until they are about six inches apart, now bring them slowly together ... then away ... then back together.

Work at this, first rubbing your hands together to create friction, then placing them six inches apart, palms facing. Pull your hands apart, then put them together, then apart, then together. Do this until you can feel an almost magnetic, pulling sensation between your hands. It will feel as if your palm centers are drawing your hands together. Continue until you can hold your hands at least twelve inches apart and still feel the magnetic energy or pulling sensations between your palm centers.

Practice this exercise every day, at least once a day, until the whole process feels natural and easy.

When asked about their first experiences with this exercise, here's what some of my students had to say. Their comments may be helpful to you.

JOAN MOULD: I first felt energy when we did the hand exercise in class. My palm centers tingled and throbbed. I felt pressure in the center of my palms, as though my thumbs were pressing a hole in them. I felt a mixture of wonder, fear, and dismay that I could feel this. The energy within my hands was like a handful of bread dough that I could stretch and contract. I was not sure if I was ready for this, and wondered why I was able to do it.

PETER BOULTON: It took several months before I was able to "feel" or "see" energy, but eventually I was able to feel it, as it was channeled through my palm centers. I could see blue spots on my fingertips. The more relaxed I became, the more I was able to play with my energy, mold it into various shapes. This was for me a wondrous experience. I felt excited that I was beginning to experience some of life's mysteries.

GEORGINA JACKSON: I first saw energy in one of Rosemary's classes. We all sat and watched as she created energy. The feelings in the room were almost tangible, such excitement and anticipation. I was surprised to see golden bubbles, like "think bubbles" in cartoons, which seemed to come from nowhere and moved toward Rosemary's head. The whole atmosphere was charged with love and light and joy. It made me feel good and left me wanting more.

When we created energy in class, using the hand exercises, it felt as if, in my palms, there was some sort of elastic, or magnet, which linked my hands together. My palms felt as if they were warm and throbbing. When I pulled my hands further apart I could feel a pulling sensation, and coolness. Describing it simply, it felt as if my hands were sucking a mint.

PAT MASON: The first time I felt energy, and knew for certain that I was experiencing something I had not experienced before, was in class, when we did the hand exercises. Having tried several times, rubbing my hands together to become aware of my palm centers, I was finally able to feel something of real substance. It seemed I was holding a "ball" of created energy between my hands. I had a slight sensation of "resistance" between my palms, similar to the resistance felt when magnets repel one another.

• • •

For me, the sensations of energy are somewhat different, less localized. I remember quite clearly on one particular occasion, in my very early days as a healer, and still very nervous and apprehensive about giving healing at all. I had gone to a meeting, not as a participant, merely as an observer. There was a group of healers, four altogether, and between them they had maybe twenty-five to thirty patients. Some new, some regular attendees. These healing sessions, held regularly twice a week, had been going on for about five years, organized and run, as most groups of this nature are, by unpaid volunteers. No advertising was necessary, it was simply word of mouth. Although I was there neither as a patient nor a healer, it was impossible for me to remain uninvolved. As each patient stepped forward for healing, I found myself asking questions of Grey Eagle. What was wrong with the patient? Was there a cure? Why had they chosen to have healing? I found myself asking these and many other questions over and over again. The answers I received varied, from patient to patient, except for one. Each time I asked my guide, "How can I help?," the answer remained steadfast. "How do you want to help?"

Those of you who know me, who have read my other books, will know that in the beginning I did not want to be a healer. I felt I wasn't a good enough person, that I wasn't strong enough, that there were others way more qualified than I. Grey Eagle, I knew, felt differently. I was learning to trust him, even when I did not necessarily trust myself. Now I was on the brink. It required only a few more small steps before I was to accept my role.

I was, indeed, a reluctant healer. Attending this meeting was one of those small steps. Still, as I watched patient after patient receive healing, I felt no desire to take any more steps that night. I was a watcher only, except in the prayers that I sent out. Until, that is, toward the end of the evening, when it was the turn of a woman who had been sitting close by me. I had not noticed her before, nor had I experienced any special feelings toward her before she stood up. But as I watched Mick, the healer, help her gently onto the bed, I leaned forward, wanting to get a better view. For no reason that I yet knew, my senses became more finely tuned, and as Mick began the healing session, my hands, my palms, began to throb so hard they ached. Then my head began to throb also, and I placed my hands, which now felt large and swollen, on my temples. Pain began to gather behind my eyes, like the beginnings of a migraine. Yet this, I knew, was not my pain, even though it felt real to me. I knew I was feeling the way Mick's patient was feeling.

Then, for the first time that night, Mick spoke directly to me. "I need your help, Rosemary," and, pointing to the woman on the bed, said, "She needs your help."

It was a brain tumor. Mick's patient had cancer and was going to die. That was Grey Eagle's answer to my first two questions. Why had she chosen to have healing? The answer Grey Eagle gave was that initially she had come looking for the miracle sought by many who are dying. After experiencing healing, she had continued to come because it gave her relief, it gave her comfort, it gave her hope. Not hope of a cure, but hope that there was more to life, and perhaps, therefore, more to dying than met the eye.

My last question, "How can I help?," was answered when I stood by her bed and placed my hands on either side of her head. She opened her eyes, looked up at me, and smiled. I smiled back, knowing that I had taken yet another small step toward my own growth.

You, too, are taking small steps, for as you attempt each exercise, you attempt growth. You grow when you attempt to discover more energy points, and you grow in trying to learn how to create energy and how to control it.

Let's take a small step further, and try now not only to be creative with our newfound energy, but to be constructive with it also.

EXERCISE 3...
VISUALIZING OUR ENERGY

Repeat Exercise 2, from the beginning, then place your hands, palms upward, on your knees. The energy points within your palm centers should be throbbing, pulsing, and your awareness of the energy you have created should be strong.

Now close your eyes, and once again try to visualize the color blue. Just as we did before, give it form, a shape, a flower, mold it into the shape of a flower, but this time, a blue flower.

Visualize your flower—a cornflower, a lily, a perfect blue rose—whatever you choose, and when you have this picture clear in your mind, visualize placing the flower in the palm of your hand.

Visualize the energy points within your palm centers, see them in your mind's eye, visualize them turning, spinning, and as they do, visualize your flower. It opens and closes, opening wide, closing into a tight bud, then opening again. Encourage the flower to take shape, to move. Visualize the color becoming more intensely blue, and watch as the flower finds life, movement, growth.

Be aware of your thoughts and feelings during this exercise, and take note of your awareness, your growing awareness of you, your own self, of your emotions, and your energy. Keep working on the exercises until you only have to look at your hand and you will see the perfect flower head.

The color blue is the universal healing color, and all spiritual healers to my knowledge use this color energy when they give healing, and understand that healing energy is often seen or felt as blue.

The power to heal, using our own energy, is not a new concept, and we are all able to do it, to a greater or lesser degree. When a child falls and hurts its knee, the child's mother automatically "rubs" it better. If we have a headache we will often "massage" the temples; we find it soothing, healing. These are natural actions . . . automatic actions, healing actions.

Visualizing energy in the form of a flower can give us a glimpse of the potential power of that healing energy, and is something that a healer will hopefully sense or see in the early stages of his or her training.

Experiencing being able to visualize or give energy shape does not make us healers. But if you want to be constructive with your newly discovered energy source, you can use it to aid your self. If you are feeling tired or depressed, anxious or tense, or if you are sick for any reason, then visualize your blue flower and let it give you pleasure. Absorb its beauty, let its healing qualities "heal" you.

This is one of the first exercises my students learn. They can look at their hands and discover untapped energy within them. This energy, combined with loving, healing thoughts (remember the power of thought?)—this energy, once we have learned how to control it, can be given out to others in a beneficial and constructive way or can be contained for one's own personal use. At least for a time.

If you would like to try to give your energy out, to use it in a healing way, it is important to remember to tell your patient you cannot promise that healing will work for them. Only God decides these things, and a healer is merely a channel, a conduit for God. As you practice, on a pet, an animal, or a relative or friend, remember to say a prayer, to ask for God's healing power, for His love and protection, before you begin. Then, first, create your energy, and, placing your hands on the subject, visualize the power and the purity of your energy. Sending out your small prayer to God and to the universe for help and guidance, give out your energy with loving and healing thoughts. Do this for about five to ten minutes. See if you can feel or sense a difference in the level or power of your energy. Try to sense whether your subject feels or senses anything.

Don't expect thunderclaps or lightning flashes, for healing is a gentle art, and in giving your energy in this way, your soul is absorbing all that loving and healing energy that you have created and is growing from it.

As you experiment with your energy, remember, you have not discovered or created anything that was not already there. You have merely tapped into and encouraged your natural energy to grow, and in the process, you have become much more self-aware.

Each time you try your exercises, write down your thoughts and feelings, being as expressive as you can. As you practice, I am sure many questions will arise in your mind. Follow the exercises slowly and carefully, and as you progress you will find that many of your questions will be answered as your knowledge expands, but as always with questions, especially those of a spiritual nature, the answers you get will only create a thousand more questions.

Some of your questions should be:

What do I feel?

How do I feel?

Am I learning?

What have I learned so far?

Only you will be able to answer, and only with time. *Be patient.* Don't be hard on yourself, the answers will come when you are ready to hear.

One of the most significant factors in your growing process is that you are beginning to question, to question what is happening to you.

Not only will you question points raised throughout the book, but you will also begin to question your own self. This is a good thing, and as you progress and learn, and become more "self-aware," you will come to understand that it is you who has the answers, you who has the ability to discover within yourself the answers to your most important questions.

• • •

I was on tour in Australia, lecturing in several cities, meeting many wonderful people, and of course it was a fabulous experience for me. At one lecture, in Adelaide, I remember meeting Chris. He had attended my lecture, then he and his friends had followed me to a bookshop where I was to sign books and generally say hello to those who had come to see me. It was to be a short visit, as I had been working all day and had to be up early the next morning to catch yet another plane. However, when we arrived, the bookstore was crammed with people, and I realized immediately that my plans of dinner and a reasonably early night were out of the question, and I knew immediately that I was going to need extra energy, more power.

One of my aims as a spiritual medium and healer is to give, to share with others, as much as I have to give. But remembering my limitations as a human being means`knowing when to stop, and knowing when to create more energy. This was a time for more power, and as always, I called out to God, to my guide, Grey Eagle, and to that universal God force. I had to "plug in," so to speak, to make sure I was truly "at home," that my door was wide open. Now it was my turn to connect with a power, an energy, which was more than I, as a mere human being, could muster on my own.

You might say I was zapped. Those of you who are hooked on caffeine might liken it to that first shot, or should I say cup, of coffee in the morning, but you would not even be close. My level of energy increased tenfold. I had the power to create more power, which I did.

My audience was warm and friendly, as were all of my Australian and New Zealand audiences, and after a brief introduction I began to give messages from the spirit world. My energy building, becoming more and more, it was wonderful to be a part of the process, seeing those in the spirit world as they were reunited with their loved ones here on this earth plane. Over and over I gave messages of love, of hope, some simple and straightforward, some more complex.

Eventually I came to Chris. He and his friends were delighted to be chosen, and explained how they had followed me from my lecture in the hopes of being given a message. But although Chris was eager, he was also apprehensive, wanting to hear from someone special, afraid that it might not happen. He needn't have worried. His lover had died of AIDS just a few months before, and as he came through from the spirit world and explained this to me, he told me, too, of Chris's love and devotion, of how, in his last few weeks, Chris had stayed by his bedside and tended to his every need.

Chris was overjoyed. To hear from his partner was more than he could have hoped for, but there was more to come. "He's moved," I heard my spirit communicator say next. "He's left the apartment we shared together and moved to a smaller one."

Chris, on hearing this, could only nod, stunned at this piece of information.

Then, "He's bought a new sofa. Got rid of the old one, and bought new chairs, too."

Chris was amazed. "But how . . . ?"

Before Chris could complete his question, his lover went on, almost confiding this next to me: "He took all the paintings down. They were my pride and joy, and he's stored them in the basement. I know he doesn't have room to hang them all, but could you ask him, Rosemary, if he'd mind hanging three or four, just for me, and for old time's sake?" Then, as he proceeded with his message, more to me than to his partner, he said, "But he's taken all my plants and moved them outside onto the veranda. Tell him I don't like them there, and would he kindly move them back inside!"

"Oh my God," exclaimed his partner as I relayed the last part of the message. "I knew he wouldn't like it, but I hate having them inside." My audience roared with laughter.

The message was so clear, so well understood by Chris and his friends, who were now all crying, as were many of my audience, and any doubts Chris may have had about life after death, in those few short minutes, evaporated.

It was at another lecture, again in Australia, that I met a young man whom we will call Neil.

I had given a demonstration of my skills as a spirit communicator, and was now taking questions from the audience, who were more than eager to participate.

Hands were up all around the hall and I went from questioner to questioner, answering as best I could, giving yet more messages from the spirit world. Finally I came to Neil, who was quite skeptical, yet curious.

"I'm not sure if I believe in any of this stuff," were his opening words, "but if it's true, how can someone be healed? You say you're a healer. How does it work?"

Although the question sounded general enough, my instincts told me otherwise. I felt Grey Eagle draw closer to me and I asked Neil if he would come up onto the stage with me.

He seemed to struggle for just a moment as he got up from his chair, and the audience murmured their sympathy as he walked proudly down the center aisle toward me, leaning on his crutch, a substitute for his left leg.

There were three steps up onto the stage, small and difficult to maneuver, but I did not attempt to get up and help him as he struggled to master them. Then he was up there with me. Tall and slim, in his mid-twenties, extremely handsome, a grin on his face, and only the glint in his eyes to give any clue as to the anger and bitterness and despair he felt. His life was over. He wanted to die, and God had placed him on the stage with me in order that I might help him.

I knew that I only had to wait. I would be shown the way.

"So, young man," I said as I pointed to the high stool, indicating that he should sit. "So you want to know about healing, do you?" Neil nodded, then said, "What I want to know is, if you had been around when my leg got crushed under my motorbike, and if you had given me healing, could you have saved my leg?" As he said this, his voice was touched with irony and there was no mistaking the bitterness he felt.

"Neil," I said gently, "I wasn't there at the scene of your accident. How could I possibly know if I could have helped?"

"Well, you're the healer," he replied, angry now, "so why don't you heal me?"

My audience gasped. This was a tragedy unfolding before their eyes. This was raw pain they were witnessing. What was I going to do, they wondered, what was I going to say?

"When you think of healing, of healers," I said, addressing Neil, but also addressing my audience, "many of you think only of physical healing. Taking away the cancer, repairing a damaged heart, giving back a limb that has been lost. And if the 'healer' can't do these things, then he or she is not truly a healer. You see only what is in front of your eyes. Only what is physical, what is material," I went on, now turning to Neil fully. "When I look at you, Neil, I see a handsome and proud young man with one leg and a crutch. But I see more, much more. I see a young man whose heart and mind are much more crippled than his body, whose soul is in torment, wishing he could die, not because he has only one leg, but because he is afraid. Afraid to live." As I said these last words, I reached out my hand and wiped away his tears. It was then I heard another voice, from the spirit world, and listening closely, I heard Neil's father.

"I died just a few months before my son's accident," he said. "It was sudden. There was no warning, my heart just gave out." I repeated the message, and Neil's father continued. "I have watched my son, seen and felt his torment. He's afraid of living his life. He feels useless, helpless. He misses me and wishes I was

74

there with him, he needs my strength. Rosemary, tell him I am with him and I will be his strength, but tell him that he is the one who holds the key. He is the one who has the power. He is the one who can unlock the door. He is a healer. Will one day work as a healer if he so wishes. First, though, he must learn to give healing to himself. Tell him his father did not die. Nor is it his turn to die. Tell him that it is his turn to live. And Rosemary," he added, "tell my son that this message is for Neil, from Neil, for Neil is my name, too."

My audience was in tears. Neil was also in tears, but as I held him, I knew that his healing had begun.

I asked for a volunteer, someone who was sick and in need of healing, and an older man came up onto the stage. "I have lung cancer," he said. "I'm not looking for a miracle cure, I know I'm dying, but I could do with a little help in the process."

I reached out and held him for a moment, then asked, "Would you mind if young Neil here gave you healing?"

The old man grinned. "I would love to be his first patient, hopefully the first of many."

I cocked my head to one side, looked at Neil, and asked, "Would you like to try?"

Neil tried to grin, but could only manage a watery smile. "Will you show me how?" he asked, and nodding, I replied, "Gladly."

Neil's father had said, "You are the one who holds the key. You are the one who has the power. You are the one who can unlock the door."

How right he was. Each of us has the choice. Each of us owns the power. Each of us chooses how to live our lives. And as I said earlier, when you become more self-aware, as these exercises will teach you to do, you will come to understand that each of us has the ability to discover within ourselves the answers to our most important questions.

Remember . . .

You are the one who holds the key.

You are the one who has the power.

You are the one who can unlock the door.

You are the one who has the power to lead yourself to the point of self-discovery.

Keep searching.

Know then thyself, presume not God to scan.
The proper study of mankind is man.

ALEXANDER POPE

CHAPTER 3

Getting to Know Who We Really Are

There were two little girls, sisters, just eighteen months apart. They lived in a house that was mostly an unhappy house, with parents who not only did not love each other, they had no idea how to show love to their offspring. There were two older sisters, and two brothers, much older, who didn't live with them and rarely visited.

The two little girls mostly played together, living in a world of pretend and make-believe, which helped them block out the sadness of the house.

Both believed in fairies, and would sometimes, before bedtime, gaze out of the window, which was partway up the stairs, to see if they could see any fairies playing around the fairy ring at the bottom of the garden. Sometimes they saw them; mostly, though, the fairies stayed hidden. Both loved to tell fairy stories and to listen to them, too. Both had dolls, and both liked to play with dolls, and they would sit on the bed, in the bedroom they shared, and would whisper and giggle, play dolls and house and let's pretend and cards and games.

When there were arguments between their parents, which was often, they were both afraid, the older one more than the younger, for they both knew that she was likely to bear the brunt of any problems. And when their father was mean to them, which was also often, they would whisper to each other all the things about him that they didn't like. And they would recount to each other all the promises he had made but hadn't kept. This helped them, somehow made them feel better. Always, when remembering their father's broken promises, reciting a long list, they would finish with the older sister pointing out to the younger, "And he never sewed that buckle on my shoe." The younger sister would always nod and say seriously, "I know, he never did."

The two little girls grew older. Their parents, their sisters and brothers, grew older, too. Nothing much changed, except that the parents became more miserable, disliking each other more, and of course, there were more things that the two little girls had to complain about to each other.

They grew older still. Sometimes the four sisters would gather together, and while reminiscing about their childhood, they would complain about their parents and the way they were treated. This was the one thing they all had in common, and in some strange way, it drew them together.

The older of the two little girls would always end any such conversations by reminding her younger sister, yet again, "And he never sewed that buckle on my shoe."

Fortunately, when she reached her thirties, although she never forgot her father's broken promises, it stopped being important anymore. In fact, she had begun to see the funny side of the situation. The truth was, she couldn't even remember those shoes, had forgotten what they looked like years ago. So had her sister.

So why had it been such a source of complaint? I look back to the time of my childhood. To those two little girls, my sister and me. She the younger. I the elder. I remember how we would sit together in those times of distress, put our heads together, and like two old grannies, bemoan our lot in life. What we were actually doing, I realize, having thought about this for some time, what we were in fact doing was sharing.

In those times of need, when we had felt the most vulnerable, the most unloved, drawing close to each other in our common hurt, our mutual feelings of rejection, we had clung to each other and embraced each other's emotions and hurt feelings. This was why we had felt comforted.

As we grew older, and with our other siblings, we did the same thing. We shared our common hurt, our mutual feelings of having each been rejected in some way by our parents. We complained, which in real terms means we expressed our dismay, our hurt.

Looking back, that old shoe buckle was the medium through which my sister and I were able to unite and express, knowing we would each accept and understand the feelings of the other.

There are the complainers of the world, those who like to moan, it might seem, for no other reason than that they enjoy it, revel in it, or that their moaning has simply become a habit. It is a very sad and lonely individual who seems to moan for moaning's sake, as what usually happens is that those around just stop listening. After all, they've heard it all before. The moaner then has more to complain about. "No one listens to me, no one loves me, no one cares," etc. The moaning becomes an even more deeply entrenched habit, a habit that can be extremely hard to break.

Most of us, though, only complain sometimes, even though our spouses or our children may perhaps disagree. Most of us only complain, or I should rather say, share our distressed feelings, when we are truly distressed.

Recently my boyfriend, Jim, and I were with friends, spending the weekend, having fun. They are a nice couple, and individually are nice people, but their marriage has had its problems, as all relationships do, and so there are times when these nice people can behave in a really not nice way to each other, and will often disregard, deliberately, each other's feelings.

We were in their car. The husband driving, with Jim up front; the wife and I in the back. The car was new, and the husband was showing off its potential. Jim was impressed. She and I were not. Racing around corners, showing how well the car held the road, speeding down country lanes, braking, then accelerating, and so on. This, I must say, is not my idea of a good time. Aside from the danger, both to ourselves and to others on the road, I never was one for fun at the fairgrounds, and the thought of riding the Ferris wheel makes me feel sick. My friend in the back with me obviously felt the same way, and after about ten minutes she asked her husband to slow down and drive more steadily. "You know I hate speeding," she said. "It really is giving me a headache. Please don't do it."

The request was put more than reasonably, but was not acknowledged. In fact, it seemed to be his signal for behaving like a real idiot, as his foot came down hard on the accelerator, and off we went again, whizzing around corners, almost on two wheels. We women gasped. The men grinned. She grabbed the back of his seat, her face pale, and I thought she was going to vomit. "Please, I've asked you once, don't do this. You know it scares me to death."

Her voice on edge, close to tears, I thought he must take notice.

"Just stop bitching and moaning," he replied. "We're almost home now anyway," and with that, he gave another jerk on the wheel. That put her over the top, and she beat her fists on the back of his seat and screamed at him to stop it. It made no difference, he refused to hear.

They had been battling through this scenario for fifteen years, I discovered when speaking to my friend about it later. She, afraid of fast and fancy cars, he buying them, driving fast, and completely ignoring her feelings.

Was she bitching and moaning?

It certainly seemed like it to him, because, boy, he had been hearing the same old complaints for more than fifteen years. But I believe she was just desperately trying to share her dismay. To express her feelings, in the hope that one day he might accept and understand that her feelings actually mattered. Even if he couldn't understand why she was afraid, she lived with the hope that it might matter to him enough one day for him to respect and love her, and act accordingly.

When does a simple act of sharing dismay and distress, become bitching and moaning? Perhaps the old adage "familiarity breeds contempt" is an apt phrase here. We become too familiar with someone complaining about the same things, and we shut off, become irritated, and instead of addressing problems, we ignore them. And in doing so, we become disrespectful.

When one person deliberately ignores or disregards the feelings and emotions of another, a thousand reasons do not make one good excuse. This is what I told my friends later that day. This is what I said to the husband. This is what I say to you the reader. This is also what I say to myself. For we have all been guilty of abusive behavior like this at one time or another.

Living your life, as I did as a child, being abused—and make no mistake, verbal and emotional abuse is just as bad as physical abuse—living this way, having to take abuse or choosing to take abuse, whichever it is, is debilitating. It takes away, lessens your power, you feel powerless in its grasp. The abuser wins, is powerful, holds power over you, and becomes the controlling force in the relationship. The truth is that all abusers, without exception, try to take control of others because their own lives are out of control. Insecure, lacking a sense of self-worth and self-esteem, they feel inadequate, powerless, and afraid. Stripping someone else of power boosts them, makes them feel more important, more powerful and in control, but only for a time.

Here is a story about a woman so out of control, so afraid

of her loss of power over her husband, so dominant, abusive, and feeling desperately inadequate, that she steps over the bounds of sane and caring emotion, and into the realms of darkness and evil.

STRANGER THAN FICTION

This story is absolutely true, and shows us again the power of the mind and how it can bring harm when used wrongly. The effects can be devastating, as you will see.

It has been more than twelve years, way back in the mid-eighties, when I was asked to get involved. Two women, both fairly elderly, came to see me. They didn't want a consultation, they said, nor did they want healing. A problem had arisen, a serious problem, but it was about someone else they wished to see me. They didn't know where else to turn. So now here we were, the three of us, in my small study in the little village of Scawby, in the north of England. They were friends, and one had merely come to hold the hand of the other, I discovered quite quickly, and they were both dreadfully upset. I could see that instantly.

"Let's start with a cup of tea," I said, hoping to put them at ease, "then you can tell me all about your problem."

As I poured the tea, Elsie, the one with the problem, began. "It's my son," she blurted out, and with that she grabbed a tissue from the table and started to cry. "I don't know what to do," she sobbed. "It's all so strange. If only you could help, and oh, if only my Arthur were here, he'd know, he'd have sorted it out long ago."

Well, none of you will be surprised when I tell you that Arthur was there, in my study, I mean, standing next to Grey Eagle, and

I was hoping that one or the other of them might move this along, and enlighten me a little. But Grey Eagle, ever-patient, assured me that all would be revealed in good time.

"He was acting so strange, you see. For over three years now this has been going on. We have always been such a close family, and then one day, out of the blue, he stopped speaking to us, even to his sister, and he's always adored her. Then, when he came back to England, we had numerous phone calls from his friends, he was always an outgoing, friendly lad. Anyway"—she paused for breath—"he wouldn't even go out with his friends, any of them. He just cut us all out of his life. Wouldn't even let us see the girls, his two girls. Only young they are, six and eight," and at this, she began again to cry.

I took her hands in mine and tried to sum up the situation. "You haven't seen or spoken to your son in three years, Elsie, or the children, is that what you're saying?"

Blotting her eyes with a new tissue, Elsie nodded. "What about your son's wife, Elsie, have you spoken to her, what does she say?"

"It's her that's done it, Rosemary, she's the one, and that's why I'm here," replied Elsie, taking a deep breath and blowing her nose.

Now this was beginning to sound like an all-too-familiar story, which unfortunately I come across often. Mother fights with daughter-in-law. Jealousy over son/husband, you know the kind of thing . . . "He was my son before he was your husband," or "Well, he's my husband now, so you're just going to have to put up with it," etc., etc. I have seen so many families pulled apart because two women can't accept each other. Was this simply another of those cases? I asked Grey Eagle. Immediately I was told that yes, in a way it was, but that she, the daughter-in-law, had taken things beyond the realm of decent behavior and into the realm of darkness.

Elsie began speaking again. "I would never have known or

understood what happened to my son Robert if a close friend of theirs, him and his wife, hadn't come to see me a few days ago. They all met while my Robert was in Africa. He lived there for several years, and is a big-shot engineer in something or other. He and his wife moved out there when they were first married, and the children were born out there. But they always came home two or three times a year to stay with us, until three years ago, that is, and we were always close. He'd call three or four times a week, especially after his dad died. Then everything just stopped. It was as if my son had died, and the grandchildren, too."

She went on, not crying now, trying to stay calm so she could make herself understood. "When they left Africa and came home, naturally I went with his sister to see him. I thought at first they weren't going to let us in the door, but they did. My Robert was always smiling, always a twinkle in his eye, and ready for fun, just like his dad. But I hardly recognized my son, Rosemary. He was thin and quiet, ill-looking, and something about his eyes." With this, poor Elsie could not help but burst into tears again, and she almost wailed as she said, "He looked dead, Rosemary, like the walking dead, and he hardly spoke a word. And *her*"—these words Elsie spat out with anger—"she just pushed us out the door."

Elsie paused again. Understanding that she had to tell this story in her own way, I sat back in my chair and waited.

"It was a few days ago, I had a visit from a woman I hadn't met before. She knew Robert and his wife from Africa, where she also lived with her husband. Ann, her name is. Well, Ann and Lena, Robert's wife, became good friends. That's how Ann knew what Lena had done. Apparently Robert and Lena were going through a bad patch in their marriage, and Robert told Lena that he wanted a divorce. He also wanted to return to England. Robert said he missed his family and friends here, and England was home. That was the last thing Lena wanted. Out there she could play the lady, be somebody, she felt, somebody she couldn't be here, and she knew that if she was not married to Robert, it would be impossible for her to stay in Africa by herself. Well, Rosemary, that's when she did it. That's when she did this terrible thing."

Grey Eagle drew close. "Listen to her carefully now, Rosemary," he said. "What she will say sounds ridiculous, but it is the truth, although Elsie does not fully understand it."

Elsie went on; her hands, I noticed, were trembling, and I'm sure she was afraid I would not believe her.

"She went to see a witch doctor." There, it was out, and Elsie stared into my eyes, wondering if I believed, wondering if she even believed it herself. "She took our Robert's photograph, and asked this witch doctor to put some kind of a spell on my son. Did you ever hear anything like it?" she asked, her head nodding, emphasizing her words. "Well, did you ever? And it worked. That's not my son, my Robert, not who I saw, and when this Ann, this friend of theirs, told me this, I knew for certain that it was true. Something, some power, some strange, evil, ungodly power, has taken over my son's mind. And that Lena, his wife, she did it, oh yes, she did it all right, I know she did." As Elsie began to cry again, her friend comforted her and they both looked at me.

"You've got to help us, please. We've heard so much about you, we know you can help."

I looked to where Arthur, Elsie's husband, stood, with Grey Eagle. He was simply nodding his head in agreement. I looked then to my guide, and it was there I found my answers, and knew that we could indeed help.

"All right, Elsie," I said, "I think we can help," and at this the two women let out cries of relief. "I need a photograph of your son, and I need your help, too." I smiled. "I am going to ask my team to help, which is why I want a picture of Robert. It will give them a mental image. They will be able to picture Robert in their minds when they ask God to send healing to him. As they pray for him—and they will pray only for God's will to be done, not theirs, not ours—as they pray, they will keep the image of your son in their mind. It will help make their prayers stronger," I said, reaching forward and holding Elsie's hands. "I will do the same. I will pray, with all of my heart, that Robert be healed, that if some power other than the power of God is oppressing Robert, then if it is God's will, I will pray that that power be removed. You, Elsie," I went on, "you must do the same, and each week, once a week, you must call me and give me a progress report. And don't worry, Elsie, your Arthur is here, has been from the moment you walked in." I laughed. "He's going to help us, too, you know he will."

"I knew it, I knew it," said Elsie, turning to her friend. "It was him, Rosemary, I'm sure, who sent me to you."

It took several months before Robert showed any real signs of recovery, and although Elsie would have wished for the instant miracle, even so, her faith never wavered. Then one day, about six months after our prayers began, I got a phone call that told me the tide was turning. "He came to visit, brought the girls, too, and Rosemary, he stayed for tea. He stayed for tea."

Eighteen months later Robert divorced Lena, getting joint custody of their children. It was two years later that Elsie called to tell me he had met "a wonderful girl." All the family liked her, and eventually they were married. A happy ending? Well, certainly good triumphed over evil; Robert was free of mind control. But was his wife Lena an evil person? I doubt it. I think perhaps she was just desperate, out of control, powerless, or so she thought, and was trying everything and anything to save her marriage. But she wanted to do things her way, at whatever cost.

The cost to Robert and his mother was great. Robert's life was taken out of his hands, controlled by dark forces. Imagine what it must be like. Your senses become dulled, the capacity to think, to feel, becomes numbed. You become a zombie, a puppet, with someone else pulling the strings. But what of the cost, the consequences to Lena? Was there a cost to her?

Remember the laws of the universe? Remember, in *Proud Spirit*, how we discovered the laws, the rules, the truths of the universe? What was that one universal law? Yes, this was it. What is given out must be taken back, must return to its source! Whatever thoughts, whatever kind of energy—misguided, unruly, or plain evil—that energy goes out and affects the person or persons it is directed toward. Then, like a boomerang, that energy, gathering momentum, gathering force, comes back and hits hard, harder at you, you who sent it out, than any who have received it. If the energy you send out is pure and good, then when it comes back to you, hits you hard, it will bring light, enlightenment, positive and pure growth, it will bring you God power. If, however, the energy you send out is selfish, self-centered, mean, or plain bad, then when it returns it will bring with it darkness, misery, destruction. And for those who have thought evil, then evil will return to you, but tenfold, and the soul will forever be in struggle, unable to see anything but the blackest black. Always powerless. Always without power.

The simple truth is that before we can become effective with others, we have to learn control of ourselves, of our own emotions and feelings. I don't mean that we should keep our feelings *under* control. That's no good, as we merely suppress who and what we are. We have to learn the best and the worst of who we are, learn to nurture the best and conquer the worst. And the place to begin is with ourselves, and then with our families and friends, who love and care about us.

• • •

Now here is one more brief story, to illustrate how mind power can and does work. Unlike the last, however, this story is mine. It happened to me.

One Monday evening, I had gone with friends to the theater, and was truly looking forward to the play, a farce. I had been told it was very funny. Good, just what I needed. We were only about ten minutes into it, however, when simultaneously I both saw Grey Eagle, and heard a voice, not his, whisper in my ear the name Michael. The only Michael I really knew was an old boyfriend. I hadn't seen him in quite some time, although a mutual friend had told me recently that Michael's mother was dying of cancer. I had left him a message on his answering machine that if I could help I would, but Michael had not returned my call, and I had forgotten all about it. Then I heard the voice again, again whispering the name of Michael, and I looked to Grey Eagle, who confirmed that it was the boyfriend, and yes, he was in trouble.

Well, I thought, there really wasn't much I could do right now, so I tried to shrug off the feeling that I should do something and went back to the play. It was impossible, however, because throughout the evening my thoughts would wander back to Michael, and each time I thought of him, my feelings about him being in trouble became stronger and stronger. He needed me, he needed my help.

I went to bed that night, and placing my head on the pillow, I asked God and Grey Eagle what I could do. "Just call his name," said my guide. "Let him know that you are there for him. His mother has died, and he has been thinking of you. In his despair he has great need of you."

So I did as Grey Eagle suggested. Closing my eyes, I thought of Michael, and silently, loudly, called out his name. "Michael, Michael, Michael."

At first it was a tiny pinprick, growing slowly bigger as I watched. It was difficult to make out, an orb, a circle, what . . . what was it? Coming close, then closer, and *whoosh*, as it sped past me, so fast at the end I almost didn't see, but seeing clearly nonetheless that it was Michael. It was Michael's face.

The next morning I told a friend what had happened, and for a time we both talked of what or why or how. Then we let it go, and I didn't give it another thought. That was on a Tuesday. On Friday evening, during a class, my phone rang. One of my students answered, looked at me, and said, "It's Michael." I took the call in my study, away from everyone else, and picking up the receiver, said, "Hello, who is this?"

"You know who it is," said Michael. "I heard you calling me, and thought you must have heard me calling you, too. My mother died last Monday afternoon. I was desperate, felt miserable, lonely, and I felt I had no one to turn to. All I could think was, 'Talk to Rosemary,' and once I had you in my head I couldn't let go." As he spoke I could hear his emotion. "I went to bed," he continued, "and I began to cry out your name. For a while the only sound I could hear was the sound of my own voice, then, clearly, I heard you. You called my name, 'Michael, Michael, Michael,' and I felt your presence in the room, and knew that you had heard me and that you were sending me a message. You were telling me that everything was okay."

• • •

How did it happen? Well, the power of the mind is our strongest possession. We just have to learn how to use it. But before we can do that, we have to accept that we do indeed own that power.

As I write this, I am reminded again of the teachings of the Native American grandfathers, who say, "There are enemies all around, outside, beyond our circle of tepees, so within your own village, where you are among friends, walk softly and speak gently." So hard to do, so worthwhile in the doing.

• • •

We began this chapter with a quote from Alexander Pope, "Know then thyself, presume not God to scan. The proper study of mankind is man."

This is partly what this book is about, getting to know and learning to understand ourselves. And in order to do that we must study ourselves, in an honest but gentle way. Not harshly; rather, lovingly and with fondness, for we are preparing the road ahead.

Few of us can see more than a mile or so, though many of us like to plan at least the first hundred miles. It makes us feel comfortable, in control, although we know that the only one who has any real control of our destiny is God. I read somewhere recently that when man talks of tomorrow, the gods look down and laugh. But we do have some say, otherwise we would be no more than puppets on a string. The say we have, the control we have, and I deeply believe this is true, is in developing the right attitude, being positive and forward thinking, creating the right kind of energy, thereby developing an awareness, a sensitivity, to ourselves, our family and friends, then, on a broader scale, to the world around us, and to the universe of which we are a part.

The stories I am about to tell involve an exercise that we can all do, either on our own or with friends, friends with whom you might be sharing this book.

The three chairs is an exercise in attitude. It shows us that there are more ways of looking at a situation than we might think. It teaches us to "try on" another way of seeing things, to look deeper, and to find, to search for, what is positive.

THE THREE CHAIRS

Already it sounds like a nursery rhyme or a fairy tale, and I considered even writing this chapter as if it were exactly that. This is an exercise I have tried many times, always with the desired results. "What are the desired results?" I hear you ask, and I smile and answer, "Don't you know?"

I especially like to do this with children, for usually children have no guile, are remarkably honest, have great imaginations, and know how to tell a good story. I hope I'm not putting you off.

My intention here is that we have fun, that we laugh, even though we might cry a little, but more, that we might learn. Before we begin, however, I must be honest and tell you that we already have confusion, for you see, even though the section title is "The Three Chairs," there is really only one.

My class was ready, eager to learn and listening carefully as I began to speak. There were about twenty of us this night, some veterans, some beginners. Brian had been my student for about a year, so he was still a novice. Having gone through a very serious illness, he had first come to us as a patient, like so many others, and had then decided after his recovery that he would like to learn to become a healer.

Now in his early sixties, Brian had experienced life in the raw. His family came from humble beginnings, and he himself as a boy worked as a farmhand, then a roadworker, digging ditches, sometimes, he had told me, chest-high in mud and freezing water. He married, had several children, worked hard, and he and his wife managed to save enough to eventually buy their own house. He was always smiling, even though life had been tough for him, and I knew that behind that contented exterior, this man had some stories to tell. I would begin, I decided, with him.

Sitting straight in my chair, aware of everyone's full attention now, I said, "Tonight each of you is going to tell me a story, and Brian"—I paused and looked directly at him—"I think we will begin with you. I want you to tell me a story, but first I want you to imagine that you are sitting in the 'sad chair,' which means that the story you must tell has to be the saddest story you can think of. As you sit in the sad chair, you must tell me a story that is so sorrowful that it might move me to tears. In the telling of this story," I added, "you must remember two things. The first, your story must be a true story. The second, it must be about you."

Brian, who had had little, if indeed any, formal education, always afraid that he would sound inarticulate, began to shake his head despairingly, sure that he would fail, and asked me how he could possibly begin. I smiled at him gently and suggested that he might try to think back on his life to a time of great pain and despair, and as I said this, he nodded, already knowing his story, for it was the one deepest in his heart. So deep, the pain had never gone away. He had never spoken of it to anyone before, not even his wife, for it had always been too hurtful a memory.

"When I was a young boy," he began a little shakily, "six years old, I became sick, and the doctors diagnosed tuberculosis, which in those days everyone believed was contagious. So I was sent away, into an asylum, a place that was miles from home. My parents were poor and could not afford to visit, except once a year, and I was there for two years. I had no books, no games, no pencils or paper. Each day I would sit and stare out of the window and hope someone would come and take me home." As he said this, tears began to trickle down his face as his memories, so many years buried, began to surface, and some of his fellow students also began to cry with him, seeing him struggle. He went on, telling us awful tales of how the other boys there, all older, how mean they often were to him because he was so small and pale and sickly. The saddest part of Brian's story, as he sat in the sad chair, was his account of bedtime, of how scared and lonely he was, and how he thought his parents had put him in the asylum for good, that he would be there forever.

It was a very moving story, a fitting one for the chair he was in, and it was several minutes after the telling before Brian was able to stop crying.

Now he thought he was done, that it was someone else's turn to tell their story, but he was in for a shock, because again I brought his attention to me as I asked, "Brian, I would like you now to tell me a story." His surprise showed plainly, and I laughed and said, "Don't worry, not another sad one. This time," I said, my eyes twinkling, "I want you to imagine that you are sitting in the 'happy chair.' This means that the story you tell must be the happiest, funniest story you can possibly tell. In fact, I would like it if you could make the story so funny I might cry with laughter." He looked at me dubiously, but I nodded my encouragement, adding, "Of course, Brian, you must remember two things. The first, that the story is a true story. The second"— and here I paused to give emphasis to my words—"the story must be the same story you just told me when you were sitting in the sad chair."

Without exception, all of my students were startled. "But how can it be?" asked Brian. "How am I supposed to do that?"

"Well," I said, "look back at that time. Think hard. There must have been some bright times, maybe some funny moments in the two years you were there. I can't believe you didn't get up to some mischief." And Brian, as he heard me say this, began to smile.

The telling of this story was hard, as, like most of us, he found it easier to remember the sad things, especially if the brighter moments are rare. But as I reminded Brian, he was now sitting in the happy chair, and in the happy chair there is no room for sorrow, only for sunshine. The story was a happy one, for Brian remembered that the older boys were not always mean to him, and that together they got up to many high jinks. Mealtimes were also often fun, and pretty soon Brian was recounting tales of the asylum that made us smile. I was proud of him; I knew he could do it, I knew he had it in him to search out the glimmer of light, even in what seemed to him to be his dark prison cell.

Now for the third chair. You remember, don't you, that there are indeed three chairs. And this, the last, could be the most difficult chair of all.

My class, understanding there was more, waited, their senses tuned to my words, my teaching. I looked to Brian. "I would like you, please, to tell me a story, and yes, you know that it must be the same story that you told in the sad chair, and in the happy chair, and yes, Brian, you know that this story must be a truthful one. But as you tell this story, I would like you to imagine that you are sitting in perhaps the most important and rewarding chair of all, the 'inspirational chair.' Tell me your story and inspire me. Make me know and feel how inspired you have become by your experience. Let me see how much you have learned in the telling of your story. Help me to see what, if anything, you have discovered about yourself in the last fifteen minutes. Be inspired by your own discovered wisdom, and allow me to be inspired, too."

And so, for the third and final time Brian told his story. He told of the lost little boy that he had been. In remembering his pain, he was also reminded of his joy when his parents had visited. Remembering these things, he realized how his experience in the asylum had made him strong, more determined in his marriage, more protective as a father. For he had grown up, truly understanding how a child could hurt. In telling his story, he also realized how this early experience had colored his thinking in many ways. He began for the first time in his life to understand why he was so stubborn sometimes, why often he had found it difficult to express his emotions. He had been afraid of hurt, and of being hurt, and of being rejected. As he talked, he became more and more inspired by his own feelings, feelings he had not allowed himself to have for so long. He laughed, he cried and laughed some more, and as he talked, each one of us became inspired by his courage, by his honesty and sincerity. And by his true humility. It was perhaps two years later that Brian received his certificate and became a full healer member of the R.A.A.H. We value him greatly.

• • •

My next story is about Tyler, a boy of fourteen who, in my opinion, began his progress into manhood as he worked with me on these exercises. Having no idea really what I was going to ask of him, Tyler thought it might just be fun to be one of the characters in my book. This was his main motivation. "Cool," he had said, when his mother asked if he would help.

Unprepared but open, Tyler was at first a little taken aback when I suggested he might imagine himself sitting in the sad chair. "Think of a sad time or a difficult time in your life," I said, "and tell me about it. Tell me a story which is so sad I might feel like crying."

He looked at his mom, who was sitting in with us, and bemused, he said he really couldn't think of a thing.

"Well," I suggested, "have you ever lost a pet, or did anything awful ever happen at school?"

Again he looked at his mom, and they had a bit of a whispering session. A couple of times I heard him say, "Oh no, I couldn't tell her that."

I waited, hoping, knowing, that something would come.

He sat back down in his chair, took a deep breath, then, "Okay, I'm ready," and as he began to speak I was reminded of a quote from Napoleon I. "Two-o'clock-in-the-morning courage: I mean unprepared courage!"

"I was caught cheating in school, last week." He lowered his head a little as he spoke the words, and I watched him as he peered from half-closed lids, looking for my reaction.

Admitting you're a cheat is hard for anyone. Harder still when you're admitting it to someone whose opinion of you matters.

I kept my face expressionless, just nodded, and asked if he would like to tell me about it.

"Remember, you're in the sad chair, so you can only tell the story if it made you feel miserable."

"It was awful," Tyler replied. "I don't know what came over me. There was another boy sitting next to me, and I could see his paper very clearly. We were in a test. When I looked over I noticed that his answers were different from mine. So I scribbled out what I had just written and copied from him. He didn't know, though, I just kept sneaking a look."

"How did the teacher find out?" I asked. Tyler replied, "She saw me, and boy, was she yelling. She just stood there and really yelled at me. And she asked me why. At first I made excuses. I really cared about being found out, about everyone knowing."

"So how did it make you feel?" I asked.

"At first I felt embarrassed, ashamed. All the other kids in class were there, which made me feel really small, stupid. Then, later, I felt even more stupid and angry with myself. When I went home I had to tell my mom. That made me feel bad. I knew I had disappointed her."

He was finished. This was a big deal, and Tyler felt that by telling me, he might lose my respect.

My only reaction was to comment on how tough it must have been to know that the whole school knew he was a cheat.

"Yes," he said, fidgeting a little in his chair, "and word got out fast, that was for sure."

"Okay, Tyler." It was time to move on. "Now," I said, "I'd like you to sit in the happy chair. Imagine you are sitting in a chair which helps you to see the happy, even funny side of things. Tell me your story again, but this time, see if you can make me smile."

Tyler frowned, puzzled a little at my request, but willing to play the game, and with enthusiasm, for this was his opportunity to lighten the situation, he began.

"Well," he said, this time with a twinkle in his eye, "you know I told you how quickly word spread, all the kids in school wanted to know the story. None of them were interested in their own test results. They only wanted to hear more about mine. Then I got to thinking about the other times I had cheated and never got caught. That made me feel pretty good there for a while, for a little while anyway."

Again I merely nodded, smiling a little; knowing it was time to move on, I now suggested that Tyler might imagine himself sitting in the inspirational chair. "What, if anything, have you learned from this experience?" I asked. "See if you can inspire me. Tell me the same story, but this time give me, if you can, a little insight into how the experience of being caught at cheating may have affected you."

Now I heard the man. "I never want to cheat again," said Tyler immediately, "and I hope I never will. Not just because getting caught is a major embarrassment, but because I don't want to live my life as a cheat. I'm not perfect, and I don't want to be, but there is a lot about me that is nice, and I want to know if I'm capable, on my own merits, of succeeding.

"I don't like it when other people cheat from me, especially when I've worked hard. I realize it wasn't fair of me to cheat from someone else. Anyway, I want it to be *my* grade, to know *I* did it.

"I told my teacher I was sorry for doing it, and sorry for embarrassing her, too. She said she hadn't expected my bad behavior. When she told me this, I realized that I hadn't expected it either. I was disappointed in myself.

"When it happened, I felt miserable and ashamed. I also felt very lonely. I don't want to live my life feeling lonely like that again. Everything I do, I want to know I did it myself. And that I was honest.

"I don't want to disappoint my mom or my dad or my brother or my friends. But mostly, I don't ever again want to disappoint me!"

I kept my face expressionless, nodded, and thanked him for his cooperation, and for sharing his story with me.

I was the teacher, teaching the student, who was teaching me. A lesson learned long ago, yet I felt value in its reminder, and I felt inspired by the storyteller.

To Tyler, my thanks.

• • •

From the woman whose fear drove her to extreme measures to control, to Brian and his story of the asylum. The story of my young friend Tyler, and the story of my friends and their behavior toward each other in the car. Then my own story, a childhood hurt, the reactions of both myself and my sister. I decided to tell these stories because they are great examples of how much we can learn when we are encouraged to look within, to rummage around in the conscious and unconscious mind. Many people consider an explorer to be that person who climbs the tallest mountain or the person who flies to the moon. Columbus is one of the world's great explorers, discovering lands and people once foreign to us all. Great men and women who found the pyramids of Egypt, the rain forests of Africa, and so on, and so on.

Reading this book, each of us can become an explorer, but like Columbus, we have to dare, for without daring, we would passively watch the world go by, and be left to wonder, as we grew older, what was life all about?

Without our explorers, we would not know the world as it is today. Some of you may think that that might not be a bad thing. But I believe that even with all the negatives in the world, I am glad that we have had, over the centuries, those many daring individuals who, with courage and determination, strong in spirit, went forth to bring us our world and all the knowledge that comes with it, for our world is a beautiful and wonderful creation of God, and of the universe of which we are a part.

In relation to this planet of ours, some would say that the individual is an insignificant speck. Certainly in relation to the universe it would seem that this is so.

In *The Eagle and the Rose*, when writing about the great men and women of our world, I made a comment, an observation born of much experience, an observation I still believe.

"It can take but one man, one voice, to rock the world."

As insignificant as we human beings may seem to be, we are truly a powerhouse. And in order to become fully operational, we must become explorers, too, intrepid explorers. Explorers of our mind, of our body, and most important, of our spirit, of our own spiritual existence, and of our power. We must dare to be. Not rash, impulsive, reckless, or impetuous, for to take that route simply spells confusion and will get us lost. The route we need to be on requires courage, a certain amount of bravery, and dedication. It also requires us to be determined, resolute, enthusiastic, and strong in spirit. This last, being strong in spirit, means understanding that the spirit can be destroyed only if we wish to destroy ourselves.

Some think that the worst that can happen is to die, or to watch someone you love die. God knows that the pain of losing a loved one, of watching a child suffering and in pain, a mother, a sibling, a husband or wife, is to suffer pain beyond description. But in remembering that the soul has lived before this time, and will survive all things mortal beyond this time, the worst thing that can happen to us, to us as souls, is to lose ourselves, to become lost in the process of life and death. To not know who we are, who we have been, who we can become. To not know what kind of soul we are.

What can we do to save ourselves, to know who we are, to find ourselves if we feel lost? For those of us who don't feel lost, what can we do to retain, understand, and remain loving to ourselves? Our next exercises might help.

They may appear at first, to some of you, designed to destroy the self. In fact they are designed to remove all unnecessary trappings, all the cumbersome emotions that are negative and destructive, and which weigh us down, hold us back on our journey toward the self and toward spiritual growth.

As you work through these next exercises, try if you can to be inspired by the stories of the three chairs. Hard as it is for us to accept, God gave us one of our greatest gifts when he gave us tears and heartache. Remember that through pain, through struggle, and through adversity come our greatest lessons.

These next exercises require honesty and truth. If you are to benefit from them at all, they require you to be brave and to dare. There can be very little that is worse than someone putting a mirror in front of you and showing you the kind of person you really are inside. It takes not only courage but great humility to be that someone, to hold up the mirror to yourself.

Before we begin, I must stress that patience is really required here. These exercises call for self-appraisal, and I would suggest that you work on and complete Exercise 1 before you even begin to attempt Exercise 2.

We are going to be making lists, and we are going to be discovering our negative and positive traits. Some of you may be tempted to ask others what they think of you, what they think your flaws and good points are. If you do this, you will completely undermine the value of the exercise and will gain no benefit from it whatsoever. Only your opinion of yourself matters here, and your honesty.

I repeat, try to complete Exercise 1 before you look at and study the second exercise. This will ensure that you will not be influenced in any way by the two example lists contained in Exercise 2.

EXERCISE 1 . . .
WHO AM I?

So far, in Chapters One and Two, we have tried relaxation and meditation, we have learned a little about energy and about our energy centers, and we have begun to explore how to use that energy constructively.

We have also discovered new potential, new possibilities, but it is impossible for us to use that new potential to the fullest until we find out who we are. How can we do that? First, we must learn to know ourselves, then we must learn to understand ourselves, after which we can then learn to like ourselves.

Learning to be tolerant of our own selves, of our shortcomings, makes it easier to accept that it is okay to be imperfect. We all have fears, but our hopes and aspirations are what really matter. We can learn to be truly tolerant of others and to fully appreciate the hopes, aspirations, and dreams of those around us, both those on the earth plane and those in the spirit world, who are with us, and see all things.

This chapter is designed to strip away the many layers of pretense and protection which we all accumulate as we grow from childhood to adulthood, and which most of us are not only afraid to discard, but the very existence of which we are afraid to acknowledge.

It might seem, as you work, that a process of self-destruction may be taking place, but what we are really doing is ridding ourselves of any illusions. After we remove the facade, whatever is left, no matter how little it may be, this is what and who you are, and what you can build on. This is how we grow, for what we have left is precious, and we must nurture it.

Don't forget the golden rule... at all times be gentle with yourself... no matter what.

You need a notepad and a pen, and you begin by writing the heading: MY CHARACTER. Draw a line down the center of the paper and head the left column MY BAD POINTS and the right column MY GOOD POINTS.

So, clearing the mind, by relaxation and meditation, find an inner calm, an inner peace, preventing any harsh, unnecessary thoughts toward yourself.

Look carefully at yourself and begin writing your list. Compile a list of points in your character that you consider to be flaws, or bad points. Don't be too hasty in writing things down. Take your time about it, and think about each point carefully.

When the list on the left side of the paper is complete, then begin on the right side. This is the side headed MY GOOD POINTS. Again, think carefully before writing anything down, and also about each point as you make it.

It is most likely that the list on the left of the paper will be longer than the list on the right. Somehow, most of us are far more ready to acknowledge our bad traits than we are to acknowledge the things about ourselves that we consider to be good. We remember the old adage "self-praise is no praise at all," or we feel uncomfortable because we might appear to be boastful or bragging. Try to overcome your embarrassment, understand that none of us is all bad, and that it never hurts to say so. If you can learn to appreciate the good in yourself, then you can learn to appreciate the good in all things.

You might want to give yourself a few days to think about your lists and to change them, but when you feel that your lists are complete, you are ready to begin to work with them.

I thought it might be a good idea to give you some examples of what it is you need to work on, and at first I considered using one of my student's work. Then I thought again, and decided that the only example I could honestly give would be my own. My thoughts, my feelings, my expressions, not someone else's. If you look at my lists, and study them carefully, you might find it easier to open your mind to a way of reasoning you may not have tried before.

Exercise 2 . . .
Why Am I?

My lists, and the detailed analysis of each point, are examples of how I tackled this exercise. If you feel that you could deal with your lists differently, then by all means give it a try. The main thing is that you look to your inner self for your answers, for as Grey Eagle will always remind me, there is not one question I can ask that I do not have the answer to, inside me.

MY CHARACTER	LIST 1
Bad Traits	*Good Traits*
Thoughtless	Sense of humor
Cruel	Quick to laugh
Selfish	Good cook
Oversensitive	Nice personality
Bad-tempered	
Intolerant	
Bossy	
Lazy	
Untidy	
Demanding	

MY CHARACTER	LIST 2
Negative Traits	*Positive Traits*
Thoughtless	Caring
Selfish	Kind
Bad-tempered	Generous
Intolerant	Selfish
Bossy	Sensitive
Lazy	Patient

| Untidy | Tolerant |
| Demanding | Assertive |

So, there are my first two lists. Notice how different they are. In list I, there are many more points in the left column, headed BAD TRAITS, than in the right column, headed GOOD TRAITS, and it would be easy to assume that the writer of this list is self-condemning. I am the writer, and I don't feel that I am self-condemning in any way, as you will see from list 2, which shows some real shifts. It could be that at this stage of the exercise we can begin to realize that there are very few issues that are black or white, and our character traits are not nearly as cut-and-dried as we thought they might be.

Let's take a closer look at the "Bad Traits" in my first example.

Number I: Thoughtless

Now, why do I consider myself to be thoughtless? Is it because I don't care about people or is it just that life takes over? After consideration, I decide that I do care about people, especially those close to me, and I am not always thoughtless, only sometimes. Forgetting to invite a friend to a party, or not always saying thank-you for a gift given. Missing someone's birthday or anniversary, that's a big one on my list. Of course, I could give myself excuses, and I often do, like, I'm really busy, have a lot on my mind, travel. All this is true. But when I don't remember a friend's birthday, for whatever reason, the consequence is that, unintentionally, I hurt my friend. Not one of the many valid reasons for my forgetfulness makes a good enough excuse.

So having thought carefully about my thoughtlessness, I have decided to keep it in the left column, as you can see in list 2, but in pondering this point I have discovered another trait in my character that I can put in the right column. I have accepted that I am a caring person. So now, making up my second list, it has already changed. And I have only just begun.

Number 2: Cruel

Putting this trait down is a really good example of how, when analyzing oneself, we can do a really good job of beating ourselves up. Of course I'm not a cruel person, but in looking at myself I know I'm capable of harsh words, and I have my share of mean-ness. Like the old story of the lion with a thorn in its paw, if I'm hurting, there have been those times in my life when I have lashed out. These are the times when I like myself the least, and even as I write, thinking of those times when I have behaved less well than I should have, and knowing better, these are the times in my life of which I have felt ashamed. But, not excusing myself, I am only human, and not by any means a saint.

I look again, to see if the word "cruel" really does apply to me. Well, I am never cruel to animals, and can be quite kind and generous. Sometimes, if I'm hurt, I can be hurtful back and I can say cruel things, but only rarely. Obviously this doesn't make me a cruel person, only human, and remembering the golden rule, to be gentle with myself, I have decided to take this point off the list altogether.

Once again, in analyzing this point, I have discovered a couple of other things about myself. In wondering if I was really cruel, I remember that I really can be quite kind and generous. Two more points for the right column. So I put these points, as you will see, in the right column of list 2.

Number 3: Selfish

Unfortunately I have no argument with this point, as I have to admit that I am very definitely selfish. But instead of just saying yes, I'm selfish, I should examine the various ways in which I am. And is this really a bad trait? Of course it is, but sometimes I feel that it is really necessary to be selfish. Surely as long as I am not selfish to the point of being destructive with other people's feelings, then isn't that all right? I ask, and now I have to do a little soul-searching, which is what this exercise is all about.

I will walk into a room and, without a thought, take the most comfortable chair. I'm told that this is a typically Taurean trait, nevertheless it is a selfish one. No excuses. I might buy a blouse for my daughter, decide I like it, and keep it for myself. When she reads this, Samantha will definitely have something to say to me.

On the other hand, I would willingly give up the comfy chair for someone elderly or frail, and I have bought Samantha many things, so the odd blouse or two I may keep are not so important.

I am selfish with my time. I need to be. I am selfish with my friends. I see them so infrequently that when I do see them, I don't want to share the time we spend with people I don't know.

One act of total selfishness happened when I hid my favorite chocolates from Jim so he couldn't get to them. One act of total selflessness occurred when my mother, many years ago, knowing I had no money, sent me twenty dollars. Five dollars for Samantha and fifteen dollars for me. It was Christmas, and this was the first time since I was a child that I or Samantha had received a gift from her. It eased my mother's guilt. She knew we were below the poverty line, and she could easily have helped us out, but chose not to. Little did she know, little did she know her daughter, for no matter how desperate we were, I would not have accepted her financial aid had she offered it, but I would have given anything for some loving support.

I opened the envelope that contained the twenty dollars, saw the note that read, "Spend the fifteen on yourself." I sighed, relieved that I now had the money to buy a nice Christmas gift for my little girl, happy to spend the twenty dollars on her. Samantha was ten years old at the time.

Selfishness in the extreme is a bad thing, but in order to be my own self I must be selfish in some things. If I were not, then that would be equally bad. For one thing, I would not be indulging in writing this book, but would be out there doing community service. So I keep this point in the left column, and endeavor, as I will with all the other points in this column, to do better. I will also, however, put this same point in the right column and endeavor to enhance this trait. In doing so, I recognize that there are certain traits in my character that can be equally destructive or constructive, negative or positive, depending on how I exercise them. This is a point well worth remembering, and I make a note of it mentally.

Number 4: Oversensitive

This point is one that I must readily put on my list, and definitely belongs in the left column. I feel sure of this because, after all, this is a fault that has been pointed out to me by many people in my life since childhood, and I have often been accused by others of being either too sensitive or oversensitive.

I must think seriously about this point as with all the others, for after all, I remind myself, that is what this exercise is about, thinking clearly.

But wait a minute; I almost fell into the trap. This is an

exercise about self-awareness, so what is important here is not what other people think I am, but what *I* think I am.

After much thought and careful consideration, I have begun to realize that without exception, all the nicest people I know are very sensitive. It is often this trait in another person's character that I look for first, and in someone else I definitely consider it to be a good point.

My biggest problem in life has been my sensitivity. Because I was born with that rare and special gift of communication with the spirit world, one of my character traits is my ultrasensitivity, without which I would indeed find it impossible to access this gift. Unfortunately, though, my "gift" of sensitivity means that I am very easily hurt by others' words or deeds. I have, in the past, been quick, often too quick, to take offense at some comment or phrase used at me or against me by some person not meaning to hurt, but not as sensitive as I. And, for many years, lacking self-worth and self-esteem, I was willing to believe the opinions of people in my life who were perhaps lacking sensitivity, and insensitive to me. People like my mother, my father, my family. Definitely my husband, who used to tell me that even though he didn't find me attractive, it was possible that some men might. How's that for insensitivity?

Having given even more thought still to this point, I realize that perhaps I have listened and believed, for too long, the opinion of some *insensitive* people in my life, and I have decided that I like being sensitive, that for me there is no such thing as being too sensitive. It is this part of my character that helps me to do my job, to be aware of others, of others' pain and anguish and loss, and to recognize the sensitivity in others that I so appreciate.

I place this point very positively in the right column of list 2.

Numbers 5 and 6:
Bad-tempered and Intolerant

Yes, I decide, I am both of these things, not all of the time, thank goodness, but certainly more often than I would like. So they stay in the left column, but I have to ask why? Why and when, and for what reasons, do I become bad-tempered, and is it that I am intolerant with others or am I also intolerant with my own self?

Well, let's see, my temper becomes frayed mostly when I'm tired. I become irritable and intolerant and unable to think clearly. Travel is the most tiring, and unfortunately I am unable, unwilling, to do too much at this time to change my life in this way. It's part of my work, it's what I do, so when I think about these traits, I know that I must simply learn to deal with the tiredness and not take it out on others. I must also learn not to take it out on me. There are those times when we must accept our human frailties, and hope that those around us accept them, too.

As I ponder this further, I also realize that I can also be very tolerant when I need to be and also very patient—a discovery. I should now put tolerance and patience in the right columns.

I decide that I will, even though when I now look at my list, it seems that I am fast becoming a saint. Don't worry, I most definitely am not!

Number 7: Bossy

The word "bossy" conjures up the image of a nagging, forceful woman who, regardless of others' needs and requirements, pushes and bullies and imposes her own will upon others. Boy, I hope I'm not like that; I don't think I am, in fact I know I'm not, mostly because I don't want to be, but there are times . . . okay, this is another of those awful traits that I readily have to admit to, but again thinking hard about this, I realize that there is a very fine line between being bossy—not a nice thing to be—and being assertive, which in my life is a very necessary thing to be. So even though bossy stays on the list because, I'm ashamed to say, I sometimes can be, once again I have discovered another point for the right column—assertiveness.

Number 8: Lazy

There are so many people who think that working for yourself, having no boss telling you what to do, must be great. And it is, it definitely is. But those who work for themselves will tell you that it is also the hardest thing. No one to blame but yourself if it doesn't work out, no one else to "carry the can." No clock to watch, no starting at nine and finishing at five. The most difficult and also the most necessary requirement for any measure of success, however, is self-discipline. This is the area I have to work at the most, and this is the area in which I most often fail.

There are days in my life when, if I could, I would do nothing except laze about, maybe take a gentle walk, watch TV. I'm a great movie fan, and I love crosswords. As hard as I work, I can also work hard at doing nothing. I'm a great "idler." I was born with an idle or lazy streak in me, which, if I were to indulge it too often, could turn me into a bore. So I make an effort to indulge as little as possible, which in turn has probably turned me into something of a workaholic.

The more I think about the hows, whys, and wherefores of my character, the more insight I have into who I really am and who I really want to be.

I am basically lazy. I have no argument with this point, and it most definitely stays in the left column.

Number 9: Untidy

I am an enigma, a puzzle. Complex, yet simple and straightforward. Unfathomable, yet easily understood in some areas. God made me different from others, yet He made me the same. This could be said of all of us.

My kitchen cupboards are immaculate, as are all the cupboards and closets and drawers in my house. A place for everything, everything in its place. Tins placed, evenly spaced, labels at a certain angle so they are easily seen. Jars in rows, like toy soldiers. I pride myself that I know, down to the smallest detail, where everything is. Mustard? Second shelf, top left-hand cupboard, on the right, next to pickles. Garlic? Bottom shelf, left-hand side, at the back. Olive oil, sesame oil, sunflower oil? All in rows, nothing out of place.

Closets. Well, let me see. Coat hangers all facing the same way, as are the clothes on them. Color-coordinated, suits all together, black on the right, leading to lighter colors on the left. Blouses on left, pants middle, skirts on right. Sweaters range from lightweight short-sleeve to heavy long-sleeve. All have their place, and are in order. I think the picture is clear. So why is the word "untidy" even in my vocabulary?

The strange fact is that everything that is unseen, closed away, is in neat order, but all else is not. I leave my papers in piles. My office desk, often my kitchen table, is covered with piles of who knows what kind of papers. Faxes, books, parts of manuscripts. I make these piles, then forget what's there, so every few days I have to sort through them. You have no idea the time I waste because of my inability to be tidy in this area.

What does this tell me about me? Totally ordered on the inside, a mess on the outside. Not quite, not really, for I am, or try to be, meticulously dressed, makeup on, hair done, even when I'm on my own and not expecting visitors. However, I do admit to a certain kind of ordered mind, and rarely will I show my emotions without careful thought and consideration, particularly when I'm working. I try to be controlled and precise of action, without being cold and indifferent to my situation. My thoughts are rarely scattered, my inner cupboard is in order, yet I will outwardly appear relaxed calm and easy, sometimes too much so.

As for the rest of it, yes, I am untidy. I intend to work on not being, but I smile as I write, for I know myself well enough to know I won't make it.

Number 10: Demanding

The last on my list of bad traits, it is true that I am a very demanding and exacting person, and this trait has caused some problems for me with other people.

I recall one particular time, a Tuesday evening, and I had decided to visit one of my healing centers, Thorne, near Doncaster, South Yorkshire, in England. This was the first of our centers, run by very capable healers, whom I trusted completely to do their best job.

It was a busy night, and there was very little time at the beginning for chitchat. A few new patients, as well as many old ones.

My visit was unexpected, although my team was used to having me drop in unannounced. As I walked into the healing room, I saw that there were about six patients, each with a healer, and three or four student healers, beginners. There was also, seated on a chair, to the side of the room, a new patient. She had been there twice before, and she was watching the healers at work.

As I always did, I quietly surveyed the scene, going from patient to patient, saying little, nodding or smiling my hellos, stopping to help, placing my hands on each one for a few minutes. My team stood, attentive to my every motion, as they had been taught, alert and watchful, always ready to learn some new thing. Mindful of their responsibilities, and wanting to give their patients the best they could.

I was their teacher. I felt and saw only their love and human kindness toward those who had come to them in need. I saw and felt only their respect for me as that someone they could learn from.

It was Robbie Burns, that wonderful Scottish poet, who wrote in his poem "To a Louse," "O, wad some Pow'r the giftie gie us, to see oursels as others see us."

Translated, it means to wish that God, or some heavenly power, would give us the gift to see ourselves as others see us. Would we be shocked, amazed, hurt, maybe awakened, perhaps confused?

I was so busy doing my job, the best I knew how, I failed to see or to be aware of the effect I, or my presence, was having on the lady who was seated by the side wall. Nor was any of my team aware of her. It was only when she called one of my healers a couple of days later that any of us knew how upset she was.

She had not seen me as a gentle healer, nor had she seen me as a stern but fair-minded and dedicated teacher. Rather, she had witnessed the reaction of my team and, in her eyes, had seen how they had stood to attention as I appeared in the doorway. She had seen me as intimidating, demanding, had seen my team fearful of my presence. In her eyes I was a tyrant.

Yes, my team had stood a little straighter, a little taller, though not from fear. They were my team, and proud to be. They stood proud, wanting my approval and my respect, as they approved of and respected me. This I know, even as I know that no organization can achieve and produce such miracles as we have done for as long as we have if that organization is fear-based, for such work must be based on love and true dedication.

"Who does she think she is?" our complainer had said of me, and, "If she's going to be there often, I won't come. It's not right that they're all afraid of her." She said this last without having spoken to any of my team, I might add.

I smile as I think back, realizing that this woman was the one afraid, not my team, and I briefly wonder, of what?

"What should I say to her?" asked the healer she had complained to, and my answer was simple and straightforward. "She wants to know who I think I am," I replied. "Tell her that I am the founder and teacher of this organization. That I am fully aware of my responsibilities to my team and to my patients. That I run the centers as I see fit, in the way that I can benefit all who come to us the best way possible. I am a medium and a healer, that's who I am, and if she would like to know more, let her come and ask me herself." Sadly, she never did.

There have been others, too, who have criticized me in my work. Recently I received a letter from two women who had come to one of my healing workshops. I was fifteen minutes late starting. I had the nerve to begin the workshop by asking everyone if they considered their lives to be dull, boring, or full. I posed the question "Is your glass half-full or do you see it as half-empty?" My two complainers found my question arrogant, offensive. They wrote that they left the workshop in disgust and disappointment. They stayed, they said, a total of fifteen minutes and couldn't stand me any longer. Sadly, they missed a really great day.

> O, wad some Pow'r the giftie gie us
> To see oursels as others see us.

Unfortunately for me, many people decide on the person I must be from reading my books or watching me on the television, and they presume that because my work is special, wonderful, and miraculous, then I must be these things also. Raised up onto a pedestal I did not ask to be raised onto, inevitably I fall off, again and again. And boy, does it hurt. It hurts and disappoints those who see me as special, superhuman, and it also hurts me, too, for all too often, when people realize that I'm just like them, that I'm human, too, they become angry with me and want to lash out. Living this spiritual life, trying to be the best I know I'm supposed to be, is really tough.

Looking at this list of negative points, seeing myself as I really am, knowing that I'm supposed to be better than I am, having to admit to the world that I am these things ... but wait. Is it what the world sees that's important? No. Is it how others view us, how others see us that's important? No again. Does it matter that much that others put me high on that ridiculous pedestal? Yes, but only in that they will be disappointed.

Robbie Burns writes that it would be a gift to be able to see ourselves as others see us. I would change his words somewhat, knowing that I am human, knowing that, yes, I am a demanding human being at times, understanding that to change is often to grow, I would have his words read: "O, wad some Pow'r the giftie gie us, to see oursels ..."

I demand high standards of myself, therefore I often expect unreasonably high and exacting standards from others. This inevitably leads to disappointments, and it has sometimes seemed to me that other people have let me down. I must work at being more tolerant of what I consider to be other people's shortcomings, and try to be less demanding of others. If I had done this in the past, in certain circumstances, I might have been less miserable.

Of all the points in this column, this is the one I feel I have to work at the hardest. I must change this, for my own sake, for my own happiness.

Although it is not complete, as I have now to reflect on my good points and deal with them in the same way I have just dealt with the bad points, let us now examine the new list, list 2, and see how it looks thus far.

Immediately we can see that the list is much more evenly balanced, and I have changed the headings, deleting the words "bad" and "good" and replacing them with the words "negative" and "positive."

Remember that this list is only an example and the comments indicate possible ways of assessing each point. This exercise has been designed to help you to reach deep into yourself in a positive way. A way that will lead to self-discovery.

You will have your own way of assessing and dealing with the points, both negative and positive, which you have on your list. The thing to remember is to try not to be influenced by what other people say or think about you, or rather what you think other people's opinions of you are. Be yourself. Good or bad. Positive or negative. Then let these self-discoveries help you. Learn to acknowledge the negative points and work toward changing or improving on them if you can. And if you can't, then learn to accept them. After all, they are part of you. As far as the positive points are concerned, learn to enhance these traits and gain confidence in the knowledge that you really do have some very fine qualities. We all have.

Your list can, if you let it, be very valuable to you. Not just for the time it takes to complete this exercise, but in years to come. It is something you can put away and not think about for a while, and then take out and study. It is changeable; indeed it must change as your character changes, and as you grow. Your list can help to build your confidence and can strengthen your resolve. It will, if you let it, help you to learn to like yourself. A most important and necessary thing to do.

Hopefully, eventually, you will, after changing your list many times, be able to say:

"I may not be the nicest person I know, but as a human being, as just one little person, I am quite nice really."

The questions I suggest you ask yourself after completing this exercise are:

1. Have I learned to know myself better?
2. Have I learned to understand myself better?
3. Have I learned to like myself better?

And the answer should be *yes* to all three, and given time and patience, it will be.

Don't forget, as with every other exercise, we expect that there will be many questions and queries concerning this chapter. Know that time alone will give you your answers. Be patient, and remember . . . *be gentle with yourself.* Your self-esteem will grow.

Did you dare? I hope you did, and I hope by doing these last exercises you gained knowledge, understanding of yourself, and compassion for yourself. Now, if you dare to advance a little more, you could, if you wish, be like Goldilocks, and try the chairs. They won't break, they won't be too big or too small, and you can sit in them on your own, or share your story with a loved one or a good friend.

First, you must sit in the sad chair, and reaching deep down inside, as you are learning to do, find the most painful and saddest of stories. We all have at least one, and even the happiest and most loved of us are no exception to this. As you tell the story, it may help if you visualize me listening to you. Of course, I am only one person and can't be in more than one place at once, or can I? But although I can't promise to hear what you have to say, I can promise that someone will. A loved one, a family member, or a good friend. We all have someone in the spirit world who loves us and is willing to listen. There are also no exceptions there either.

Sit in the sad chair, and in telling your story, bring out all the old buried hurts and pain that have been stored inside, just as my friend Brian did.

Sit in the happy chair, and in telling your story, search out those small rays of sunshine, and the silver lining that is always there if we look hard enough, even behind the darkest cloud.

Sit in the inspirational chair, and in telling your story, like our boy Tyler, be inspired that not only did you survive your pain, not only can you smile a little despite your pain, but that your pain, your experience, has helped make you stronger and more sensitive to other people's pain.

As you sit in your inspirational chair, be inspired, too, that even as I write, my heart goes out to each and every one of you who has dared to explore the depths of your soul. I send my loving and energizing thoughts to you, and will remind you, if I may, that as you tell your story, there are those, above and beyond all others who are listening to you, God's messengers . . . your angels.

You are already in touch with your world, through books, radio, television. Now you are learning to be in touch with yourself, and inevitably, you will learn to be in touch with your spirit, and with that place beyond our earth, which we call the spirit world. As you strive to learn, feel your power grow. As you grow, feel yourself become more powerful.

It is important to be "at home," to be welcoming and receptive to the spirit world, to our spirit nature. But it is imperative that we are "at home," welcoming in thought, receptive to our own feelings, knowing who we are, so that we can know our power.

Two may talk together under the same roof,
Yet never really meet.
And two others, at first speech, are old friends.

MARY CATHERWOOD

CHAPTER 4

Fields of Light Are Fields of Life

Is it an accident that the paintings of the Madonna and Child, the Annunciation, which shows the Angel Gabriel and the Virgin Mary, and the Pietà, the Virgin Mary holding the dead body of Christ, painted by Botticelli, show the holy figures with a light behind them? Or that *St. Anthony Healing the Youth's Leg* and *Presentation of the Virgin*, painted by Titian, do the same? Many religious artists, great painters of religious or holy pictures, all depict saints and holy men and women with a golden aura.

An accident?

I don't think so. More probable, I feel, is that these artists, involved as they were in their craft, became so close to their subjects that their sensitivities became heightened as they were painting. It was then possible for them to become attuned to the power and energy of their subject, and therefore able to see, to visualize in some way, their aura, and to paint it.

Most, if not all of us, are born, I believe, with the ability to "see" or to sense auras. Many would agree, but suggest that this is perhaps for most a lost art. I am more optimistic, and firmly believe that this art is not lost to us, merely mislaid. That if we search in the right way, it is more than possible for us to rediscover it.

We know that every living thing has an aura, an energy field. Every plant, every tree, every insect, fish, fowl, all that breathes, including us humans, of course.

Since I can remember, I have seen energy, in the form of color and light, around people. Not knowing that it was "auric energy" I was seeing, and not realizing that others could not see, I never took much notice. It was natural for me to see, but my ability to see auras was not especially well developed, as I didn't exercise it often. My fault. I pushed it away, as it was too confusing and simply added to the terror that was my life as I was growing up.

It was only after I had met Grey Eagle that I became more curious about auras, and the energy that we all have, and I began to make more conscious efforts to "aura-spot." Then, after talking with Grey Eagle about flying insects, which the Native Americans call the "Tiny Winged People," I became somewhat more intrigued by the auras of insects, beetles, spiders, and such.

I have written previously about the time when, quite engrossed in some movie, something, a flicker of movement to my right caught my eye. I turned, and there, crawling up the wall, next to my chair, was a tiny wood louse. As I watched, I became fascinated, not by the wood louse, but by the tiny pinprick of light that followed it, like a bright shadow. As this little creature crawled slowly up and down the wall, the light hovered over and around it. That light, its aura, was pure and uncluttered, very different from that of a human aura, which has many colors, many shades. I was thrilled to see it so clearly, and I promptly forgot the movie. This was much more exciting, and I remember reflecting later how, in the greater scheme of things, in God's great plan, how even the tiniest and seemingly most unimportant of His creatures has its place, and its energy.

I also remember the first time I saw a spider's aura. It was just the same, an intense bright light, bigger than that of the wood louse, like a spotlight, moving as the spider moved, pure and bright and uncluttered, following, sometimes hovering, right above the body of the spider, sometimes seeming to trail a little behind. But always with the creature, a shadow part of it.

I remember a friend of mine once asked me, a little ruefully, as she inadvertently stepped on an ant, "Rosemary, what happens to it now? Does it go to the spirit world?"

Even as she asked the question I heard and repeated Grey Eagle's answer. He said simply, "It becomes light."

Imagine the earth without light—or worse—without energy. Instantly we think, no light, no heat, no industry or cars, no means of transport. No cardiac machines or incubators, no TV, radio, communications systems, radar. No press, no news, no contact to or from countries outside our own. No telephones or computers.

Albert Einstein writes, "It has become appallingly clear that our technology has surpassed our humanity," and it was written in the 1978 *Farmer's Almanac*, probably by some frustrated computer buff, "To err is human, but to really foul things up requires a computer." True, but still, what would our lives be like without energy? No freezers or refrigerators, no ovens, microwaves, kettles. How would we boil water? Oh yes, some of us would manage, with difficulty of course. Our survival instinct is great, and when stretched, the human being can be very resourceful and creative. But our world would be different, more uncomfortable, and survival over a long period of time would be for most impossible.

Now imagine the human being without energy. Instantly we think lethargy, no willpower, only sleep, sleep, just sleep. If you've ever been sick, you know what that feels like. But it would be more than that, much more. For science tells us that matter is energy, that every living thing has an aura, an energy field, which surrounds us and extends out from us by several feet. We as individuals are a power source, a living, breathing mass of energy,

energy of various kinds and strengths. What if that energy was suddenly lost, gone, moved somehow, somewhere else? I believe that when we die, the soul, which is the source of our energy, removes itself and takes its energy with it. So if our energy was to disappear, would we die, or would we become zombies? Breathing, just, but unable to think or talk or walk, or be anything but a lump of unmoving flesh.

When I have debated the issue of life after death, and have talked with the spirit world about life here on this earth, it has sometimes been said that those in the spirit world are often more alive, more vibrant than those of us so-called living, and that some of us on this earth plane are more "dead" than those who are in spirit.

How? Why would this be? I have asked, and the answer is simple. Energy. Those in the spirit world have it and use it. They know how. And those of us on this earth plane have it, and have little or no idea how to use it. Some of us, even understanding that we are energy, have never thought or wondered, even mildly pondered the question, could we use it, could we use our energy?

If the earth was without energy, how would we communicate? Drums, carrier pigeons, some of us could use telepathy. We are all capable of it to a greater or lesser degree. And how would we survive? Simple, we would use our instinct. We all have it, some more than others. But we can survive only if our energy is positive, powerful, at high speed, and in good working order, with no blockages.

Put the kettle, full of water, on the stove, set at number two— a low setting—and yes, eventually the water will boil, only it will take a while. Set higher, at four, the water boils quicker, but at eight, we reach our goal in no time at all.

If we look at the energy level of the human being, we could say that the average setting is between four and six. We can tell this by examining the human aura, our energy field. Judging the high setting, I'd say the most powerful rate of energy is number twelve. This means that most of us work on roughly half our full capability. If we tried to boil a kettle constantly on high, the oven, man-made and fallible, eventually would overreach its capacity and burn out. Not so with energy that is of man, not physical energy, but energy of the spirit and God-given. The more we use our inner resources, the more energy we create, the more power we have. We can never reach a stage of burnout, only burn-on and on and on. We own the power, and the more we use it, the more it grows.

Not all psychics see auras, but with practice I believe that we are all able to develop a sense of sight or an awareness of our own energy, our own aura. Of course, this statement begs the question, How? And the answer, Time and patience. Oh, how irritating those words can sound, but along with time and patience, there are some valuable and constructive exercises that we can have fun with. First we begin by exploring the aura a little. There have been many books written about auras or energy fields, explaining their existence and nature. Mediums and psychics have been aware of the existence of auras for centuries, but scientists have only relatively recently accepted them as fact, thanks to a Russian-born husband and wife, Semyon and Valentina Kirlien, who developed a special type of camera and perfected the techniques of Kirlien photography, which is used to photograph the aura.

In this chapter we are going to explore the aura in relation to the self, to learn how to use the knowledge we are gaining from self-exploration, to discover a new depth, a new dimension of our own selves, of our spirit selves, and of our energy, and if we succeed we will inevitably become more spiritually attuned.

Let's look at a few facts:

1. The aura is associated with all living things; every living thing has an aura.
2. The aura is made up of different types of energy.

3. This energy manifests above and beyond the surface of the skin.
4. The aura is a very subtle interaction of energies, and surrounds the human body for a distance of yards.
5. There are many layers, colors, shapes, and patterns to the aura.
6. The characteristics of the aura change according to the mental, physical and spiritual, or inner state of a person.
7. The aura is a pure field of energy.

So our aura is energy that moves, changes shape, forms patterns. But how and why does the aura change?

When we first examine the aura, it might seem as if attached to us is an energy field that moves, or bounces around of its own accord, with a mind or will of its own. Yet if we study fact 4 very carefully, we can see that there must be a connection to the aura through our state of mind or mood. How else can we perceive this point? Our aura changes as our mental, physical, and spiritual states change.

This is not a new concept, far from it, in fact. How many songs talk about "the blues"? Are you feeling blue, are you feeling down, miserable? Haven't we heard the phrase "he saw red," meaning angry, or "green with envy"? If we refer to someone's yellow streak, we mean that they're cowardly. And what about when someone chokes? "Well, she turned purple." Of course she didn't, or did she? Is it possible that her aura turned purple?

These are clichés, and perhaps they come from someone years ago who was able to see auras, or maybe just flashes of energy around people, flashes of color.

Auras change as our moods change, and this fact brings us to the conclusion that the mind of the aura and the mind of the person are one and the same. Therefore, we can assume that our thoughts affect our aura. Or, indeed, that our thoughts are our aura, or at least part of it. We discussed earlier in the book that each tiny thought is a small pulse of energy, but that no matter how small the thought, the energy that comes from that thought is powerful.

Accepting that our thought energy is connected to, is indeed part of, our aura, we can begin to understand that if we exercise control over our thoughts, then we can deliberately bring about effective changes to our aura by changing the type of energy we emit.

But why would we want to change our aura, an energy that most of us cannot see or sense or feel or smell? An energy that we seem to have no use for anyway.

We see the need to change it only when we begin to understand its importance as the life field that surrounds us. Our aura acts as a mirror, the mirror of our soul, our spirit, of the very depth and being of our personality, of our inner self, of our power. It is our aura, our life force that attracts the spirit world, makes that God force, God energy, want to draw closer to us or to pull away from us.

When I see a person's aura, I can clearly see what kind of soul type they are. Are they loving, caring, kind, compassionate? Greedy, avaricious, mean, unkind? The aura shows it all, and although we might not be able to see, God sees, our angels see, our loved ones in the spirit world also see. When we talk about changing or enhancing our aura, we are talking about changing and enhancing that energy that we have created by our thoughts, by who we are.

It is easy to become a bad-tempered, mean old grouch, or to become a complainer, a nag. Life sometimes throws such turmoil at us that in our fear for survival, we develop habits that, with a little thought, we might wish we didn't have.

I was in an airport recently, and my companion, with no thought for anyone but himself, began stomping and yelling at one of the women staff who was working at the desk. I couldn't find my pass into the airport lounge. Not an especially big deal, but definitely frustrating, and entirely my fault. "I'm really sorry," she said to me, "but without your number, there's nothing I can do."

"This is outrageous, ridiculous," my companion complained loudly, in a rude and abusive manner, and proceeded to try to bully both the assistant and me, insisting that I must have my ticket somewhere.

Horrified and embarrassed, I apologized for his behavior. He, however, felt it was enough that he later came to the counter, put his head in his hands, and said how very tired he was. An explanation possibly for his bad behavior, but definitely not a good enough excuse. True, he was under pressure. Travel is pressure for everyone, and because life pressures us, it is easy, when those habits show themselves, for us to shrug off our bad behavior, to excuse or ignore it, pretend it didn't happen, and hope that not too many people see us as we really are in our bad moods. But ignoring never makes anything truly disappear. Ignorance really isn't the bliss the old saying makes it out to be. One day, whether it is a day we have on this earth, or if it is the day we leave here and move on to the spirit world, there will come that day when we have to face ourselves. So why not make sure we see something good when we look into that mirror? Why not take control of who we are, and who we want to become?

We need to build and to mold our energy, and we can begin by changing our thought process. But before we begin to explore the ways and means of changing our aura, there is another aspect of this energy that we have not yet approached. We have not yet dealt with the fact that the aura, our energy field, is made up of many colors. Now, this is not surprising, as nature itself is made up of many colors. Blue sky, green grass, golden sun, silver stars, and so on. To help us understand or "read" a person's aura, we can easily relate a state of aura with a state of nature.

If we look up into a sky that is dark and cloudy, we can see turbulent and distressing energy. This energy creates unhappy weather conditions, which in turn can make us feel cold and miserable. But if we look up into a sky of clear blue and filled with sunshine, then we can see calm and peaceful energy. This energy creates good weather conditions, which makes us feel warm and happy.

In the same way that nature needs good and bad, positive and negative weather conditions, in order that it retain balance, so we in our learning process on this earth plane need to experience both positive and negative conditions, to eventually achieve a balanced state of mind and being. A balanced state of spirit. Although intellectually we can see that an equal amount of positive and negative action gives us balance, reason, and a chance to grow, for most of us, when we are going through the bad times we do not want to hear some sanctimonious-sounding do-gooder telling us that this is our learning process, and good for us. Even though they may be right.

Clients of mine lost their business. A cheating partner ran off with the money, leaving my clients to face the creditors. It was a nightmare for them. They lost their house, too, and had to stand and watch as the bailiffs came and took away all that they owned. Left with virtually nothing, in their early fifties, they thought starting over was impossible. But both were strong, strong-minded, and their attitude was that at least they had each other, they had the kids, and they all had their health and strength. They had balance.

Everything is attitude. The ability to see the silver lining in the blackest cloud. Is my cup half-empty or is it half-full? God leaves no one with an empty glass.

Our lives are as delicate and intricate as a fine clock. Our emotions are the pendulum, swinging first one way, then another. But if the pendulum swings too far one way or another, if it is erratic, then the workings of the clock go haywire. The clock needs balance. We spiritual beings, having this human experience, we need balance. Pain and pleasure mixed. We need to control our pendulum.

When our emotions, our thoughts, swing too high one way or another, or when our thought process is at full speed, erratic and out of control, our energy becomes a huge steaming kettle, like a large boiler, and unable to contain the steam pressure, it begins to rock. Sparks fly. Red, green, purple flashes, then red and more red, our energy, our thoughts, flow from us, showing themselves in the energy field around us, our aura. Mini-explosions, black clouds form, we become depressed, it shows in the darkness of our confusion, in which we have become encased.

Our positive and negative thoughts and feelings show themselves in our aura in the same way that nature shows its conditions in the sky. Although, unlike the weather, over which we have little or no control—or do we?—it is possible to have a great deal of control over our own aura. We must learn to control our thoughts—and what a thought that is.

Before we go further, let's look at the various colors in our spectrum and see what those colors mean to us.

Most of us will have a favorite color. Mine is green, although I rarely dress in green, and almost never use green furnishings and fabric. My love of green comes from nature and the peace I feel when I'm surrounded by green hills or walking on grass that is lush and rich in color. And, too, I was born with green eyes, as was my daughter, Samantha. When she was a baby and I would look into the clear deep green of her eyes, each time I knew a miracle.

We all have color preferences. It shows in the clothes we wear, the way we furnish our homes, and most of us acknowledge that there are some colors we surround ourselves with which make a decided difference to our mood. But let us explore the subject of color a stage further and bring to it something of a more spiritual nature.

As a medium and spiritual healer, I find the use of colors to be an integral part of my daily work. As a healer, I use color energy, healing energy, not only with all my patients, but with all my students as well. Now we need a guide, a definition of the meaning and type of energy that each color is perceived as. The color chart I used in *Give the Gift of Healing* is just such a guide to the type and use of color, and is very helpful in our search in understanding our aura.

Each color reflects a certain type of energy, and using certain colors in specific ways can be extremely beneficial to us, as you will see.

Let's begin with the color *blue*... Blue is the universal healing color, and to my knowledge, blue healing energy is used universally by all healers, even those healers who do not work with auras and colors.

As a healer, I might suggest as I give healing that my patient visualize herself lying under a beautiful blue sky or wrapped in a soft blue blanket. This is a color that brings comfort and aids relaxation, a most important ingredient in aiding the healing process.

Moving now to the color *green*... the color that denotes peace. Certainly I would use this color to help stem anxiety and bring about calm. The color green aids in harmonizing and uniting the soul, spirit, and body. How might I suggest my patient visualize this color? Perhaps the best and most effective way I have found is to imagine, visualize, slowly walking in my bare feet on soft, lush grass that has been warmed by the summer sun. One of my patients was so soothed by this that he walks barefoot on his lawn most days as part of his health regimen.

Red... The color red seems to be the total opposite of that wonderful peacemaking green energy, as it is a color of vitality, of stimulation. I advise great care in the use of this color and will sprinkle it oh so gently and sparingly if my patient is suffering from depression or extreme tiredness. If you are lacking energy, in need of a little vitality, then a good exercise is to visualize a tiny speck or two of red, just a splash, dancing in your aura. Don't overdo it, though. You don't want to be dancing on the ceiling!

One of my favorite colors now . . . *rose pink* . . . the color of warmth, of warm affection. In a world where there is so much heartache, so much pain, this energy is most needed, for it is the color that aids in matters of the heart and emotions. It is said, and I know this to be true, that a broken heart can be a most painful thing, that it can even be a terminal illness.

There was a time, many years ago, when I was twenty years old, seriously ill and in hospital, when I met a woman. She, too, was sick, and had had many tests, but no one could discover the reason for her sickness. I was in bed, unable to move, and in great pain. She—I have long since forgotten her name—came to hold my hand. I remember her as quiet-spoken and gentle, and I remember that as she sat by my bed, she told me her story. Her husband had died suddenly and unexpectedly, six months previously. They had no children; just the two of them, a devoted and loving couple. As she finished telling me this, I remember her pausing, smiling a little, then saying simply, "I have no reason to live without him."

The next day she was wheeled to the operating theater for a minor exploratory operation. She never came out of the anesthetic.

I look back on that time, thinking, If only I had known about healing then. If only I had understood how easy it is for us all to give a little healing, both to ourselves and to others. Well, first I would have held this lady's hand. Then, having sent out a prayer to God, to the universe, for help, I would have visualized my patient wrapped in a soft wool blanket the color of summer sky blue. I might then, knowing her sickness was of the heart and emotions, have visualized tiny threads of silk, the color of the most delicate and delicately perfumed soft-petaled rose, rose pink. Gently, and with great care, painstakingly and lovingly taking my time, I would have woven those perfect threads, in and out, back and forth, through the blanket. Weaving the energy up and down, around and around, building a protective and healing cocoon for my patient to lie within.

This method of healing, visualization, is very common and also very successful, for both the patient and the healer. It is a method I have encouraged my students to use, and I would urge anyone wanting to try self-healing to use this approach. Thoughts are powerful pulses of energy, remember.

Would my healing have saved her? Who knows, except God. Maybe it was her time, it surely must have been, for she chose her path, her future. A better question, then. Would my healing have helped? I know without a doubt, and from long experience, that it most certainly would have. But I must not dwell on what I didn't know, nor on what I couldn't do. I must look to now, to the future, and simply learn from the past.

Let's move on then. Now to *mauve*...a deep and penetrating color. A color that can promote the desire to understand the mind. As a healer, I would use the color mauve for any type of mental stress, from depression on to the more serious diseases, such as schizophrenia.

Stress is also a sickness, as it is a confusion of the mind. I have many patients who come to me for help because they have a need, a desire, to climb out of the confused, stressed state that they are in and stay healthy. We can, any of us, I believe, do this only if we gain some understanding of who we are, how we think, and how we allow circumstances around us to affect our mental health. I would use the color mauve to help to improve any mental condition, and as with all color, all energy, I would use it gently, lovingly.

A great exercise for management under stress is to spend just a few minutes every morning before work, and every evening after work, visualizing the color mauve. How you do it is up to you, but I personally might do it this way. My most indulgent time of the day is when I stand under the shower. It relaxes me, warms me, and if I feel mentally exhausted, I will visualize the water as it cascades over me, and I will visualize the water as a delicate and healing shade of mauve. I begin then, naturally, to unwind, to relax. I let my body, my mind, act like a sponge, and I throw myself wholeheartedly into the exercise of soaking up this powerful and positive energy. As I allow the process to take place, I can actually feel that energy penetrating right to the heart of me, healing my soul.

So on to *purple* . . . a color we see a great deal of in our churches and places of worship. This type of energy is powerful and can be used to promote strength and growth, both spiritually and emotionally. Purple is the color of encouragement, so if I had a patient who was feeling, for whatever reason, helpless, hopeless, and with no strength to fight his or her condition, I would reach out into that mass of universal God energy. Taking hold of that vital purple, drawing it to me, I might visualize it as many ribbons, soft, silky ribbons, dancing around and around, over and under, penetrating, becoming part of my patient's aura. My aim would be to give my patient strength, not just physically but emotionally and spiritually, too. If a patient can feel this strength as it enters him, then he might feel encouraged, his feelings of helplessness and hopelessness will, hopefully, diminish a little. Growth takes place. My patient, feeling this encouragement, is more in control, feels more powerful, more purposeful, and is able to move forward.

The sun, with all its power, all its warmth, deep and penetrating, revitalizing, speaks for the color *gold*, the energy of wisdom, joy, hope, laughter, and happiness. Gold is a color of great strength and opportunities, a color that shines out from most of our children, from their energy, their aura, which surrounds them. In a school playground, the park, anywhere we see groups of children, even on the dullest day, if we could see energy, see auras, then we would see a mass of gold, a live, shimmering, unrestrained mass emanating from our youngsters. There is not one of us who would not want this color, this energy for ourselves, as this is the color of life.

It was over fifteen years ago that I first saw the aura of the wood louse, and although it may not have seemed much to you as I recounted it, to me it was a great discovery. Would I want to be a wood louse, my aura, pure and beautiful? The answer: no, I like being who I am, a human being with clutter. But I could do with a little more gold in my aura, a little more purity in my heart, in my mind. I guess I'll just have to keep working at it. Maybe one day . . . with God's help.

Finally, last but by no means least, the color *silver*. This color, in all its beauty, can be used to bring about the enhancement of spiritual love. What does that mean—spiritual love? To understand, we have to remember the philosopher Pierre Teilhard de Chardin and his words, which I quoted in my first book, *The Eagle and the Rose*, "We are not human beings having a spiritual experience; but spiritual beings having a human experience."

And Christ said, "Love thy neighbor as thyself." And we are all of God, even the woman who was rude to us as we shopped in the supermarket. Or the driver who screamed obscenities, or the man who practically knocked us over in his rush to catch the train, or my companion at the airport. What I'm trying to say is that we all speak of tolerance, knowing we must strive to practice it, knowing that sometimes we find it impossible. We speak, too, of love, of giving, of friendship, yet we limit these things. To have spiritual love, to give spiritual love . . . is to give someone a smile because you have it to give, not because you want it returned. It is to put out your arms to someone and be unoffended if that person seems to turn their back on you. To do a good deed for the pure sake of it. Not requiring appreciation or acknowledgment . . . simply giving from the heart, because you have something to give.

The color silver. This energy, fluid, liquid strands that move through the universe, silent, noiseless, and pure. This is the energy of purity.

• • •

One day she woke, feeling sick. Perhaps it was the beginning of a cold, or a migraine? Knowing she must go to the office, that a day off was out of the question, knowing, too, that she was in need of a little healing, she picked out the softest pale blue sweater. As she put it on, instantly she felt much better.

Next day, in turmoil, having had an emotional and somewhat upsetting argument with his boss, knowing that the rest of the day was going to be difficult, and seeking some inner peace he knew he was in need of, he was glad that he had chosen to wear his favorite shirt. A rich subtle green soft cotton. As he ran his fingers over it, he let out a sigh of relief.

Going out, tonight of all nights, having been on her feet all day, feeling totally worn-out, she knew that if she was going to make it, she would have to get an extra spurt of energy. A red scarf with that little black dress would be just the thing.

It was an exciting day. He had just received the news that his daughter had given birth, his first grandchild, a girl, and he was sure she would be beautiful. Hurrying to the car, he tightly clasped his small parcel, remembering his wife's last words when she had called from the hospital to give him the news. "Don't forget to bring the blanket," she had said. How could he? They had gone out and chosen it together. Soft and pure white, with fine strands of rose-pink ribbon threaded through it. They wanted to give the baby something special, and what could be more special than wrapping the baby in a blanket of love?

All I want, she thought as she hurried home from work, is to put my feet up and watch TV. Opening the door, however, she was immediately bombarded by her children. Mark, age twelve, eager to talk about his soccer game, and how he wished she'd been there to see him score a goal. Cissy, beautiful fifteen-year-old Cissy, who was in tears because she was off to a sleepover and had nothing to wear. And Matt, the oldest, seventeen, on his way out for a driving lesson, but hungry, and waiting for Mom to come home and feed him. All this, and she hadn't even taken her coat off yet. It was nine o'clock before she finally sat down, cozy and warm in her soft fur slippers. She smiled a contented smile, feeling the stress of the day leaving her, as she pulled her robe more snugly around her, and sighed a sigh of pure heaven. She loved this robe. It was old and a little worn, but the color, it made her feel so good, it was the softest and most delicate shade of mauve.

In need of strength, he stood by the graveside, wondering, as he watched the coffin being lowered into the ground, how he was going to manage without her. All his life she had been there for him, loving him, scolding him, sometimes smothering, but mostly mothering him, in the very best way. Feeling the tears on his face, biting down hard on his lip, he reached for her scarf, which he had kept in his pocket since she died. He pulled it out, crushing it in his hand, and began to wipe away his tears with it, whispering, "Mother, Mother, Mother." The scarf brushing his face, he could smell her, a comforting mother smell, and opening his hand he looked down fondly at the delicate piece of chiffon. Deep purple and seeming to shine, it was his mother's favorite. "Makes me feel closer to God," he heard her say, and smiling, he remembered that she always said that when she tucked the scarf into her coat. He lifted his head and was surprised to see the sun shining so brightly that it made him squint. "Mother," he whispered again, and clutching the scarf now more tightly as the rich purple seemed to seep through his skin, "Mother, your scarf makes me feel closer to you."

It was her wedding day. A day of love and joy and happiness. The service was wonderful, their vows had been said, and it was as they exchanged wedding rings, as she looked down at the pure gold band that was now shining on her finger, symbolizing all that she was feeling, all her hopes and dreams and aspirations, it was as she gazed at the band of gold that she really understood how truly alive she was.

His wife gone more than eight years before, his children grown and busy celebrating the holidays far away, unable to get home, the old man pondered what to do. He was on his own. It was Christmas Eve, and as he sat in his comfy old friend of a chair, memories of earlier Christmases came to him, when the kids were young, and the house was noisy with excitement. Anne would round them up and get them off to bed. Then it would be their time. A ritual glass or two of homemade apple cider, cookies, fresh-baked from the oven, Anne laughing as he struggled to get the box from the attic, and the old worn tree, which wasn't so old and worn back then. The ritual decorating of the Christmas tree. Chuckling, a single tear falling from the old man's eye, he heaved himself out of the chair and made his way slowly up the attic stairs. The box and tree were just as he had left them last year, and the year before, and all the years since Anne had gone. It was his ritual now, and he had never missed a year. Pulling the tree and box, which had become so much heavier now, it seemed, down the attic steps, he could hear his Anne laughing. "Come on, old man, I want my tree." Her laughter rang throughout the house. "Well, come on, old woman"—he chuckled as he puffed his way into the living room—"don't just stand there watching, give me a hand." For a moment he sat, catching his breath, the only noise the sound of the clock on the mantel, *tick, tick, tick,* and for a brief moment the loneliness and emptiness of his life overwhelmed him. He heard her voice again, loud as could be, as if she were standing right next to him. "Come on, my love, I want my tree," and the force of her, the force of her spirit, her love, propelled him out of his chair. Kneeling in front of the box, he reached inside with his trembling old man's fingers, and for a long time he reached in and out, and hung baubles on the tree. All memories, every one, and then the last, the crowning glory. A silver star, shiny and glittering. With aching bones he reached high up to the highest branch of the worn old tree and balanced the star on the very top. Exhausted but pleased, he sat again in his comfy old friend of a chair, and gazed, as he always did, with wonder and delight at the Christmas tree.

"Well, my love," he said to Anne, "what do you think, then?" He heard her chuckle. "Well, my love," she said, "you've got silver from the star on your fingers, and silver in your hair, and on your face. And I've got it all over me, too." And the old man looked, and the old man saw, for he, like his wife, had silver in his heart and silver in his soul. And it was another happy Christmas.

Reading these stories, we can see how color can and does, often without our realizing it, play a big part in our lives. We can see, too, how we can consciously use certain types of energy to enhance, help, and aid our lives. My team of healers has been trained to use color energy, not just with and for their patients, but also for themselves, which they do on a regular daily basis. You can do this, too.

Remember that each color has a variety of shades and hues that we can use. Colors that combine and, as energy, make up the aura.

This next exercise deals with how we can learn to develop a constructive use of color, energy, and thought, and to bring about certain changes in our aura, and therefore, as the aura is a mirror image of our inner selves, change our own selves for the better. In doing so, we go even one step further toward our own discovery. The discovery of the self, the awareness of self, the awareness of our spirit, and the awareness of our power.

MY OWN FIELD OF ENERGY

Through visualization and energy creation, we can, with lots of practice, create an aura that is full of vibrant, brilliant color, full of life. We can, if we persevere, create beautiful, positive, and constructive energy, and in so doing, discover a way to create inner peace, harmony, and light . . . the essence of being.

Never forget, when doing these exercises, that the aura mirrors the inner self. By creating the pattern, shape, and characteristics of your aura, you will begin to shape your own self. Remember, do this with love and yes, here's that word again, gentleness.

We begin Exercise I, as always, with meditation, achieving within ourselves a state of calm well-being. Breathing gently through the solar plexus, we then reach a state of awareness of our own energy as we learned to do in Chapter Two.

Take a few moments to enjoy the feelings and sensations of the exercise and stretch your senses as an athlete might flex his muscles, or as a cat might stretch and purr with ecstasy when basking in the warm sun.

Now, your eyes closed and your mind alert, begin to visualize your own energy field. You may at first find it difficult to see anything more than an almost indefinable mist, but reach out with that part of your mind that desires knowledge and learning. That part of you that inspired a desire to reach out to do these exercises. Visualize your aura in a rainbow of color, moving, dancing, full of life. And breathe deeply yet gently, becoming calm. Try doing this over a period of a few days until you feel that you have achieved some small state of recognition of your aura. Then allow yourself the luxury of enjoying the sensation, repeating the exercise daily, over a period of a few days or even a week or two. Do nothing but relax and enjoy the experience, and don't try at this stage to change anything, just get to know and to recognize that your aura exists and is you. Don't push for more yet. Be patient, more is on the way.

Patience really is needed now, as there is often within us the urge to learn more and more, and to race ahead before we are ready. A child, having watched someone more experienced mold clay into something fine, will dive gleefully into a pot of wet clay, expecting to do the same. All that happens is that the child gets messy and the clay is ruined. A good teacher will show the child slowly how to be constructive and creative with his clay.

Although these exercises seem to be teaching you, the fact is that they guide, steer, and gently prepare you to come to the realization that you yourself are the teacher. Eventually you will learn to sense, to feel, to see, to be more aware. Not just self-aware. You will begin to notice, more acutely, the many things that are around you in your daily life, things you might have taken for granted before you started to fine-tune your senses. Becoming more aware of your own emotions, you will also be more acutely aware that the people around you are also sensitive and emotional beings, even those who don't show it, and you will begin to be more tolerant of the moods of others. Most exciting, though, is the possibility of your becoming "in tune" with the universe. "At home." You are fine-tuning your senses, which means that you are getting ready to sense, to see and to feel, many things you were not able to before, things that are of the universe and of the spirit world. As you begin to understand, you will teach yourself, but being too eager or too impatient is foolish, for in rushing ahead, you will miss the finer points of the experience your exercise will give you, and you will only create a sense of frustration and confusion, because you were unable to find the right frequency that enables you to tune into your own self, let alone anyone or anything else.

Give yourself two to three weeks, continuing this exercise on a regular daily basis, then the chances are that you will be ready to go further.

• • •

Begin Exercise 2 once again, with meditation, and continue with the exercise until, through visualization, you see your aura bright and clear.

Now, using your thought process, let's see if you can change the color and pattern of your aura.

Remind yourself of the eight colors we used earlier and ask yourself which of these colors is the most likely to help you achieve a state of peace and harmony. It might be helpful to read some comments from a handful of my students. When asked the question "Have you visualized your own aura?" here are their answers:

Georgie Jackson, a healer, and my student of many years, says, "My aura seems made up of layers of color. Pink in the middle, then green, over which is a wider layer of blue, over which is a wide, luxurious layer of sparkling gold. It took me more than two years before I could see my aura, and it still surprises me that I can see anything at all. When I feel down, I visualize filling myself up with the sun or wrapping myself in a gold blanket. It makes me feel comforted, warm, safe, and happy."

Jeanne Hinsley, also a healer, and student of many years, says, "After a long time of searching, I finally saw my own aura. It was like a shadow, a dusty haze, surrounding my whole body, making me feel warm and cosseted. I tried 'painting' pink into my aura and the results were great. I felt a tingling sensation which went from the top of my head to the tips of my toes. I felt as if I glowed, and I felt cherished."

Lynn Bolton, wife of the chairman of the R.A.A.H., and a full-fledged healer for many years, had these comments: "Although I have never seen my own aura, which disappoints and frustrates me at times, I do feel it. When I am happy and bright, the air or energy around me feels warm and as light as a silk scarf as it wraps around me. If I am depressed, that same air feels cold and dingy. Painting my aura is an uplifting experience that gives me a warm and comfortable feeling inside. It makes me feel loved and important."

Many of my students have never seen either their own or anyone else's aura, and so when they work on altering or changing their energy, they use the visualization techniques we have been using and will use here. We were all born with a certain amount of creative imagination, and as we develop this, particularly with our aura exercises, our visualization skills will improve.

As you begin, remember to be positive and constructive with your thoughts, and start to create a state of harmony and peace within your energy.

If I were doing this exercise, I might choose green, rose pink, or silver. However, don't allow yourself to be influenced by my choice, but make your own. If you do choose one of the three colors that I favor, then it must be because you feel that this color is right for you.

Let's go ahead, then, and experiment a little with our choice of color. Think of yourself as an artist. Don't worry about how good you can be, but with controlled confidence—remember, you are in charge—visualize the paintbrush lying on the table in front of you. Take a deep breath, pick up the brush, and begin to paint. What color did you choose? Visualize it. Dip your brush deep into it, then begin to "paint it" into your aura. Imagine that you are standing upright, floating two feet from the ground, and that you are painting the space around you. Keep dipping your brush into the paint pot, but use it sparingly at first. Test it out, "see" how it "feels." And when you become used to the "feel" of it, and only when it "feels" comfortable, then you can reach for another color to "paint into your aura." You might want to visualize wide, bold streaks of color around you. Or you might prefer to "paint" spots or splotches or other shapes. A house, a dog or cat. Stars or leaf shapes, flowers, anything you like.

Through a process of creative thinking and visualization, you can now "paint your picture." Fill your aura with bright and positive colors. First, create peace and harmony within your aura, using the colors that work best for you, then, slowly, build in vitality and purpose, love and life, and above all, light.

Each color has a certain type of energy all its own. Blues and greens will give you harmony, peace, and healing. Put in a little red, maybe orange, pink for love, and for the light in your life, which we all need, gold and silver, maybe in the shape of the sun and moon. Experiment with the colors, with your energy, and have fun.

This is an art, and in a way that you have never done before, perhaps never thought possible before, you can become more creative and constructive. You can learn to build the finest masterpiece, the most important work you have ever done, or will ever do, because you are learning to construct and produce your own energy field, thereby dictating, taking charge of who you are, what you are, and even why you are. You can learn to be anyone you want to be.

Own your power. Look on this as a great adventure, perhaps the greatest adventure you've ever had, through which you will stumble upon even greater discoveries. The best and most important discoveries, discoveries of the self. Many of us are afraid to learn, afraid to know, afraid of so many things. But fear can be a destructive emotion and therefore very negative. Hopefully, through your learning process, as Grey Eagle and I guide you through your exercises, leading you gently toward yourself, you will come to understand that the only thing in life we have to fear is fear itself.

Face it, look it straight in the eye, and you will find that it simply disappears.

There is not one among us who does not have the light of love, the light of God, within us somewhere. Reach for this, and you will find that the light will burn ever brighter as you recognize it more and more. And it will be mirrored in the energy field that surrounds you. The energy field you will come to know as you come to know yourself.

So, paint your picture, using the colors you choose carefully and gently. Expand your picture, allow it to grow and take shape. The pattern will alter as your thoughts alter, but you are the artist, you control the brush, and you are the one responsible for your own creation. Make your picture the brightest, clearest, most positive and beautiful work of art ever. It won't turn out to be perfect, but it will be your own, and of your own making.

Before you start on this part of the journey toward yourself, try to remember this:

We are, all of us, able to give something of inestimable value to others—namely *love*.

First, though, we must learn to give it to our own selves.

• • •

Hopefully, you have now completed the exercises in this chapter. Possibly, hopefully, you have done them many times, and are achieving great results.

Before we move on to Chapter Five, I would like to take a moment to reflect on what I last wrote, the part about giving love to ourselves, and also to suggest another exercise you might want to try.

Why is it, I wonder, and have wondered over the years a thousand times and more, why is it that we find it so difficult to give love to ourselves? Why, I wonder, was it so hard for me? And in pondering this question, I find myself, as we all will do, looking back, reaching into the past to try to discover the clues that will help me find the answers.

My guide draws close to me, and I visualize that ocean of emotions that as a child, and as an adult, were my great turbulent sea, and wonder briefly, could I have drowned in that sea, could any of us drown? Grey Eagle, laughing at my thoughts, is quick to explain to me that we can drown only if we create a whirlpool, if we refuse to allow our emotions to flow, if we trap our energy within us. Then yes, he says, then we will drown in the despair of loneliness and isolation, for our whirlpool will become the wall that will inhibit our growth.

Looking back over my life, I see how many times through the years I have almost drowned in my own personal river of misery and despair, often causing myself more pain than necessary because I would not share my emotions. It is easy to figure out why I couldn't share, why I always showed a good face to the world, even when I felt my sanity going.

Remembering, I hear the taunts from brothers and sisters, mother and father, "Crybaby, crybaby, leave her alone, don't talk to her, miserable crybaby."

Remembering myself at age sixteen, I see my father standing in front of me, a large round smooth stone held in the palm of his hand. As if it were yesterday, I clearly hear him say, "See this stone, see this stone, take a good look. Hold it, feel it." And he pressed it into my hands. "Make your heart like this stone. Make yourself hard. Don't cry for anyone, and never cry for yourself."

What my father said was not just advice, it was an order. It was a shock, but used to obeying his orders without thought, I learned to hide my emotions, not realizing that sooner or later they would swirl around and around inside me, and eventually rise up to choke me, that I would almost drown. So I built my wall, bigger, thicker, and stronger than any wall could possibly be, as many of us have done. Keeping my fears and pain, my thoughts and feelings, especially my feelings, keeping these things inside, and consequently, everyone and everything else out.

Many years and a great deal of learning later, having knocked down my wall, I began building again. That's what this book is about, and that is what life is about, but many people feel they don't have the tools to build, or the capacity to design. So to help us with our work I thought I would tell you John's story, and how together, he and I, how ... well, let's see.

• • •

I first met John when he came to one of our centers for healing. He was just eighteen years old, and very curious about my work. After a year or so he became a student, joining one of the classes of the R.A.A.H. One day he came to me expressing a desire to know more about himself. He was twenty-one years old and was looking to his future, but not in the way most of us do. He was not concerned about his career prospects, nor was he too concerned at this point in his life about girlfriends, although he made it clear that marriage and children were important to his future at some time, but not yet. John's concerns were more to do with what kind of person he would become as he grew older. Contentment and happiness were key issues, and he had learned enough to realize that he would only achieve these goals by looking within himself and by building a good and strong character. His problem was how to do it, and so he sought my advice.

We decided to meet once a week on Wednesday evenings, a huge commitment for me as my workload was already full, but I felt John was worth my time and effort. I knew also that the exercise we were about to undertake would be a great healing process for both of us. And so it was that I, the insightful one, taught insight. And so it was that I, the designer, created in John a great architect. And so it can be that if you follow along closely, you, too, will find insight, design, and, hopefully, just in the way my student gave inspiration to me, this story will give inspiration to you.

"We are going to build a house," I said, that first Wednesday evening. "Each week you must make notes, write down your thoughts and feelings, and from week to week you must work on those thoughts, consider your feelings, until you have what you

145

want." John looked at me as if I was a little nuts. What was I talking about? How could we build a house, a ridiculous suggestion, except . . . he had been my student for over two years, and he trusted that I knew what I was doing.

"Okay, then," he said brightly, "where do we begin?"

"Well, first"—I laughed, pleased with his confidence—"before we build the house, we have to design it. And before we design it, we have to decide on a site. The nice thing about what we're doing here is that there are no restrictions. We can build anything we like, choose any materials, and we can build where we like. Our choices are wide open."

"Well," said John, "I've always wanted to live near the sea. Not too close, but if the house were on a hill, I could have a great view."

"So, then, views are important to you?" I asked. "What else is important? Do you want to build your house away from other houses, or do you like your neighbors nearby?"

"No, I don't want to be on my own. I would definitely like houses on either side, close by. Not too much land, just a small garden back and front."

"And would you grow flowers or vegetables or both?" I asked.

"Both," replied John quickly, not having to give any thought to the last question at all. He was getting into this now. It was fun. He could have anything he liked, and he liked that idea.

"So, you now know roughly where you want your house to be. You have chosen the site. Nice views, neighbors, small garden, flowers and vegetables, right?" I asked. And John nodded.

"Let's look at these things, then, and let's see what this tells us about the kind of person you are. You want a view, so this tells me that you don't like confinement. You need to be able to stretch. You want neighbors, which speaks to the fact that you like people and want to be around them. How am I doing so far?"

146

John again nodded his agreement, adding, "I want a garden, and flowers and vegetables. Does this mean, then, that I want to grow?"

"Well," I said, "it could mean that, and it could also tell you that you like to be productive, and that it is important for you to see the results of your labor."

"I get it," said John. "We are going to build a house, but really I'm the house. We are going to build me, right? And the site, well, that can tell me whether I'm a loner, if I need people in my life, and how clearly I need to see where I am." I smiled, knowing that he understood, knowing that he had already made progress.

Over the next several months John and I painstakingly erected his house, I guiding, John building. He chose the materials carefully, and believe it or not, this taught John a lot about his vanity. It was important to him that his house looked good from the outside. That he looked good from the outside, but the real work came as we began to design the interior of the house. A bathroom, of course. A living room, kitchen, and a bedroom. We now had to consider, however, not just the necessities of living—this was the time for John to consider his emotional and spiritual needs, his many facets both as a human and a spiritual being. I reminded him again that his house could be as large or small as he wanted, and he could decorate it any way he pleased.

"I want a music room," he said, and he discovered the need within him for music and for rhythm.

"I want a games room, a room for fun," and in voicing this, he discovered within him the need for laughter.

"A study, yes, a room to read and to be quiet," he said, acknowledging within himself the need for quiet meditation.

Every time we created a room, we would carefully furnish and decorate, using colors that were appropriate to the specific needs of the room. If he was feeling depressed and needed uplifting, he would mentally "step into" the games room. The decor must be appropriate, light, bright, sunny. The study must be a room of calm, no bright colors here to detract from quiet meditation.

And so, the months turned into a year, then more, as each week we worked to build. Some of you may wonder why we took so long, some of you may have already guessed the answer, for do we ever stop building? Only if we stop growing, only then.

"I think I'd like a nursery," said John on one of our Wednesday nights, many months into our project, and I smiled a secret smile, for this lovely young man, who at this point in his life did not have a girlfriend, was, I knew, acknowledging his need to one day share his life, his house, himself, with someone special. To have love in his life, and to have a family. At that time he felt that love was a pipe dream, that it was a dream he would perhaps never realize, but I encouraged him to include his nursery, knowing that one day in the future he would become a father.

It was I who introduced them. Claire was a student, and while studying, she stayed with me for several months. For her it was love at first sight; for John, well, he was a little more cautious, it took him a little longer. As soon as I saw them together, I knew they were meant for each other. I also knew that John knew himself, he knew more than most men his age the kind of person he wanted to be and the kind of life he wanted to have. He had grown in confidence, he was happy with who he was, knowing he would change and grow more with time.

They were married, and about eighteen months later their first child, a girl, Lucy, was born.

All that time ago, when John first came to me to ask for my help, his key issues were that he attain contentment and happiness. We all know that these two things can be elusive. But in building, in working on himself, my friend has discovered these things, for he has discovered that contentment and happiness come from within.

• • •

Now it's your turn, and to help you I thought I would give you an example or two of the rooms you might want to build. You will see as we decorate what an important role color plays in our lives, and so we must make it work for us, just as we did in our earlier exercise in this chapter. We are, through visualization, trying to create rooms, spaces, within us, which, as we did when we painted our aura, our external energy, we can now do with our internal energy. As we go along, I will remind you of the color guide we used, and we will color our rooms accordingly.

A most important room for many people is a family room. Some might say this room is the heart of the house, where loved ones come to be together. To sit with one another, to talk and express themselves. The family room that we would build within us might be a room large enough to house the emotions and feelings of others. A place where we might "think" ourselves if we wish to contemplate the needs and requirements of those around us, whenever we desire to care and share ourselves with them. It should be warmly painted, maybe a soft blue, with sunlight-yellow drapes, and gentle spring-green sofas with deep and soft welcoming cushions.

This is a room that must be immediately calming and relaxing, where any tensions or fraught emotions can be calmed. It is a room we might enter when considering the needs of our children, our spouse, and our parents. A room of decisions, sometimes difficult ones. Often a room where painful emotions dwell, not just our own emotions, but the emotions of our loved ones. And, of course, this is a room where we can contemplate and remind ourselves of our joys and blessings. We must furnish it in a way that feels good to us, somewhere we can sit and unravel our jumbled and often confused thoughts. Visualize walking into this room. Make it a room where common sense, good thoughts, and lots of love prevail, against any odds. Love for ourselves, as well as others. Visualize sitting on those sofas, sinking into their warmth and comfort. This room is a place that will help you find peace and joy, and gentleness.

In our family life, when situations arise, we often see ourselves as being too close to the issue, to the person. We can become confused with our emotions and irrational in our thinking. Our internal family room can solve this problem. Entering it, we can learn to think rationally and lovingly, and without harsh judgment.

The colors I chose were blue, gold, and green. If we look at our color chart we can see that first our room is full of wonderful healing energy. The warm soft healing color blue. If we surround ourselves with the color blue, we bring an energy that is calming and peaceful, enabling us to stem anxiety. Gold is the energy of wisdom, of joy and hope, of laughter and happiness. Certainly in our family room we need this energy, and the strength that it gives to us. Finally I used the color green, and as we visualize ourselves deep in the comfort of those wonderful green sofas, we must remember that the color green is the energy that aids in harmonizing the soul, the spirit, and the body.

As I have been writing I have also been visualizing, and the effect of this has been great. I feel calm and rested and at peace in my mind. Try it. Be patient, you can do it, and I truly believe it will work for you.

As you are visualizing, remember that not only are you using your own energy, which you can build more of, you are also drawing into you that external, universal, or God energy, which flows into and out of the body, through those spiritual centers that we call chakras. We have already talked about chakras, and in fact learned in Chapter Two how to use three of them. The one seated close to the solar plexus, and the two placed within the palm centers.

Let us, briefly now, take a look at another of the rooms we might need within us. The bathroom. Our house would not be complete without one, but obviously the function of our inner bathroom would be somewhat different than the function of a bathroom used for physical cleansing. In our inner bathroom, we would want a facility for mentally cleansing ourselves. Getting rid of all those harsh and confusing thoughts that create such a jumble in our heads.

My inner bathroom would comprise simply a shower. A large, roomy cubicle, maybe with a seat in it. The showerhead would be large, the faucet would be powerful, and the temperature of the water would always be the same whenever I stepped into the cubicle and turned on the taps ... the water would always be perfect. I would color the inside of the cubicle the palest pink, and the color of the water as it streamed over me, I would color the palest, purest, gentlest mauve. For in standing under my man-made waterfall, I would need not just to be cleansed, but to be loved and healed. This, for me, would be one of my most important rooms, as even the thought of spending some "me time," in this way makes me feel warm and soothed inside, just the same way that indulging in a piping-hot mug of chocolate on a cold, cold day does.

Of course, no house would truly be complete without a room of quiet. A room to rest, to meditate, to read or simply take some quiet relaxation. You could call this room a library or a reading room, a music room, or, like me, a study. For me the idea of a quiet, cozy little study sounds like heaven.

A fireplace with real logs, nothing fake. Two comfortable Victorian leather armchairs, the color of warm russet. And a footstool, for when I really relax I like to put my feet up. I would color the walls cream and give them the texture of rough burlap. The drapes framing the two long narrow windows would be tapestry, birds and leaves, and warm autumn colors. And whenever I went into this room, the fire would always be lit, the flames leaping up and over the large rough-cut logs and reflecting in the heavy brasswork around and in front of the fireplace. The carpet, the same pattern as the drapes, would be of the most luxurious deep pile so that when I entered the room, in my bare feet, I would feel instantly pampered.

Each of us as human beings has many facets, many sides, rooms within. What better than to create a sanctuary of rooms that we can visualize, mentally step into, and use to benefit us? What better than that each room be changeable, as we change? What better than that they are our own?

In one of my workshops, in Manchester, England, I formed about eight groups of around twenty people each, and gave each group a choice of four rooms. Study, bedroom, bathroom, and family room. Six of the eight groups chose either the study or family room, feeling that the others were a less than exciting project. Of the two groups left one chose the bedroom, one the bathroom. The consensus of opinion generally was that the bathroom was the most limiting. Not so, however, as the results of the exercise showed.

Each group was asked to develop, design, and be as creative as they could be with their room, bearing in mind the needs of the individual when entering the room, and also bearing in mind that they could have within that framework anything they wanted. No expense should be spared.

Our group with the bathroom astounded us all. They built nothing short of the most luxurious Roman spa. Beautifully tiled, a sauna, hot tub, and bathtub. A shower to die for, large, soft towels, the palest blue. Sofas and loungers. Creams and soaps of the most delicate fragrances. Candles everywhere, giving out a soft light that took away the harshness of the white tubs. Ooh, just imagine, just visualize . . . a busy day at the office, sitting in rush-hour traffic, surrounded by kids and problems.

"I'm just going to take a bath," you might say, at the end of such a day. You go into the bathroom, climb into the tub, close your eyes, and escape. Take a brief mental step into your sanctuary, into your inner bathroom, and cleanse and pamper yourself until you feel restored. Give me that Roman spa any day of the week. It certainly works for me.

And as she looked about, she did behold,
How over that same door was likewise writ,
Be bold, be bold, and everywhere be bold.

EDMUND SPENSER

CHAPTER 5

Joining Forces with the Spirit World

The title of this chapter might suggest séances, tarot cards, dark rooms, and eerie whisperings, as for many, the idea of joining forces with the spirit world means having to go into some trancelike state. Far from it, although speaking of such things reminds me of the first couple of experiences I had with a Ouija board.

My husband and I had gone to a friend's house for dinner. I was just twenty at the time. Our friends Clary and Jan were a little older than us, and had two young sons, who were both sound asleep in their beds.

It was Clary's suggestion. Apparently he had wanted to experiment for a while. My husband thought it was a riot, Jan thought it might be fun. I was the only one unwilling. "We need four," said Clary, putting his arm around me. "Come on, be a sport, what can it hurt?"

We got the glass and placed it upside down on the table, the letters of the alphabet written on scrap paper, placed around the

154

edge, forming a circle. Clary took charge, behaving as if he had done this many times before.

"Forefingers lightly on the glass," he instructed, placing his own finger on, and looking to the rest of us to follow suit.

"Not me," I said, already very nervous and not really wanting to play.

"Oh, come on," said my husband, "don't be a scaredy cat, it won't bite you." And he and Jan followed Clary's example, although I had the feeling Jan wasn't too keen either.

Clary gave me a hard look, but I stood my ground. He shrugged, closed his eyes, and in his most dramatic voice said, "Is there anybody there?"

Nothing happened. We waited a few moments, and then he tried again, his voice sounding even more like something out of a horror movie. "Is there anybody there?" he called dramatically, and again, no movement, no sound, nothing happened.

Clary was disappointed and frustrated. I was relieved until he said, "Now look, Rosemary, it's obviously not working because we have a broken circle." For someone who had never done this before, he was beginning to sound like an expert.

"You're just going to have to help. Put your finger on the glass with the rest of us. Be fair. We all want to do this, so stop being a wet blanket."

In those days, when I was just a young woman, insecure, afraid of not pleasing, it was easy to persuade me that I was spoiling everyone's fun. I was easily embarrassed by most things, and so I put my finger on the glass. Despite my fear, despite my headache and my pounding heart, I put my finger on the glass. Immediately, it began to move, circling the table, at first very slowly, then moving faster and faster, so that it was difficult to stay with it. No one was given time to think, to ask questions. We were all stunned into silence.

Abruptly the glass stopped. Taken by surprise, each of us took our hands away and sat gazing at the table. Then: "Come on, Clary," my husband said, laughing. "That was a good trick."

"I didn't move it," replied Clary indignantly.

"Well, I didn't," said Jan, and "Nor did I," I said, then, "Let's not do this anymore, I've had enough."

"If none of us moved the glass, and we all swear we didn't, well then," said my husband, "I'm with Clary. Let's see if we can get it to move again. Maybe spell something out for us."

"I'm game," said Clary eagerly. "Come on, you two," referring to Jan and me. "Let's try again, only this time I'll ask some questions, right."

Tentatively we placed our fingers on the glass. Nothing happened.

"It's waiting for a question," Clary said confidently, and once more, closing his eyes, and in a trancelike way, he repeated, "Is there anybody there? Is there anybody there?"

The glass seemed to jerk a little. Someone's pushing it, I thought. It jerked again, and involuntarily I blurted out, "If anyone's pushing it, they'd better stop right now." My nerve was cracking and it was showing. All my life I had spent my energy trying to ward off these external and unseen forces, unseen by most, that is. Why would I want to call them to me? This was crazy. But I was too afraid of upsetting my friends to stop.

Slowly, very slowly, the glass began to move, circling the table once again, and again, really into this now, Clary asked, "Is there anybody there?"

We watched with bated breath, my heart thumping loudly in my chest. The glass, still moving, seemed to me to be seeking something out. It speeded up, slowed, then stopped in front of the letter *C*.

"Write it down, write it down," cried Clary excitedly to Jan, who had a notepad and pencil in front of her, and she dutifully did as he said. The glass moved again, circling 'round and 'round. Fast, then slow, fast again, searching. Definitely searching.

I wanted to stop, but now I was just as fascinated as the others.

The glass stopped in front of the letter *L*, then *A*, then *R*, *E*, *N*, and *C* again, then stopped at the letter *E*. It had spelled out the name Clarence.

"That's me, that's me," cried Clary. "It wants to talk to me."

NO. The glass had shot over to the left of the table, where between the letters was written the word NO. On the right of the table, between letters was written the word YES. This, Clary had explained earlier, was so that any spirit wishing to communicate would find it easier to answer simple yes and no questions.

Moving, circling, the glass once more moved to the word NO, and instinctively I knew we had a presence. Someone who called himself Clarence. Now I really wanted to stop, in the worst way. I was truly afraid, yet my finger stayed firmly on the glass, and it was me who asked the next question, and the next.

"Your name is Clarence?"

"Yes."

"What do you want to say to us?"

A mind of its own, yet somehow directed by the four of us, the glass moved around the table, seeming to gain more confidence as it did so. Spelling out several words, and even though this happened so long ago, I still remember everything clearly.

F-I-R-E ... F-I-R-E
C-A-R ... C-A-R
A-C-C-I-D-E-N-T
K-I-L-L-E-D ... K-I-L-L-E-D
B-R-I-D-G-E ... B-R-I-D-G-E
B-R-I-D-G-E

Jan had written down the words, but there had been no need. We could all see the message quite clearly, although none of us could see the point of it.

I took my finger off the glass. "That's enough," I said shakily. "I agree," said Jan, "I don't like it. It's spooky."

The men saw things differently, and desperately wanted to continue. My husband was convinced that one of us must be pushing the glass. It was fun. He wanted to see how far it would go. Clary, however, was totally convinced, as I was, that there was an entity, a spirit, in the room with us. Furthermore, because of the name, he felt that this spirit must connect to him. In that assumption, I totally agreed.

So we had a stalemate. The girls wanted to stop. The boys wanted to go on. Eventually we came to a compromise, but only because Clary was pleading. "Just once more. Just one more question, please. Let's just ask if it wants to tell us anything else. Come on, girls, one more question, okay?"

Giving in, we placed our fingers on the glass one more time, and Clary asked the question.

Moving slowly, no jerking, no hesitation, the glass went from letter to letter. First, *D*, then *A*. On to *V-I-D*.

"David," cried Clary, "it spelled David." But the glass did not stop. *S-I-M-O*... "No more, no more," cried Jan, and she swept her hand across the table in fear and panic, knocking the glass and the letters to the floor, ending the "game." Then, jumping out of her chair, she ran upstairs to her two sleeping children to make sure they were safe. She need not have worried, the boys were curled up in their beds, safe and sound. Her two boys, David and Simon.

It was several weeks later before we mentioned that night again, and it was after Clary had been home to Yorkshire for a family funeral. At the first opportunity, he had cornered his mother and asked, "Is there another Clary in the family?"

"Not really," she replied, "except, of course, for your great-uncle Clarence, who you were named after. He died just before you were born. Terrible tragedy that was. He was killed in a car accident. Hit a bridge and the car exploded, burst into flames.

But that was years ago. Nobody ever really thinks about it these days."

But Clary thought about it, for a long, long, time. So did I.

Four years passed. We were still friends with Clary and Jan, although we didn't see them as often as we used to. I had been sick and had undergone surgery. Also, we had been trying, unsuccessfully, for a baby, and I had already had two miscarriages. It seemed so unfair, and was made even more difficult to handle as women all around me were either pregnant or pushing baby carriages around, as if there was a childbirth epidemic.

My husband and I were at a neighbor's party. It was fun; everyone, it seemed, was having a good time, until the hostess suggested we "play" the Ouija board. Once bitten, I was having none of it, but my husband and several others thought it was a great idea, and immediately set about clearing and preparing the table. More than twenty sat to play. Others surrounded them, standing, watching, suggesting questions.

I sat as far away from the table as I could, not wanting any part of it, although my friends kept calling me over. "If you don't want to sit in, at least ask a question," one friend said, and as I watched the glass move, I tried to warn them to stop. But it was fun, a game, a party, and first one question, then another and another were asked. There was laughter and friendly banter, and it seemed there was nothing to be afraid of, yet I was afraid. They were messing with something they didn't understand. Please stop, please stop, I silently begged, while my friends were laughing more and more.

"Come on," they called, "don't sit over there, come on, ask a question, ask a question," but I would not move.

"I know," I then heard a girlfriend of mine say. "We'll ask a question for her." I leaped out of my chair and raced to the table, meaning to knock the glass away, but my friends, laughing, held me back. "It's only a bit of fun, don't be so silly," and the question was out before I could stop them.

159

"Will Rosemary have a baby? She really wants one."

And . . . and the glass began to spin. Around and around the table, with what seemed a malevolent force, faster, faster, slowing a little. I watched, eyes wide, not struggling now. The glass shot over to the left of the table, and everything went quiet. No laughing now. Not funny anymore, and I closed my eyes to stop the tears, but they came out anyway as I got my coat and left the house. It took less than ten minutes to walk home, but it seemed like forever. I so desperately wanted a child, had cried and mourned the losses I had had. What if it was right? What if the glass was right? What if the answer was *no*?

While I was carrying Samantha, all through the nine months of my difficult pregnancy, each time the doctors gave me my weekly shot, then when the ambulance raced me into hospital with toxemia, dangerously high blood pressure, discovering at seven months that they had failed to protect my baby from a possible problem, due to my rare blood type, all that time, in the back of my mind I was scared that something bad would happen. Every twinge, every small problem became exaggerated, because every so often I would see the Ouija board, remember the glass next to the word NO, and remember the question, "Will Rosemary have a baby?"

The Ouija board was wrong, is often wrong, due mainly to the fact that those who use it have no idea what they are doing. They have no idea of the power and energy of the universe, which is not to be used as a toy, as entertainment. They have no idea of the mischief and malevolence that is waiting for some naive and unsuspecting individual or individuals to trigger.

When most of us think of the spirit world we think of God, of the light and pure power, of the wonderful God force that surrounds and protects us. But we should be ever mindful of the face of evil, and the terrifying and malevolent force of evil. To forget or ignore its existence would be, at the very least, foolish, and for those like myself who work constantly with the many forces of the universe, it would be downright dangerous. Protection is simple, though, and requires only a small prayer and a pure and good heart, for though the face of evil is one that most of us are fortunate enough never to encounter, we must guard against its diligent and watchful gaze, as it waits its opportunity to enter a welcoming heart.

The story I am about to tell will give you perhaps a small glimpse of the enormity and potential of both negative and positive power, energy that can be directed in any way we choose.

FACING EVIL

It was a long time ago, about two years past the beginning that it happened. We were in my study, in Epworth, in the north of England. Five besides myself, all experienced, had experienced Grey Eagle, had experienced trance work, and so knew what to expect and how to behave, as I did, or so we all thought.

At first it was just as it usually was. A simple trance state, very peaceful and easy, as I had long since stopped struggling for control. The others, part of my team, were there watching attentively, listening carefully, and the tape recorder was on. Grey Eagle was close by. I could feel him standing behind me, and I felt perfectly safe, until... "What was that?" I had seen something, a shadow, an image. A flicker of something dark. And the room grew cold, as cold as ice. Still in a light trance, but totally aware of everything around me, my senses finely tuned, I heard a sound, a gurgling, growling noise, and at the same time I became aware of a smell, an acrid, bitter smell like rancid meat alight over a charcoal flame. Then I saw the smoke, or what looked like smoke, a swirling, spiraling circular mass larger than a football, which was perhaps five feet in front of me. I heard the noise again and realized that the sound had come from the center of the mass.

Now there was another smell, the terrible and unmistakable smell of fear, and it was coming from me.

"Grey Eagle," I whispered, "what is it, what is that thing? I don't like it. Make it go away." But from my guide there was only silence.

I heard the noise again, coming strange and low, as if from the depths of the earth, or some strange and terrible doorway of the universe, best left unopened and forgotten.

The smoke, the mass, seemed to have a life of its own, did have a life of its own, and as it moved and swirled, it seemed to change in color, going from gray to gray black, to blue gray, blue black, becoming more and more threatening. And then I saw the face, and ice ran through my blood and entered my heart, for I had seen nothing like it, and nor do I wish to see it, or anything like it again. A pernicious, evil thing, wishing to destroy, and I knew that it meant to destroy me.

"Grey Eagle, Grey Eagle, help me, help me," I called as I watched the "thing" creeping slowly forward toward me. And in a voice as calm as a still pond on a late summer evening, as if nothing was amiss, he replied, quietly, "Rosemary, you must deal with this yourself."

How could he, how could you? my mind screamed out. Can't you see that thing? Help me, help me. But although I felt my guide there, close by, only silence came from that quarter, and I knew I was on my own.

My friends, the five who were in the room with me, had said nothing, done nothing so far, but even though they could not see as I could, they all knew that a terrifying and terrible entity had entered the room. Each one of us could feel the cold, smell the odor, sense the evil. They were ready to protect me, to protect themselves, to fight. But how does one fight the unseeable, the unknowable? What were they to do? They could only trust. Trust in God, and trust the process.

"Its" features changed as the smoke, "its" energy moved, swirled about. Sometimes "its" mouth was a grinning open cavern, a snarling twisting thing, sometimes smiling its cruel smile, ecstatic in my fear of it. "Its" nose (did it have a nose?) a blur, a smudge of gray, shapeless, no shape at all. But "its" eyes, dark, piercing, penetrating, burning coals, they never changed at all, at least not till the end.

The five gathered close around me now, forming a tight circle, with me in the center. Now the "thing" let out a loud cackling sound and, without seeming to move, lunged toward me. Its evil power was overwhelming as it wrapped itself around my mind. Energy that wasn't mine, and from no good source, entered my hands. My fingers began to curl, my hands to take the shape of claws, and I watched as they lifted from my lap toward my face, my eyes. Talons, my fingers became talons, and terrified, I realized the "thing" was forcing me, willing me, to claw my eyes out of my head. That's when I began to fight.

Until this time I had been stupefied, rendered insensible, paralyzed by fear. Now that same fear moved me to action. I screamed out, "Help me, God help me!" and with all my will, I began to force my hands back down.

Whack! A blow to my head. *Whoosh...thud,* a force, so strong, now in my chest, rocking me backward, almost out of my chair. The face, now so close to my face. "Its" eyes, glittering, cruel, hard, triumphant, piercing my brain.

"Grey Eagle, where are you? Why won't you help? God, oh Jesus, oh somebody, please help."

Screaming, kicking, yelling, I tried to fight, but slowly, slowly, my hands, clawlike and dangerous, began to rise up again to my face. My team of five were with me, holding me down. Two of the men, realizing instinctively that some unseen evil force was somehow manipulating me, grabbed my arms, and tried to hold them down. Together we struggled, but it seemed that we were

163

losing the battle. I was losing, for "its" eyes held me in their grip, and the force of "it" was reaching into me, taking me over.

"I can't win, I can't win," I panted, crying, almost exhausted, as my fingers, my fingernails, came closer to my eyes. And sensing my weakness "it" roared and swirled in a maddening, frenzied dance, growing larger and larger, feeding on my fear.

Then a voice, "its" voice. Finally heard. "You are Miss Goodie Goodie, too strong, too nice. Likes dogs, likes cats, likes babies. I will destroy. For I am *hate.*" "Its" voice was slime, old and cracked as time itself, dripping bloody filth from every syllable. Purring, slurring, halting sound. And in "its" simpering, whining, miserable tone, I heard "its" weakness and knew my strength.

I stopped fighting. My fear dissolved, and in that quiet moment I heard a voice, another, this one recognizable. It was that still small voice within me. Not God, not Christ, not Grey Eagle, but perhaps some measure of all three ... that voice was *faith.* A memory came, carried on the wings of faith, from long ago, from yesterday ... "and as I walk through the valley of the shadow of death, I will fear no evil. For thou art with me." The Twenty-third Psalm.

I looked at the thing, the "it" that was so malevolent and terrible, but now I looked with steady eyes. My fear, not gone, no ... never gone completely, for I would always remember, but now not the driven, crazy thing it was.

"It" looked back, eyes hard and mean as ever, but sensing change, not understanding yet, it paused in "its" movement. I smiled then, and mine must have been a terrible smile, for I saw "its" eyes as fear crept into them, for now I was the death of evil, and "it" knew that death was near. The final blow, and fatal, as I spoke these words: "You cannot harm me, for I am light, I am of God, and all good things." Those words, spoken softly, but from my knowing heart, were like poison to it, and I watched it squirm and scream, not now in ecstasy, but in agony, as it grew less and less, slowly diminishing, until finally it was no more.

Afterward, we sat, my friends and I, for more than thirty minutes, in almost total trembling silence. Only the sound of my sobbing could be heard. It was my worst nightmare come true, and I was never to speak fully of it to anyone, not even now.

Cranial knowledge is a wonderful thing. We read, we learn, we grow. But there are some things we can only fully understand through experience. I had to, needed to, learn about evil. It would not have been enough to talk of it, to read of it, to sit with others debating it. I needed to taste, to touch, to hear, see, sense in every way I could, so that I could fully appreciate my own power, my own strength. Who knew when in the future I would need to know these things? Well, God knew.

The very next day after my ordeal, the phone rang. It was obvious from the tone of her voice that the lady who had called was not just scared, but very, very afraid. "Please help me," she sobbed. "There is something terrible in my house. It's evil, evil, and I don't know what to do."

My guide drew close to me, and I felt his strength, his voice, calm as a still pond on a late summer evening, he whispered gently, "But you know, my little flower, you know. You know exactly what to do."

Do I believe in the devil? The simple and honest answer is no, I do not. Not as in Satan, with his forked tail and furnace of hell. I do not believe in a supreme spirit of evil. I do believe, though, that there are beings who are full of evil, who live and breathe all that there is of evil, and as I write, some of those names spring to mind. Hitler was one. Then there was Himmler, Pol Pot, Tamerlane, the Duvaliers, Idi Amin, Bakhasa, and more recently, Gacy and Bundy. These were men of evil, each in his own way a devil.

And I do believe that out there in the universe there is an evil force, a terrible and negative energy we might call it. But that force, no matter how savage or brutal, no matter how nefarious its intent, that force cannot harm us in any way unless we allow it to. Only if our hearts are dark, if we are black souls, can evil enter. Only if our soul allows, is welcoming, will evil feel a welcome. Evil feeds on fear, and all of us who are sane fear evil to some degree, but if there is light in our hearts, if our soul welcomes God, then that force that is dark and destructive will find no room to dwell, no room to grow, and will ultimately die.

I have seen the face of evil, and nothing I can say will show you truly the sadistic, insensate, and wanton cruelty of it. It is to be feared. It is right that we should fear it, remember its presence, so that we can always guard against it. And all we have to do is simply keep God in our hearts.

Gerard Manley Hopkins wrote, "The world is changed with the grandeur of God."

I would go further. I would say that God changes not just the world, not just the universe. Where God enters, then all there becomes light. And knowing that, I know that I can smile at the face of evil, and it will wither away and die.

We all know the rules. If you play with fire, expect to get burned. If you use fire carefully, respect and treat it as you should, then it will give you warmth and comfort. Any energy, any power should be treated respectfully. Our own power, that which God gave us, which we are born with, that innate force that is in each one of us, must be used in a way that will not only warm and comfort us, but that will make us strong.

When we join forces with the spirit world, we want to understand our power, and the power of spirit. We want to be unafraid, and we want to make sure that we join forces with that power that is God, pure, and of the purest light.

This next story is an example of how creative and constructive we can be with our own positive power, and what good results we can achieve when we combine our power with the power of the universe, the power we call God.

• • •

I was in Arizona, giving a lecture, and there were over a thousand people attending. It was question time, and I was walking up and down the aisles, the microphone in my hand, going from person to person, trying to answer as many questions as I could. About halfway through the evening there was a question from a man who said he needed to know about his brother who had died. "Is he all right, is he happy, and is he with our father?" was the question.

As soon as I had begun to listen to the question, my door opened wide; "at home," I was tuning into the spirit world, using my power. Grey Eagle was at my side, and my mind, my senses became fully alert. At first I didn't see the brother; instead, as often happens, I found myself in another place, another time, even though I was still almost fully aware of the lecture hall, and my audience. I was in a plane, flying with many other passengers. The flight seemed full. There was some noise, laughter, chatter, and the ride was smooth. The first sign that something was wrong occurred when I smelled burning, and it was at precisely the same time that I connected with the brother of the man who had asked me the question. "I was one of the first to smell it, I think," he said as I felt him draw close to me. "At first the smell was quite mild, then it became stronger." He continued, saying, "I saw smoke, and almost immediately I heard a cracking sound, so loud, and instantly knew we were in trouble. It took only moments," he went on, "then the explosion, and that was it." As he said this, I, too, heard the cracking sound, both saw and heard the explosion as if I was right at the heart of it. I felt the heat, though I wasn't burned. The sound, though deafening, didn't deafen. And then I heard the sound of laughter and chatter, of people calling out to one another. I saw a reuniting as I had rarely seen before, a reuniting of souls. Families and friends from the spirit world had come to welcome all onboard, except that we were not onboard anymore, seeming just to be. I heard crying, soft and gentle crying, as people held each other, rocked each other, joyful in being together again. And I heard the sound of laughter, the sound of joy for a joyous homecoming for everyone on that flight.

All this took only moments to experience and to recount to my questioner, and as he and his family, all standing, arms around each other, supportive and loving, heard my words, I heard their crying, too. Soft and gentle crying, it was the sound of joy for a joyous and wonderful message. "My brother is safe," my questioner said. "That's all I needed to know."

That air crash was the TWA Flight 800, of which there were no survivors. Afterward FBI investigators took four hundred and eighty-five days, interviewed seven thousand witnesses, and spent millions and millions of taxpayer dollars trying to discover the cause of the crash. They came up with a two-page report and no conclusions.

There were no survivors, no one lived to tell what happened! Did I say that? Oh no, not me, for I believe, I know, that they all survived, that they all live, and there are those among them who could certainly tell us more of what happened. The brother of the man in the lecture hall told us a little of what he knew, which was more than any of us here on earth had known before. He really did come back to tell us, and I am sure, given time, he could have told us more.

When we think about the spirit world, many of us cannot conceive of communication in any but the simplest of ways. It is hard for us to imagine that our loved ones can tell us anything other than that they are safe, that they love us, and that they survived death. Joining forces with the spirit world means much more than that, however. It means making a mind/spirit connection that goes way beyond mere mortal understanding. As yet no scientist has discovered a means to measure, to test, to prove, or to disprove what I am saying. The power of God, of the universe, and the mind, spiritual or human, if indeed they are separate and apart, that power is incomprehensible to us. Our human concepts, born of our earthly and spiritual experiences, are so narrow, so limited, that we can only guess at the potential of the mind, and of the spirit that we all are.

For those of you who are doubters, bear with me. Forget for a while your earthbound reasoning, your so-called common sense. Suppose for a moment that what I believe is actually a fact. That not only is there continuing life, that we don't die, but that the universe holds a life force so powerful, so all-knowing, that if we join with it, we, too, can know that power for ourselves, and we, too, can become more knowing, more at one with the universe and all its secrets. Think about that. Could it really be? And if I am right, and what I say is so, where do we begin?

Not all-knowing or all-seeing by any means, but maybe knowing more than many, because of my experiences, that the power of the universe is already a power that we own, I would suggest that we begin our connection with the universe, with the spirit world, by developing our connection with the mind.

This chapter is about just that. Making a mind connection, and discovering ways to strengthen our mind power.

Once, with a group of students, I asked where they thought the mind was. Most said "in my head." "Oh, really," I mused, giving them time to ponder, to maybe doubt their answer. "Have any of you seen it, then, or felt it?"

"Well, no," said one, "but it's part of the brain, isn't it?"

"I don't know," I replied. "I've never seen or felt it physically, I don't know how big or small my mind actually is, and I'm not sure if it is inside my head or if it's somewhere outside of my physical body."

These comments from me started up a debate, which in the end became rather silly and pointless, as each of my students came up with another possible place other than the brain where the mind could be situated. It was fun, but after a while I pointed out that it really didn't matter much where the mind lived—in the head, the heart, the butt, what difference did it make, as long as it *was*, as long as it existed, as long as it was alive and working, and working well?

When I connected to the man who had died on the TWA flight, we were of one mind, connecting minds, using our power, using our mind energy, our constructive thought process. We had discovered the power of the mind and the power of positive thought. What we need to do here is to discover the power we already own.

• • •

It is my belief that we all have potential, that we are all potentially great men or women, but the concerns and fears that our lives create make us doubt. There are always moments when we doubt ourselves. Even the greatest men and women had their doubts and fears, but it could be said that some people have a greater capacity for overcoming trials and tribulations than others. I feel that the only thing that the great men and women throughout history have that others of us don't have is right thinking, the right attitude toward determining their own future. They discovered the power of the mind, the power of positive thinking. And they were not afraid to use that power.

It was Ralph Waldo Emerson who wrote, "They conquer who believe they can," and it was Dr. Karl Menninger who said, "Attitudes are more important than facts."

According to the Bible, Matthew 9, verse 29, "If you have faith nothing shall be impossible unto you." Maybe he was talking about having faith in God, in the Scriptures, or in Christ, which is great, but aside from our faith in God, I believe that we also need to have faith in ourselves, and that can be really hard. To learn to trust our own judgments, to believe in our own power, to truly acknowledge that we have potential and that if we explore, we can fulfill that potential—accepting these things as facts can be a very hard thing to do.

Wherever we look in the world, there are people who are afraid. Maybe they don't appear to be, but yet inwardly they fear. People who hide from life, suffering quietly from a deep sense of insecurity and inadequacy. Those who doubt their own strength and who mistrust their ability to meet responsibilities and to grasp the opportunities that life presents to them. I have been one of those people, and, perhaps, so have you.

If we want to change, to grow, first we must develop an attitude that is positive. We must ask ourselves every day . . . is our glass half-empty, or is it half-full? Are our personal skies really so dark and gloomy, or are there maybe one or two rays of sunshine in our day?

In those times that we are in emotional struggle, it is so easy to see our glass as half-empty, to never see the bright rays in our lives.

When I was going through my divorce, oh so many years ago now, my struggle was great, my struggle to smile even the smallest smile was great. Not only had my husband cleaned out our bank account, left thousands of dollars of debt, and refused to pay any support for me or our child, but I was the one who had to deal with the debt collectors. Many times I would hide in the house with my daughter, Samantha, then just eleven years old, while the debt collectors banged at the door. Twice the bailiff tried to break in while I was out, only to be stopped by my neighbor, who threatened to call the police if they didn't leave. These were just a few of the things that made it difficult for me to smile. The worst was not having enough money to feed my daughter properly, not to be able to buy her Christmas or birthday gifts, to see her when we were out grocery shopping, never asking for an ice cream or candy like the other kids did with their moms. That was a heartbreak. Watching her as she became more shy, more introverted, as she, too, struggled to smile. But there were those precious moments, when despite the struggles, we would find ourselves giggling together over the smallest thing, finding fun where we could.

It was because I had Samantha, because I had to be the best example for her, that, on the surface at least, I pasted on a smile and put forward an attitude that said, "My glass is half-full!" Inside, though, like so many, I feared, I was miserable, and my skies were very gray.

I worked in a pub, serving drinks behind the bar, and at lunchtimes helping the landlady cook and prepare food. The pub was always busy, and for the most part the locals were friendly. Each day, no matter how I was feeling inside, I would walk out of my front door, put on my smile, and go to work. It was hard, always seeming to smile, always trying to show a good face. I remember one day, coming home from work at about four in the afternoon, stepping through my front door into the hallway, sitting on the stairs, still with my coat on, crying because I couldn't take the smile off my face. I had pasted it on so well, had done such a good job, that my face had frozen into position. Even while I was crying, that wretched smile stayed put.

Every day was the same, seemed the same, and the months turned into a year, then two. I was still smiling the false smile, still struggling to feed my child, each day was a battle, and I, well, I felt like the lone soldier left on the battlefield. It wasn't true, though. I had made new friends, I had found Grey Eagle, and I had begun the most important work of my life, and without my realizing it, things had begun to change, and change for the better. It was on a day in early spring, the weather was mild, and there was a watery sun hiding behind wispy white clouds. I don't remember where I was driving or why I was in the car that day. The radio was on softly and music was playing. The stretch of road I was on was straight, with fields on either side. Just motoring along, going from home to somewhere, I leaned back against the car seat, looked out at the day, and smiled. A moment or two passed and I heard a voice. Not the voice of my guide, or the voice of someone in the spirit world, but that still small voice inside me. "You're smiling," it said, and for the first time in what seemed like a lifetime of pretending, I was shocked to realize that my smile was for real. I felt Grey Eagle's fingers gently brush my cheek as he wiped away my tears, then I began to laugh and laugh and laugh. Finally, I realized, my glass was full, so full, it was truly overflowing.

• • •

All of my exercises have been designed to help us recognize and face our inadequacies and our insecurities, our negative energy, and also to recognize our positive energy, our adequacies, qualities such as kindness, caring, determination, showing that with positive thinking we can and we will meet and also deal more than adequately with our fears and insecurities. Creative and thought-provoking exercises help give us confidence in our own selves so that we can more easily grasp the opportunities that life presents us with both hands, willingly and eagerly.

Meeting our responsibilities, we learn that our first responsibility is to our own selves. We have a responsibility to grow, and to discover ourselves and our own potential, for without growth, not only are we not much use to ourselves, we are also less than we can be for those around us.

THE POWER OF POSITIVE THINKING

This is the one chapter that totally and completely unifies all the other chapters in the book. Making the exercises one whole instead of seven separate stages.

Let us look at the previous four chapters, and take from each a key point. As you read, take note of these words: thought, awareness, mind, visualization, think. See how a thread runs through the book. Thinking, thought, mind, equals mind power.

In Chapter One, as we learn to relax, we discover, using our thoughts, visualizing, centering our minds, a great way to relax, and control our mind, and our emotions. "Using gentle mental massage, visualize, and become aware of your chest, your lungs, your arms and hands. Wriggle your fingers, talk to your body lovingly, bring your thoughts to your neck, your cheeks, your lips. Become aware of the top of your head. Using gentle mental massage, center your thoughts on your temples, and visualize all the tensions of life, and all of the impurities of your body, wasted away!"

Chapter One is about you, learning about you, discovering and becoming aware of the deeper part of you, the very essence of your being, your spirit.

Chapter Two is about palm centers and the solar plexus, about our awareness of our energy. When we start to explore the area around the solar plexus, we begin: "Now, placing your hand, palm down, on your stomach, over that sensitive area of the solar plexus, close your eyes and concentrate your 'mind,' your energy, on the area around the solar plexus." We go on, further through the exercise, to talk about being constructive with our thought process, that thoughts are energy. It is important to understand, I write, that each "thought" we have is a tiny pulse of energy. And that "collective thought" equals more energy, a mass of energy.

Chapter Three, healing the self, is all to do with finding the tools that build and strengthen us. This is the chapter in which we make our lists, where we must "think" hard about our character traits.

When I was writing my personal list, it is interesting to note that the first negative I included was "thoughtless," which means that I don't think, don't use the power of thought as far as others are concerned, as much as I should. As we go through each character trait, I suggest that we should use our thought process. This chapter is all about the power of the mind, in relation to our growth process.

Coming then to Chapter Four, we find ourselves yet again working with visualization, mind techniques, thought and energy in acknowledging our aura. When we begin to paint our aura, to control our energy, I refer to "a process of creative 'thinking' and 'visualization.' " In this chapter we talk further about awareness, of becoming aware that our auras exist, and we come to this passage.

"There must be a connection to the aura through our state of 'mind.' Now, let us see if we can change, by 'thought,' the color and pattern of our aura. With eyes closed, 'mind' alert, 'visualize' your own energy field. Reach out with that part of your 'mind' that desires knowledge and learning."

So now we come to Chapter Five.

It could be said that all we are is thought. It could also be argued that all we have been, and all that we will be, is thought. For, after all, without the ability to think and to process thought, we become empty, nothing.

I can remember a very sad case of a young man in his early thirties who was a patient of mine. He was married, had two small children, a girl and a boy, a great job, and everything in his garden was roses. Until his accident, that is. He ran his car into a tree and he was plummeted straight through the windshield, and as his head connected with the tree trunk his skull was split wide open. His injury wasn't fatal, but the central part of his brain was severely damaged. He became not much more than a vegetable, or so it seemed to the doctors and to his family.

He is brain-dead, the medics diagnosed, for he showed zero response to all the tests and all the machines. Nor did he respond to touch, to sound, to his children or his wife, or to his parents or his siblings.

But he did respond to me. Oh no, I did not produce a miracle cure, make him walk again, or talk again. But we did talk, he and

I, yes, we really were able to talk. We found a mind connection, a thought connection, similar to that which we understand twins sometimes have, or people we are especially close to. We can "read" their mind; they can "read" ours. My patient's name was Ivor, and I found him to be anything but "brain-dead." And for those of you who might think that Ivor's mind, his thoughts, were trapped inside his physical body, you would be incorrect. Ivor's mind was alive, active, his thoughts were acute, his senses had become ultra-attuned. He knew he was going to die, that physically he would eventually weaken, even with the aid of his life-support machine, that his body would waste away, and he was right. It took over a year, but eventually he suffered a serious lung infection, and that was the end of his life here on earth.

It was during our conversations, Ivor's and mine, that he told of his growing awareness of the power, the energy within him, and he came to realize that the death of his body was by no means the death of him. As his body weakened, his mind power became stronger. Ivor came to know that he was an indestructible being.

There are also many cases of babies who are born "brain-damaged," with apparently no thought process, no ability to feel, to experience emotion, to hear, to understand anything. I know, too, that this is not so. In *The Eagle and the Rose*, I tell David's story. How, even though he was born totally damaged physically, seemingly unable to communicate in any way, shape, or form, David was aware, his psyche absorbing every day of his earth life. His thoughts, his mind, his soul indestructible. This is what hopefully, here in this next chapter, you are going to discover.

Most of us develop a pattern of thought from an early age and we stick to that pattern until such time, often a time of crisis or confusion in our lives, that we are jolted or nudged into re-thinking. There are those of us who never ever consider altering or changing the pattern of our thoughts, but follow the established pattern of a lifetime. Switched on to automatic pilot, we become robots, slaves to a lifestyle and to the mind we have forgotten how to use, or have never learned to use.

In Chapter Four we learned to create a new pattern of energy, using colors, visualization, and our mind power, in a positive and constructive way, to change the pattern of our aura, our energy field, to form this pattern to suit us. We found a way of using our energy that made us comfortable, and that hopefully taught us to be creative.

Now, in this chapter, we are going to explore the possibilities of changing our thought pattern for another reason. We can discover that by changing, in a constructive and positive way, the pattern of our thoughts toward our own selves, we will automatically become more confident and much more self-assured, as well as becoming more self-aware. We are going to build on our self-esteem and our sense of strength.

Knowing that we must be responsible, that we must all take responsibility for our own selves is one thing. Actually responding to this awareness and taking responsibility is something else entirely. It is easy to blame others, to blame circumstances for a lack of progress in your career or a strained personal life.

It might be easy for a man to say his wife is difficult to live with when, because of his womanizing, drinking, or bad habits, she has laid down certain rules in the relationship that she will not allow to be broken. For if those rules are broken, she herself becomes damaged. The rules are for her protection, but may make her seem harsh, controlling, and demanding. It is not so easy for the man to accept that he alone and his behavior caused his wife, indeed, forced his wife to make the rules. He might say of her: she is controlling, demanding, nagging. She may even have become these things in order to keep her relationship. However, if he were to face the fact that it is up to him to change, and if he were indeed to change, then none of the rules his wife made would apply. They would become obsolete.

It might be easy for a woman to feel victimized in the workplace when her boss is constantly complaining about her attitude. It might not be so easy for her to accept that she is consistently late—let's blame the kids, they got up late, which in turn makes her late. It is not so easy for her to accept that her standard of work might be poor because "it's that time of month," another great excuse. That her mind is often not on her work but on her home life or her personal life. It is much easier to blame the boss. She might say of him, he's a male chauvinist, he's ruthless, he doesn't care about his workers, and horror of all horrors, that most male trait, he's insensitive. He may be all of these things, he may certainly be all of these things to her. His attitude may well have been colored by the fact that he's getting a second-rate job performance from her, but is paying a first-rate salary.

If only she could face the fact that she and she alone is responsible for her boss's attitude toward her, that it is up to her to change, that if she did indeed change, then maybe her boss, and her situation, would also change, and for the better.

Of course, there are wives, and husbands, for that matter, who are controlling and nagging for no reason other than that they have allowed their own personality traits to be molded that way, and no matter how good their spouse is, their glass is always half-empty. They have an attitude of dissatisfaction, no matter what.

And, of course, there are women and men who are truly victimized in the workplace for no fault of their own. Being a woman, I know all about P.M.S., indeed have suffered with it from time to time, as most women have. So please don't misunderstand my two examples. I realize in all situations there is more than one side to a story. What I am suggesting we do when we find ourselves in any situation that involves behavioral struggles is to look to ourselves and our own behavior first, instead of readily pointing the finger somewhere else. Questioning why someone behaves in a certain way toward us, questioning our own behavior and our responsibility can only help us handle our difficulties in a more reasoned and adult way. This is where growth takes place.

She doesn't understand me. He doesn't understand me. I don't understand. They don't understand. How many times have you uttered at least one of these phrases? All of us who admit to being flawed human beings will admit to using one or more of these phrases fairly often in our lifetime. And we may have been correct. We may truly have lived our lives being misunderstood. So who must we look to, who will we say is responsible?

I remember as a child being sent across the street to a neighbor's house for shilling pieces. That was in the days of gas meters, or in our case, electricity meters. Every household had a stash of coins, "a shilling for the meter," we used to say. Of course, quite often we would run out of shillings, and so I or one of my sisters was then sent to a neighbor's house.

None of us liked going to this particular neighbor. Not that she wasn't nice, just that she couldn't hear. She was deaf, stone-deaf, couldn't hear a thing. We knew that no matter how loudly we shouted at her, she would never understand what we were trying to say, and it would take ages before we could get her to understand us, using sign language that only a ten-year-old could possibly decipher. Even though we knew this, even though my mother knew this, she also knew that Mrs. Smith never ran out of coins. She was a certainty and always had a shilling or two to spare. The interesting thing is that although we knew she was deaf, knew she couldn't hear a thing, nevertheless, every time we were sent over we would try to communicate with her in the same way. Our way. We would begin by asking for a shilling in a loud but polite tone, and always end up yelling our heads off. When I think about this I can see her face, the struggle in her eyes as she tried desperately to understand us. I remember, too, the smile of recognition on her face when finally she got the message.

Never once, in all the years and all the many times we went to Mrs. Smith's house, did it ever occur to any of us to try a different approach. How much simpler and easier, and how much terrible aggravation could have been saved if we had just taken a piece of paper and a pen and written out clearly, "Do you have a shilling for the meter?" Can you imagine how much easier that would have been. And whose responsibility was it to ensure as little confusion as possible? There are some who would say, "Well, you would think that Mrs. Smith would have had a pad and pen at hand, for she must have encountered this situation often. So let's point the finger at her." There are others, myself included, who would say that if you want to be understood, it's up to you to find a way. If you want to have good communication, and you don't have it, then learn to speak a language that others might understand better, instead of continuing to speak, in what sounds to some, double Dutch.

When we try to communicate with the spirit world, we need to be so aware, so sensitive to what they are communicating to us, and it is very easy to get it wrong, to mislisten. Often in relationships we miscommunicate what we are actually thinking, and we also mishear or mislisten to what others say to us. How many times have we said, "But I didn't mean that," or "Oh, I thought you meant such and such"? This business of communication can be tough. This is why to set us on a clear path, it is important to communicate well, at least with ourselves. To know what we want, to know what we mean, and to learn to express ourselves clearly, with as little confusion as possible. If you are confused about yourself, you can expect to be misunderstood by those around you. You have to set your mind straight, and that is a task that no one else can undertake for you. Others can help, of course, but only you can determine whether you succeed or not. The responsibility lies with you. This is where the buck stops, with you. Understanding the power of the mind, you begin to understand your own power, your own potential. Setting goals and achieving these goals is your aim. You can do it if you set your mind to it.

The mind creates thought, and as we learned earlier, just one single thought represents a small pulse of energy. Imagine how much more energy there would be if we were to deliberately construct positive thought, if we were to take responsibility for our own thought processes, if we were to take control of our mind. What a powerhouse we could be. Of course, we must also realize that our thoughts, used negatively, can be just as powerful, and when we do realize this, we are able to evaluate how much we can damage ourselves by the use of negative and therefore destructive thought.

There was a man, we'll call him Mr. Jones, who, having felt unwell and suffering with stomach pains for several months, finally went to see his doctor. After several tests and a short stay in hospital, Mr. Jones went back to his doctor for his results. The doctor, in the most sensitive and sympathetic way, informed Mr. Jones that he had terminal cancer. Too late for treatment, his body, riddled with disease, he was given three months to live.

Mr. Jones, devastated, went home, told his wife and family, put himself to bed, and proceeded to die. Within two weeks he was little more than a skeleton, in great pain, taking morphine, and everyone knew he would not survive too much longer.

Then one day the doctor arrived for his usual daily visit, but on this occasion, Mrs. Jones noted, as she let him in the door, the doctor seemed somewhat strained and ill at ease.

"There's something wrong?" she asked, and he, nodding, said, "Let's talk about it with your husband."

Now, almost four weeks since his diagnosis, Mr. Jones, frail and sick, lay in his bed, unable even to lift his head from the pillow as his wife came into the bedroom, followed by his doctor. The doctor sat down next to him on the bed and took hold of Mr. Jones's hand.

"I don't know where to begin," he stammered. "There's been a mistake. I gave you the wrong diagnosis, got it muddled with another Mr. Jones."

"Well, what does this mean?" asked his wife, startled and a little fearful.

"It means," said the doctor, taking a deep breath, "it means that your husband isn't dying at all. That's the size of it, he doesn't have cancer, just an ulcer."

"But, but," said Mrs. Jones, "look at him, look how sick he is, of course he has cancer."

"Such is the power of the mind," replied the doctor. "I've seen this sort of thing before. Tell a man he's dying, if he believes it enough, well, then it can happen."

You'll be pleased to hear that Mr. Jones made a complete recovery. Even his ulcer healed. Such is the power of the mind, and mind over matter.

Another story, which my own doctor told me, concerns a widower who had been left with six young children to raise. When the man was told he had terminal cancer, he replied, "Don't be ridiculous, I can't die, I've got way too many things to do, and too many people relying on me." He lived for more than twenty years. My doctor lost track of him after that. "Who knows"—he laughed as he recounted this story—"he's probably going to outlive me."

Such is the power of the mind, that under extraordinary circumstances that power can be an indomitable thing. If only we could learn how to exploit it.

Once we realize that determined positive and constructive thought energy can counteract negative thought energy, then we are all well on the way to producing a state of personal well-being within, and growth takes place.

A good example of what I mean about counteracting negative energy is the story of a friend who recently called. She was experiencing some difficulties in the workplace and had found herself having to deal with problems created by someone else's incompetence. Feeling down and inadequate, unable to function properly, she asked, "Rosemary, what can I do? I feel utterly despondent and negative, really depressed."

This was a situation that, for the time being, was in the hands of others, as she personally could do nothing to rectify it. However, she could begin to plan for the time when her hands were not so tied. She could begin to take action in her mind. Easier said than done. But no one promised that the exercises I suggest are easy. "Begin first," I said, "to work at the things in life you value. Look at, make a list even, if it helps, of all the good stuff, both in your working environment, and at home. Then ask, is my glass half-empty or half-full?" I already knew the answer, so did she. My friend's glass was more than half-full. This moment in her life, however long a moment it might seem, would pass, was a minor glitch, and not worth all the negative emotion she was feeling. "Your glass is half-full. Now be constructive, be positive with your thought process. Think beyond the negative, the impasse, think to the time when you can be actively constructive, but for the moment be content to be mentally constructive. In doing so, you create a powerful and positive energy that will not only affect you in a good way, but will also touch those around you."

"But that's so hard to do," came her reply, and smiling in understanding, I replied, "When your back is against the wall, there are two choices. You can slip down onto the floor and lie there until, if you're lucky, someone comes and picks you up, or you can stay against the wall until you have built up enough energy, enough mind power, to take a step or two forward. Your choice." But, I ended by saying, "I know which way I would go."

As a healer, I am very aware that constructive and positive thinking can be used to aid spiritual awareness, and I have been privileged to help many, many people who have been sick, some dying, many recovering. It is always amazing to me how, in the face of adversity, so many human beings are able to draw on an inner strength, an inner power, that they never realized was there until they needed it. Very few of us, when faced with death, take the news lying down. Somewhere from within, I have seen people muster enormous strength and courage in the face of death, and having to confront their worst fears. Thomas "Stonewall" Jackson once said to one of his doubting generals, "General, never take counsel of your fears." Well, Stonewall Jackson was an unusual man, of unusual strength of character. Most of us mere mortals do take notice, and are affected by our fears. But as a healer, I have heard cancer patients who say God gave them the greatest gift when He gave them their sickness, as Carol did. Carol was a member of a cancer support group in Hong Kong, and on one of my visits there, I was invited to be the guest speaker. As always, when I'm involved with support groups of any kind, I come away inspired and awed by the strength and determination of its members.

Recently I was invited to go to a women's breast-cancer support group, in Manchester, Vermont. A patient of mine, Kathy, invited me, and it was a wonderful experience. Talking with women of great courage, whose need to share, whose need to be heard, was surpassed only by their willingness and compassion to listen and to hear the others in the group. To be, if they could, of some help and comfort to others, even while seeking help and comfort for themselves.

I have seen men, women, and children, often in great pain, still able to give a smile or a reassuring squeeze of the hand to their families and friends, whose fear is showing. I have seen the sick and dying make up their mind to get well, or to cause as little pain and grief to others as possible. And I have been witness to and understood the power of the mind in such circumstances, and have been proud to be a small part of it.

Positive thinking can be used to create a greater sensitivity toward one's own feelings and the feelings of others, and collective thought, collective energy, lots of people working together for the same reason, having the same thought, is stronger than one single thought and can produce miracles. For instance, many people throughout the world observe the healing minute—a particular time each day when each individual takes one minute of his or her time to sit and pray for all who are sick, and for all sickness in the world. Some may take a moment or two of that minute to remember someone particular, a loved one, a friend. We in the R.A.A.H. take perhaps five or ten minutes each day to send out our prayers and our healing energy to all our patients around the world. We join forces with each other, and with God, and with all those in the spirit world who wish to unite with us in our goal. Joining forces produces tremendous power and energy, and the results of such combined efforts are incredible. We get letters and phone calls from thousands of people who feel the benefit of being on our healing list, and many write to tell us that they actually feel a presence as they sit with us in prayer. A presence of positive, often energizing, and definitely healing power.

I was browsing in a store recently and came across a plaque I loved, which read, "Life is fragile, handle it with prayer."

If we all pray, and pray together as we in the R.A.A.H. do, then we can see that this collective energy is very powerful, as the results of our efforts have shown. Receiving testimonies from all over the world thanking us for our help, and asking for our continued support, both encourages us and shows us that prayer really works.

As we pray, my team always tries to use clear positive thoughts, and our positive thought patterns create powerful, pure, and constructive energy, producing a ripple effect, like throwing a pebble into a pond. One positive thought extends out to another and another, and so on. It is easy to see how we must become more aware of our own thoughts, our thought process, our thought pattern, to become more aware of our own ability to control and direct our thoughts, our energy.

Yes, it is easy to see. But how do we begin? First, learning about your negative thought process, and finding out at what times and for what reasons your negative thoughts take place, that's a start. Then looking to discover what it is that triggers negativity within you. It might be that you allow other people's moods to affect you. It is easy, if we have a friend who is depressed, to offer help, even if that help can come only in the form of listening. Before your friend begins to tell her sad story, you might be in an up mood, but after your friend is finished you could feel just as depressed as he or she. You have allowed her negative energy to "rub off" on you.

Or you could be the kind of person who finds it hard to "lighten up" when you're in a really depressing situation. Ask yourself why that is. Some people just like being miserable. Are you one of them?

I was recently a guest on a TV talk show, and during the break was talking to a woman, we'll call her Margaret, who had sadly lost her husband. "My life has been miserable," she said. "I have had such a hard time and there has never been any joy, nothing that I could take pleasure in." As she said this, I knew she expected that I would be sympathetic and commiserate with her, but I had just been speaking with a family who had lost their eleven-year-old boy, who was very tragically knocked down by a car. The mother of this boy, Timmie is his name, although completely distraught, had told me how grateful she was that God had allowed her the gift of her child, that her boy had been their sunshine. So when I heard Margaret complain that her life was nothing, although I was indeed sympathetic to her loss, I could not help but compare attitudes, and gently told her so. "You say there has been no sunshine in your life," I replied, "but we both know that this is far from true, for you have experienced many wonderful things. The trouble is you don't recognize the good things because your attitude is so bad. You close your eyes and refuse to see. Your glass is always half-empty, never half-full. Nothing is enough for you, and you are full of self-pity."

Margaret liked being miserable, some people just do. They are never happier than when they are complaining. Are you one of these people? It's hard to imagine, having read the book this far through, that you are, but it wouldn't hurt to ask yourself the question, and it would be good to find the true answer. Do you like being miserable, or have you allowed your attitude to become negative, always looking on the dark side—your glass half-empty? Be honest with yourself, but don't be hard on yourself. We are all flawed beings, every one of us. Think about how your mind works, try to understand why you have your particular way of thinking. Once you begin to understand your own thought process, then you can learn to use it to your advantage . . . *positively.*

The power of thought is the most powerful energy source we have. If we learn to use it, to use it as a tool, creatively, positively, it would be to our advantage. The ability to possess and to utilize faith or belief, whether that faith or belief is in God or in your own self, and to gain the release of the power that this provides, is a skill, and like any skill, it must be studied and practiced often, in order to build on and to grow.

These next exercises will help us to achieve such a skill, but as always, how much you gain from them will depend on how much time you are prepared to give, and how determined you are to succeed. There are those of us who are so blinded by pain and hurt and anger that we cannot see the beauty around us, for we live too much in the past, and it is so hard to break the pattern. The blows of life and the accumulation of difficulties tend to sap our energy, leaving us spent and discouraged. When this happens, the true status of our own power is obscured. So that we can feel, see, and understand our power, we must learn to change our pattern of thought from negative to positive. The negative is "We won't get a table, the restaurant is always too full," or "I bet I've missed the bus (or train or plane)," "She's sure not to be in," or "There's no point asking, he's bound to say no." The positive is "Let's try for a table, there could be a cancelation," or "With a bit of luck the bus (or train or plane) will be held up." "Let's call, it doesn't hurt to try, she might be in," or "You know, it never hurts to ask. He could say no, but we could find him in a good mood. He could just as easily say yes." Instead of thinking thoughts often based on fear, of defeat or ineffectiveness, we get better results by thinking thoughts of faith, faith in our own selves. Learn to believe in yourself, and create thoughts of courage.

A positive or negative way of thinking is not to be confused with an optimistic or pessimistic way of thinking, although optimism and positive thinking, and pessimism and negative thinking, are very similar. An optimist, in the doctrine set down by Leibniz, believes that this world is the best possible of all worlds, and that good will ultimately prevail over evil. A total or foolish optimist, blinded by his or her inability to acknowledge anything but the best in any situation, will often do nothing to bring about change, believing that good prevails without any personal effort.

A positive thinker knows that often, personal effort is required in order to bring about change. A positive thinker accepts that not all situations are as we would wish them to be, but determines to "*positively*" make the best and the most of whatever situation they are in.

A pessimist has a tendency to take the worst view, to expect the worst outcome, and believes that this world is as bad as it could be and that evil dictates all things. The eyes of pessimists are closed, and they live in darkness.

A negative thinker is not so bad, but does allow him- or herself to lean toward a pessimistic attitude, and presumes that any personal effort to effect change is not likely to succeed.

Having a positive attitude will not always give us a perfect life, will not stave off the inevitable dramas and traumas that are meant to be our lessons in life. Will not necessarily mean that we are going to win the big prize or take home thousands of dollars at the gambling tables. But a positive attitude enables us to cope better, face our trials and difficulties in a way that is more constructive, more powerful. A positive attitude makes us stronger, and at the same time more realistic about the things we are able to achieve.

As a positive thinker myself, I believe that the only way we can fail in life is if we don't try. How does anyone know what things are possible in life unless one makes an effort to work, to see, and to experiment a little?

Changing our thought process and building a creative attitude means learning to create a good, positive mental image of ourselves. Again, easier said than done, an art in itself. Positive thinking is a skill, and as with any other skill, only study and daily practice draw us closer to our goal.

Here are a few simple and straightforward exercises that, if tackled with a positive and determined mind, will help you to master the art of self-creating a positive self.

EXERCISE 1 . . .
UNDERSTANDING OUR THOUGHT PROCESS

Let us look at the negative list first. Sit quietly and contemplate for a few minutes each day some of the negative thoughts you have had during this day.

An example:

Meanness
Anger
Frustration
Irritation

189

Unfriendliness
Disgust
Loneliness

Now ask yourself what it was, and why it was, that you allowed these negative thoughts to enter your mind? What was it that triggered these thoughts?

Example: Today I was sitting in an airplane waiting to take off. My trip to California had been tiring and I longed to go home. Then the announcement came. "There is a delay due to problems with the rear doors of the aircraft. We are experiencing a difficulty, etc., etc., etc." *Frustration* was very definitely my immediate reaction. However, I was having a good day and was able to quell my negativity by controlling my thought process. Turning my thoughts around, I became more positive, asking the spirit world, asking my guide, for help. The doors were fixed, the delay lasted only half an hour, and we were off.

When we arrived in New York, however, another challenge presented itself. It was one A.M. and the car we had booked was not there. Frustration, and this time, irritation, both negative emotions welled up, and I can tell you, at one in the morning, after hours of travel, it really is hard to remain positive, as I'm sure you will all agree. I failed, but Grey Eagle did not. A man with a limousine whose passenger had not turned up offered the car to us, at a cheap rate, and we were home in no time.

• • •

When you are thinking about your day and working out what and why you allowed negative thoughts in, it might help to use a notepad and pen to jot down those thoughts. At the risk of suggesting that you make too many lists, I will add that making a list of your negative thoughts, and a list of the reasons you suppose that they have been triggered, can be very beneficial. Ask yourself, did you have good reason to feel the way you did? Could you have been more tolerant, nicer, a little more patient, perhaps more positive?

This is a tough thing to do, but beginning to understand why a problem occurs can give you a jump on solving the problem, and negative thoughts can be a major problem, making any difficult situation worse, for you are creating and drawing to you a great deal of negative energy, which will take away your power.

EXERCISE 2 . . .
CONTROLLING OUR THOUGHTS

First, make a list of the various effects that you believe positive thinking can have on other people's lives generally, and then make another list of the effects that positive thinking can have on your own life in particular.

For example:

General	*Personal*
1. Cheerfulness	More determined
2. Inner calm	More positive
3. Positiveness of action	More self-respect
4. More determined	More confidence
5. Satisfaction	Friendlier
6. Better health	Happier

Then read the lists out loud, stating each point, until you begin to feel in a really positive and happy frame of mind. Remember that when you do this, you are beginning to create a real, powerful, and positive energy. As you state each point, it might be good to remember some small thing that occurred in the day that made you feel good. It might be something that happened to you or some small event you witnessed. A child holding its

191

mother's hand, a bird landing on the branch of a tree outside your window, a kind word, a smile.

Example: As I was heading out of a TV studio in Los Angeles on my way to catch my plane, I turned to wave goodbye to a couple who had lost their son. They had been on the show with me. I saw them hugging each other, the husband gently wiping a tear from his wife's face. But they were smiling, happy to have been with me. I felt good, my energy was positive, my thoughts were positive. I thanked the spirit world, and as I climbed into the car, my head aching, tiredness overwhelming me, I was smiling.

EXERCISE 3 . . .
CREATING POSITIVE MIND POWER

Make another list, this time based on the ones you made in Chapter Three, but this time list only the good/positive factors in your personality and makeup.

For example:

1. Gentle
2. Caring
3. Sensitive
4. Kind
5. Hardworking
6. Thoughtful

Then find a special time each day, allowing a few minutes for this one exercise, and again, state each point out loud and in a very positive way. But this time, begin each sentence with *I am.* Do this firmly and with confidence, and when you have finished reading out loud all the points, end with the same statement *I am.*

Example: I *am* a gentle, caring, and sensitive person. This is what I want to be. This is who and what I *am.*

By doing this, not only are you creating powerful, beneficial and positive energy, you are also making an affirmation. I am, I am, I am.

In the spirit world, just being is enough. We don't need the fancy car, the big house, the prestigious job, or the right friends to boost our ego and make us feel better about ourselves. We discover that simply being, existing, is everything. That through our own self-growth we become more of who we are, who we want to be.

There was a man whose name, well, let's call him James, James Jackson, of the Jackson family, heir to a fortune, known to all the so-called best and wealthiest families. James Jackson was a boaster and a braggart. His father had made the family fortune and James had, as the eldest son, been expected to do equally well. He did, and in the eyes of all who mattered—well, all who mattered to him, anyway—James Jackson was successful, except, that is, where his father was concerned. James Jackson's father was proud of his boy, but never told him so, and when singing his praises to others would say, "But don't tell him I said so." So James grew up with the feeling that no matter what he did, he would not be good enough. He could not impress his father or make him proud. So he began to boast louder, loud enough that his father might hear of his achievements, of his friends, of his success. By the time his father died, boasting had become a habit, a way of life, and a crutch for James to lean on, for inside himself, he believed that he could never live up to his father's standards, therefore he was a failure. And as he grew older and felt more and more inadequate, the louder he boasted and the louder he bragged.

Then came the day that James Jackson died, and as it is with all of us, his angels came and carried him home. There waiting for him was a man whom James could not remember seeing before, and the man said, "Who are you?" James Jackson lifted his head and looked the man right in the eye. "I'm James Jackson of the Jackson family. My family is one of the wealthiest in the Western world, and, and . . ." And then he paused, for he noticed the man was staring hard at him. Then, "I know you, you're little Jimmy Jackson," said the man, and smiling, continued gently, "You are my son." Little Jimmy Jackson looked again, and seeing not a mogul, not a tycoon, but a simple and humble man, reached his hands out to his father, and through his tears, he cried, "Why yes, I am."

Throughout his life James Jackson had boasted and bragged about who he had pretended to be, all the time simply wanting his father to acknowledge him as a son he could be proud of. Most of us have a need to be recognized and accepted. A good wife or father, a successful homemaker, a successful anybody. We have a need to be acknowledged. First, though, before anyone else can truly see us as we are, we must acknowledge ourselves. I am. I am. I am.

Earlier in this chapter I quoted Dr. Karl Menninger, "Attitudes are more important than facts." In that, I believe he is right, but facts count, too. It is a fact that we are all spiritual beings having a human experience, and it is our human behavior that often holds us back, blinds us to who and what we really are. Therefore we should try to train our mind to work in the way we want it to work, and not in the way it has been conditioned to work.

Look again at the positive factors in your personality and makeup. List those positives, and for a few minutes each day state them, out loud and positively. I am gentle, I am caring, I am a sensitive person. Then state again positively. This is what I want to be. This is what I want to be more of. This is what, and who *I am*.

This is how you can learn to control your thought processes in a positive and constructive way.

Exercise 4 . . .
Mantra

This next exercise is probably the easiest, but most effective, and requires the use of a mantra.

A mantra is a word or phrase many people use to help with meditation. Words, arranged in a certain way, for chanting. This is not the point of the exercise for us, however.

You can learn to use a mantra on a daily basis, at any time of the day, and in any situation, for a mantra is simply a sequence of words of power. Words of power. I will, I can, I do, I shall, I am, etc.

Finding your own mantra is easy, but as a guide, I offer you here some examples of mantras that I have suggested to other people, those who for one reason or another have been unable to take that major step toward self-discovery on their own.

> I *will* find joy in my life, and all good things *will* come to me.
> I *will* lift my face to the sun and bring light into my life.
> I *can* be happy, I *will* be happy.
> I *will* smile, I *will* smile, I *will* smile.

The words that I have used here correspond to certain issues in other people's lives, and are not necessarily connected to the issues in your life, although you may find some similarities, and you may even want to use them yourself.

• • •

The power of the mind, word power, mind energy, is the most powerful energy we have, remember, and we shouldn't be afraid to use it.

Embarking upon these exercises can help you to change the pattern of your thoughts, just as you were able to change the pattern of your aura. It will help build a creative attitude toward yourself and your life, and will *enable* you.

Learning to create a mental picture of yourself as succeeding in your goal helps you to be more positive. Try never to allow that picture to fade.

The Chinese use many symbols in their lives, and for myself, there are two—the dragon, symbol of power, and the phoenix, the symbol of new life beginning—that have special meaning. These two symbols used together spell out double happiness.

This is my mantra and I use it daily: Double happiness... double happiness... double happiness.

Finding your own words, your own mantra, should not be too difficult a task, but if you are finding it a struggle, take a look once more at the examples I offered above.

Example:

I *will* achieve... I *can* achieve.
I *will* grow to be more confident... I *am* more confident.
I *can* do anything that I set my mind to.
Be bold... *be* strong... *be* true. *BE.*
I *will* lift my face to the sun, and I *will* find happiness.

Whatever mantra you decide to choose for yourself, remember, the power that comes with it is yours. Think carefully before you decide. These words, chosen by you, can change your life.

For your mantra to work effectively, it must be repeated ten times, three times a day, each day. If you discipline yourself, your mantra *can* and *will* improve your attitude, and will help to make you a more positive and a more confident person.

• • •

I had been to the Far East, to Hong Kong, several times, and on one of those visits I had acquired what I can describe only as a hanging ornament. It is typically Chinese, a large, round piece of jade, like a big disc, half an inch thick, about a foot in diameter, ornately carved, with a phoenix on one side and a dragon on the other. Double happiness. It was set into a wood frame, also ornately carved, and hanging from the bottom was a long red tassel. I loved it. It was my mantra. It reminded me of my power, so I brought it home and hung it on the wall of my study, where I could see it every day.

Some time passed, a year, maybe two, and I had redecorated my bedroom. There was one wall that was incomplete, you know how that is, it just needed a picture, or, well, something. Then I thought, the ornament, that would look perfect, so I hurried to the study to fetch it. On my way back up the stairs I took with me a large pile of laundry, mostly towels on top of which I had carefully placed the ornament from the study. It was heavy, and I didn't want to drop it, so I went cautiously up the stairs with my bundle, into the bedroom, and gingerly I bent down and placed the towels on the bed. It was as I straightened up that the towels tipped, and the disc slipped off the towels and landed on its rim, and with force, right across the toes of my right foot. The pain was excruciating, and I let out a yell of agony and grabbed my foot in my hands.

Samantha immediately came running, for having heard me scream out, she thought I must have had an accident. She rushed into the bedroom and couldn't believe her eyes at the sight of her mother, hopping on one foot all around the room, tears spurting from her eyes, gritting her teeth in pain and spitting out the words "double happiness, double happiness, double happiness."

It didn't help the pain, but it definitely helped me see that the situation could have been worse. The disc could have landed on *both* feet, now, couldn't it? My glass was surely at least half-full that day.

• • •

The power of the mind, the connection of the mind to universal power is extraordinary, and it is important therefore to remain always mindful of the reasons we want to learn. Only for our spiritual benefit, for our own growth, never to change others, to interfere with someone else's mind power. Here is a story that illustrates the worst of what I mean by that.

A HAUNTING

Woken from a sound sleep by someone tugging at his arm, he half opened his eyes, turned toward his wife, who was lying next to him in their bed, thinking it was her. But she was fast asleep. He shrugged, thought he must have been dreaming, punched his pillows up, and closed his eyes. Boy, was he tired. Just beginning to doze off, he felt the tugging on his arm again, and shrugging again, tried to ignore it, but it was persistent. "Oh God, what is it?" he mumbled to no one in particular, and in reply he heard a whispering and felt the bedclothes pulled back. He flopped over, onto his back, opened his eyes, and found himself staring into a woman's face. It was so close he could feel her breath on his cheeks.

Great dream, he thought, closing his eyes, and grinned as she began to stroke him, at first gently, then stronger and harder, her hands all over his body. "You're mine," she whispered then, and his eyes flew open, reality striking him hard, and he pushed himself up in the bed, throwing her off as he did so.

"It's a dream, it's a dream," he told himself, closing his eyes tight and rubbing his face with his hands. "It was just a dream," and as he said this, he was sure that when he opened his eyes she would be gone.

He lay there, his heart pounding, trying to pull himself together, and it was just as he was about to open his eyes that he heard her chuckle. "I told you"—her voice was hard, determined—"you're mine, Richard, you belong to me, and no one else is going to have you."

Terror struck him, somewhere there was a pain, his chest? His stomach? He felt cold, clammy, and afraid. Afraid to open his eyes. "Come on, Richard, I've come for you," and again he felt her hands, stroking his face, his hair. Her voice, now soft, wheedling, she began making cooing noises. "You're mine, you're mine," he heard her say again, and involuntarily his eyes opened, and there she was, in the bed with him, a terrible grin on her face as she looked into his eyes . . . and he began to scream.

• • •

Sarah had called from her home, a large old house once belonging to some rich family estate, somewhere close to the Scottish border. Immediately the scene is set for a real live ghost story, and in its way, that's just what this is.

"It's my husband." I could hear the panic in her voice. "He doesn't believe, always treated the idea of an afterlife with utter disdain. Now, well, now I'm afraid. He seems on the edge of a nervous breakdown. You must help us, please, please, we'll do anything."

"Calm down, start at the beginning, and tell me what all this is about," I said. "Just tell me what has happened."

"It began a week ago. We were in bed asleep, when suddenly I was woken by my husband, who was screaming, 'Go away, go away.' It scared me half to death, and I thought he must be having some sort of bad dream. He was sitting bolt upright, his back straight against the wall, his eyes bulging, then he began to cry. I tried to calm him down, but he wouldn't be calmed. I went downstairs to the kitchen to make us both a cup of tea. When I arrived back upstairs he was still crying and shaking from head to toe."

"Was it a nightmare?" I asked.

"No," she replied. "He is adamant. He says he was woken, that someone, a woman, shook him awake, kept talking to him, smiling at him, a terrible smile, he says, kept touching him, and just wouldn't go away. Finally I managed to calm him and he went back to sleep. The next morning he laughed it off, told me he must have been dreaming, and went off to the office as if nothing had happened. However," she continued, "that afternoon he decided to take a nap. Worn out from the events of the previous night, he went straight to sleep, having had his secretary hold all his calls. He believes he was asleep for only about thirty to forty minutes when he was shaken violently awake. This time he didn't see anyone, but there was a strong and familiar smell of a woman's perfume, and—and again he swears this is true— he felt a presence, someone standing close to his chair. He was so spooked that he raced from the office, telling his secretary that he wasn't well and was going home. But he didn't come straight home. He rode around in his car for an hour or more, not know-ing what to do. That night he hardly dared to go to bed, and it took a while before he went to sleep. It must have been three or four in the morning when I woke again to hear him yelling in a terrible and frenzied voice, 'Go away, go away, leave me alone, please leave me alone.' "

She paused, a small sob escaped her, then she continued, telling me how, night after night, for over a week now, the same thing kept happening. "He's at the point where he daren't close his eyes, he's afraid to sleep, won't go into the office, can't work. You have to help us, Rosemary, it seems as if the house is haunted by an evil woman who keeps attacking my husband."

To get to their house was a two-hour car journey, and I was accompanied by my friend and fellow healer Ann. It was three days since the telephone call and the only real question I had was, could this man, a very successful and powerful business mo-gul, simply be having nightmares that were maybe stress-related, possibly a midlife issue, or was his ghost real? Well, we would soon find out.

The house was indeed perfect for a ghost story. Big, old, Victorian, and somewhat isolated.

She answered the door immediately, took our coats, and showed us into a large, comfortable sitting room. Her husband, tall, slim, graying hair, somewhere in his early sixties and quite distinguished looking, stood as we entered the room, but made no forward motion to greet us.

He's afraid, I thought, but what of? and instantly I heard Grey Eagle's voice. "Of you," he said quietly in my ear. "He's afraid of you."

I smiled brightly and taking the initiative moved across the room toward him, holding out my hand as I did so. "I'm Rosemary, and you must be Richard." Then turning quickly, I introduced my friend Ann.

"I'm, er, well, well," Richard stuttered. Not used to feeling awkward, usually in complete control, the man was totally lost as to how to behave.

"Why don't we start by sitting down," I said gently, and turning to Richard's wife said, "Perhaps we could have some tea. It's been quite a long journey."

She nodded, pleased to have something to do, and bustled off to the kitchen, returning very quickly with a tray of tea and biscuits.

While she was gone, Ann and I made small talk, chatting about how beautiful the house was, asking questions. How long had they lived there? Had they kept the original fireplaces?

Richard became more at ease, and as we drank our tea, he began telling us about the house, which he obviously loved. As the chitchat continued, although I seemed, to the couple, to be part of it, Ann knew that I was looking for any signs of an unwelcome force or entity, but so far I could see none.

Then, without warning, I reached across to Richard, who was

seated in the chair next to mine, took his hand, and said quietly, "I'd like you to tell me what has been happening to you. I realize that you are nervous and upset, that you may find it difficult to talk, but I need to know from you what you think is going on."

His immediate reaction was to take a defensive pose and I caught a glimpse of the businessman as his tone and manner became somewhat bossy and a little pompous. Pulling his hand from mine and looking across at his wife, he said, "Sarah has told you all there is to tell. Surely it is not necessary for me to enlighten you further."

My voice, still quiet and gentle, but now firm, I told him that yes, indeed, it was necessary. That I needed to know the details from him. I had his wife's account, that was true, but maybe there were some things he had not told her, maybe some things had slipped her mind or his in his recounting to her. "And I also need to know," I added, "if in the last three days the happenings have continued, and if so, in what way."

Used to having his own way, Richard was not about to give in. "Look, I don't believe in ghosts, I don't believe in you. In fact, I didn't want you here. This is my wife's idea, not mine," he blustered.

"That's fine," I replied, my voice and demeanor still calm. "I came here, Richard, because your wife insisted that you needed my help, that you were desperate. If, however, that is not the case, then I'm pleased, pleased that things are better, and I am happy to leave." At this, his wife started to cry and yell at him all at the same time. "Just swallow your wretched pride, man, tell her, tell her. Admit you're scared and need help." And Richard, hearing his wife, slumped in the chair, put his head in his hands, and began to sob.

I listened for over an hour as he told me pretty much the same story his wife had, adding that over the last three nights it had become much worse, as each time he was on the edge of sleep "she" would come to his bed, shake him awake, touch him, stroke him. She had even lifted the bedclothes to climb into bed beside him, and he had also begun to hear her voice during the day, as well as at night, calling his name, he said, and over and over he heard her say, "You're mine, Richard, you're mine, you belong to me."

Listening intently to his words, and watching him closely, I noticed, as he repeated "her" words, a certain reserve in his voice, a flicker of fear or confusion or both in his eyes. There was something he wasn't telling, but I knew that Grey Eagle would help me find the missing pieces of his story.

Now, turning to my guide, I asked, "What do I do now, where do we go from here?"

Even as I asked the question, I saw her. An elderly lady, well into her eighties, small and slight of build, with snow-white hair, she was standing next to Grey Eagle. I looked to Richard, to see if he could see her, but no one else in the room could see what I could see, nor could they hear our words as we spoke.

"Are you the one?" I asked the old woman. "Are you the one who has been haunting him?"

"No, no." The old one chuckled. "I'm his grandmother, I wouldn't do that to him. But give me a while, child, and I'll tell you who it is. First"—and she pointed at Richard—"let's give him another shock. I want him to know I'm alive, you know, still living on, and I want to make sure he doesn't forget in a hurry either." She winked at me, as if to say, "Know what I mean?" and I did know what she meant. She wanted to give him real evidence of her survival, and she wanted to make sure he was in no doubt that his grandmother had come to visit. I liked her immediately. There was in her a great sense of fun, and it felt as if we were like children, conspiring, but I knew she was here to help her grandson and to put things right. Grey Eagle had brought her here, and I had every faith that I would leave this house with the problem solved.

Turning to Richard and Sarah, I explained that I had been

talking with Richard's grandmother, who now wanted to talk to him. I smiled at the look of total disbelief on Richard's face, thinking how sad it was that some people just can't accept, no matter how much evidence they receive to the contrary, that there is no such thing as death, that strange happenings do have explanations that are not necessarily of this earth, but of the universe and of God.

"Come on, girl, let's get on with it." I heard her voice, impatient now, as I was, to begin, and for the next thirty minutes I recounted, as she gave it to me, her story. Scottish-born, she married a Scot, gave birth to two sons, one Richard's father. Richard himself, as a boy, until the age of ten, lived with his parents and grandparents in his grandmother's house, which of course she described in great detail. Fast and furious the evidence came through, and Richard, at first dumbfounded, speechless, finally found his voice, and forgetting the terror and trials of the last two weeks, became excited, immersed in the wonder of the grandmother's all-too-obvious presence. Asking questions, enthralled at the answers, wanting more, until finally I heard Grey Eagle's voice. "Time to stop, to take a break," he said. I smiled, thinking he was thinking of me, of my need to replenish my energy. I felt fine, could have gone on longer, but knew better than to argue with one who knew better than I.

All the time I had been communicating with Richard's grandmother I had been looking, too, for the reason we were here, the "ghost" who had begun this nightmare, but I had not had even the slightest glimpse of her. Well, not so far, I thought, not yet, but the night was not over yet.

More tea, more biscuits on the tray. Then Sarah, excusing herself, said apologetically that she really must walk the dog, and she hoped we didn't mind. "I'll be about half an hour," she said as she buttoned up her coat. And as I replied that she mustn't worry, that she should take her time, I knew instantly that this was all part of the plan.

The door had barely closed behind her when I heard Richard's grandmother again. "This is it," the old lady said determinedly, "now it's time for the truth," and I listened quietly as she quickly told her tale. Then, "All right, child, you better tell him what you know."

I looked at Richard, took a deep breath, then, "Richard, how long have you been having an affair? Five years, perhaps a little less, your grandmother says."

"You don't know, you don't know, you can't, you can't, it's not possible," he moaned, realizing as he said it that I did know and that it was more than possible. I went on: "It would be good to get this part out of the way before your wife comes back, right?" I looked hard at him. "She doesn't know, does she, and I'm not going to tell her. Enough hurt has been done. But tell me, Richard, you know who the woman is who is haunting you, don't you? It's your lover, isn't it?"

"But how is it possible?" he cried. "I knew it was her, I tried to push her away, but I just can't get rid of her."

He went on to tell me how, over the five years he had known this woman, he had tried several times to break off the relationship. Each time she had threatened him. She would tell his wife, kill herself, ruin him, ruin his business. This was one person he had not been able to control; in fact, he had allowed her to take control of him.

"Four weeks ago I broke it off, finally, once and for all. I told her I didn't care what she did, it was over. I was not going to see her again. I thought she had accepted it, then, two weeks ago all this started happening. I was so afraid, am so afraid. How is it possible that she can come into my bedroom, like a ghost in the night, and haunt me this way? I've even thought I must be going insane. Things like this just can't happen. They just can't."

"Well, Richard," I said, "now you know that things like this really can happen. Obviously this woman is very strong-minded and very determined to have her way. The emotional power of her feelings toward you is so strong, and she is exercising that power over you. She is trying to control your mind, using the power of her own mind."

I asked him if he'd ever heard of out-of-body experiences, and explained to him how it was possible, unbelievable as it may sound, for someone to leave their body and to travel to other places. "I do it all the time." I chuckled, seeing the confusion on his face. "I have patients the world over, and so it is impossible for me to physically visit everyone, but I will often travel out of body to visit my patients who are sick and dying, and who need me. Some of them actually see me, just as you have been seeing your girlfriend. The difference between what I do and what is happening in your case," I continued, "is that I use my mind power, my energy, for the good of the one I am visiting. My intentions are the best for my patient. Your girlfriend, however, has a different agenda. It is doubtful that she understands or realizes the full extent of what she is doing. However, her intention is to force you to think of her. She wants you to be totally unable to think of anyone but her. She wants to make you want and need her, as she wants and needs you."

"My God," Richard spluttered, taking in all that I'd said. "Well, how do I stop it, how do I stop her?"

"It's simple, Richard, once you realize that all that is happening here is that your girlfriend is forcing her will on you. She can only win if you want her to. If you truly don't want this relationship anymore, and," I added sternly, "for everyone's sake, especially your wife's, I strongly suggest that you don't want this relationship to continue, well then, the remedy is simple. When she comes again, mentally, emotionally, with all the power of your mind, turn away from her. Refuse her, and send her away. If you really mean not to see her again, then close your mind to her and to all that you have found attractive about her. Use your thoughts. Use your power. Send her away."

Richard sighed. "It really is that simple?" he asked, and I nodded.

"Mind over matter, Richard," I said. "Mind power over matter."

Hardly had these words come out of my mouth than we heard the kitchen door open, and a breathless Sarah came almost at a run, worried that she had been away too long. I assured her that she had not, and told her we were going to talk some more to Richard's grandmother. As it turned out, we talked to Sarah's father, too. He had died some several years before, very suddenly, and Sarah was overjoyed to hear from him.

Not too much more was said about the ghost. I assured Sarah that Richard's grandmother had taken care of the matter, and Sarah, relieved to know it was over, didn't ask too many questions. It was six weeks later when Richard called. "It works, Rosemary, it really works. Thank you for everything, thank you." And as he said this, I smiled as I was reminded of his grandmother's last message.

It was just as we were leaving when I heard the old woman's cackling laughter for the last time, as she gave me a final message to give to her grandson.

"Richard," she said, "remember me, know that all of us here love you. And Richard, remember, I'm watching you, boy, I'm watching you."

Beloved Pan, and all ye other
Gods who haunt this place,
Give me beauty in the inward soul,
And may the outward and the inward
Man be at one.

PLATO

CHAPTER 6

Savoring Our Common Senses

The price of good mediumship is sensitivity and loneliness. This is what I was told more than eighteen years ago by my friend and colleague Mick McGuire, who was himself a healer. I remember nodding as he said this, knowing yet not knowing, understanding yet not understanding. How could I? I had hardly yet begun.

Loneliness was something I was used to; having always been "strange," being lonely came with the territory. It hurt, but I had learned to live with it. When I heard Mick's words I already knew loneliness, I just didn't know it well enough. Over the following years it was to creep up on me at so many unexpected times and places, wrapping its painful arms about me as if it were my closest friend, almost comforting in its cloudy familiarity. An ever-present companion.

I accepted my loneliness, knowing it was impossible for others to understand me, to understand the way my mind works at times, the strangeness of my living in two worlds, my ability to see the unseen, the often unfathomable "other side." This was a price I accepted and could not quibble about. A price worth paying. But what of sensitivity? Could I or anyone pay that price? Of course, it's easy after eighteen years of learning, growing, discovering. It's easy to understand why being sensitive is so important, but it is not so easy, though, to handle. That I should deliberately make myself even more sensitive than I already am could be construed as madness. Though not only must I try, on a daily basis, to be more sensitive, I urge my students to heighten their level of sensitivity also, and now I'm asking you the reader to come and join us.

Why would you want to? Are you mad, a masochist? We all understand that if we open ourselves up to become more sensitive, then we inevitably open ourselves up to more pain, deeper hurt. We become more vulnerable, and why would you want to do that?

We all know about pain thresholds; some of us have a high level, which means we don't feel as much pain as someone who has a low level, a low threshold. Not surprisingly, I have an extremely low threshold of pain. I suffer the merest cut or bruise badly. Just the sight of a needle makes me wince, and often I have had to clamp my teeth down hard so as not to scream out in agony before the needle has even pierced my skin. Some would say I'm simply a big baby. They would be right. Others would say that I am merely ultrasensitive. They would be right also.

A low threshold of physical pain indicates a high degree of sensitivity—physical sensitivity, that is. In much the same way, a low threshold of emotional pain, the ability to be easily emotionally wounded, indicates a high degree of emotional sensitivity. So I ask again, why would any right-minded, sane individual want to put themselves in the position, deliberately, where their tolerance of emotional, mental, and spiritual pain is lessened?

Actively seeking to increase our level of sensitivity means this. An increase of pain. An increase of heartache. An increase and deepening awareness of our feelings. An increase and deepening awareness of others' feelings, others' pain, others' heartache. If we were not careful, surely we could own the pain of the world, as it rests heavily on our shoulders.

Why would we want more pain? But isn't pain our greatest gift from God, our often-present teacher? And why would we want more heartache, and what could we gain from a deepening awareness of our feelings, and the feelings of others?

Increasing our level of sensitivity, however, also means that we are more aware of the beauty of the world around us. Of the sunrise and sunsets, the sight of sunlight dancing across a still pond is more breathtaking to us, we feel more deeply the hand of God or some power greater than ours. Yes, pain is felt more deeply, but so is joy, and laughter is more appreciated the more we cry.

Some would say that we are instruments of God, and this might imply that we are inanimate beings waiting on the will of heaven. But I am not an inanimate being, nor do I believe that any of us is just such an animal. God gave us a free will, a mind of our own to use. We are our own instrument, the machine and also the machinist, the fiddle and the fiddler, the singer and the song.

Most of us were given five common senses. Sight, hearing, touch, smell, and taste, and every day of our lives we use those senses naturally, easily, without thinking. They are second nature to us, and it is only when one of our senses fails us that we give any thought to the blessings we have had, or how we could live our lives without them. But rather than dwell on being without any one of our common senses, let us try to concentrate our mind and efforts on making our senses more sensitive, more finely tuned than they already are. What effect could that have on our lives?

• • •

A musician trains his ear to the point where he is sensitive enough to hear not just his music but also his instrument. He or she can tell in a fraction of a second if his instrument is sound or needs adjustment. Likewise a hunter trains his senses. The instrument he uses, his own self, his sensitivity. Using sight, hearing, even his sense of smell, he seeks out his prey. And what of the artist, and of all things that require our creative nature? The best chef is the one who not only is in tune with the taste and smell of his food, but with the color and texture. All of his senses must be in harmony and totally attuned.

So the chef, the artist, the hunter, the musician, writer, poet, sculptor, creator, all must finely tune their senses. Become more sensitive. The result? Yes, an increase in temperament, more pain, more struggle, more heartache, and yes, of course, a deepening awareness of our own and others' feelings, which may well be tough to handle, but what better art, better food, more enjoyment, more beautiful music, poetry, writing, sculpting, what greater pleasure in the very process of our creativity. How can we gauge great joy if we have no yardstick, if we have never known despair? Who can tell what love is, or to what depths we can love, without the experience of receiving and giving love, feeling both the pains and pleasures of love? How do we know how high our spirit can soar, if we never give our spirit wings or room or opportunity or even recognition? How far can we go, how will we know, unless we dare to step out? And how will we know when we have arrived at the many good resting places there are along the path we will take, unless we are in tune, tuned in, to our senses, our sensitivity?

We cannot hope to be a great musician or sculptor or writer if we don't train ourselves, and we all know that thorough training doesn't just take months, it can take years. Years of dedication and hard work. However, most of us don't want to be great at anything. We are satisfied to live ordinary lives, striving the best we can simply to be decent, honest, and nice people. And most of us, recognizing that we are spiritual beings, don't necessarily want to gain second sight, explore the universe, or become great

211

mediums and healers. We would be content just to know a little more than we do now about our spirit, to strive just a touch harder in getting to know our spirit, that spiritual nature and what it might mean to us, how it might help us. And many of us would like to discover how we could help ourselves and our loved ones in times of sickness, distress, or pain. Could getting to know our spirit selves give us more insight, help us be stronger, give us more tools to enhance our own and other lives? Most of us don't want to be great, we just want to do our best with the gift God gave us, the gift of life. It doesn't take years and years of training to do this, but it does take a certain amount of courage, determination, and perseverance.

Every exercise so far has encouraged us to stretch our emotional, mental, and spiritual senses, to discover the power within us. But we must not neglect the fact that, after all, we are human, physical beings, made of flesh and blood. We have five common senses, directly connected to our physical selves. Sight, touch, hearing, smell, and taste. These senses are what steer us in our lives on this earth plane. Not all of us have all five senses, of course, but often, when we lack one or more of them, those others we have are more acute, and in some ways compensate for the lack of that which we are missing.

If a man is blind, how is it that his hearing is often more acute? When a woman is deaf, what is it that enables her to see things, her vision more acute than if she were both a hearing and seeing person? The answer is simple. He needs. She needs. And their needs drive them to train that which they do have, to become more sensitive. A person who cannot speak, and who does not train himself to learn another way to communicate, is someone who lives in his world alone, is someone who does not recognize or wish to be a part of our greater world. Likewise, she who does not train her senses to see, to hear, to taste and smell and touch more than this world of ours requires, is someone who does not recognize, or wish to be a part of, our greater universe.

I remember a night, many years ago. It must easily have been maybe three or four in the early hours. Something woke me, and I turned from my side, onto my back. Groggy, sleepy-eyed, I half wondered, but was too tired to take any thought I might have further. Sighing, I flipped myself over to the other side of the bed, my eyes already tight shut, sleep fast closing in over me, when something again caught my attention, and my eyelids fluttered open for a few seconds more. A smell, strong, perfumed, and very familiar. Brylcreem. My father always used it on his hair. It washed over me, covering my face. I smiled, snuggled deeper down in the bedcovers, my last thought rocking me softly back to sleep. "Daddy's here. Daddy's here." I knew it to be true.

My sense of smell is especially acute, which has often, throughout my life, been a source of some difficulty. There is a downside to most things if we want to look for it. The upside, however, is that I can often tell if someone from the spirit world is around, long before I see them. There are certain odors that we can recognize our loved ones by, a favorite perfume, hair lotion, hand cream, pipe tobacco, or cigarettes. These are the scents that are familiar to us.

A client of mine lost her husband very tragically. His death was sudden and she not only mourned the fact that he was gone, she also mourned the fact that she was not there with him at the end. They had a very close relationship and had had a very rich and long marriage. Her favorite flowers were freesias, and every year, on her birthday, he would fill their house with them.

It came to the eve of her first birthday without him since their marriage, and as she went to bed that night, she dreaded the thought of facing the next day.

The sun, bright and strong in the early morning, forced its way through the crack in the drapes and sought her face. Bright light filtered through the blindness of her nighttime slumber, and she squinted to try to block it out. Half awake now, her mind opening to a new day, she remembered, and tears flowed steadily down her cheeks as hard realization struck her heart. "It's my birthday, and I wish so much that you were here."

As if in answer, it seemed, a faint breeze entered the room, carrying with it the most gentle of perfumes. "What is it?" she wondered, and through that thought came her answer. Jumping out of bed, fearing it to be her imagination, she went out into the hallway, then through to the living room, the kitchen and dining room, and then back into the bedroom. She had begun to cry again, but this time not with that most utter and lonely despair which had caught her in its grasp as she had come awake. This time her tears were mingled joy, happiness, disbelief in the miracle she must believe in. The scent of freesias . . . all over the house.

If each of us could develop our senses to the degree where we might make such connections, how much effort might we make in our training process? And where would we begin? How can we make our senses more sensitive, more acute?

Well, throughout this chapter I have laid down some guidelines, suggestions, exercises that are not only fun but can be very productive in showing us how to fine-tune the gifts that we already own. In this chapter we are not looking for something new, we are building and training that which we already know we have. We just don't know how much of it we have.

So, first, briefly, let's look at our five senses and remind ourselves of their functions.

A child will, from day one, reach out to *touch*, using this sense to seek out its mother's breast. We test, by touching, to see if something is hot or cold. We touch each other to give affection or comfort.

The most incredible and wonderful touch I ever felt in all my life was that first touch of my baby's hair, as it brushed against my cheek while I held her in my arms. Soft as soft. Softer than down on down. If I close my eyes I feel it still, even after twenty-eight years, I feel it as if it were the first time all over again.

Taste is something any cook will use, and I know for myself that if I am cooking a meat dish and therefore cannot *taste* to see if there is enough salt or seasoning, I feel somewhat handicapped in my culinary skills. Of course, that is my time to ask Grey Eagle, to be "at home," connect with his thoughts, and he always helps me out.

Especially good *smells*, like homemade breads, nice perfume, are great. One of my most favorite smells is the smell of a child dusted in baby talc. Nothing else can make me feel so broody or mumsy. That's when I wish most to be a grandmother.

Those of us who have good *sight* take it so much for granted. We read, watch TV, revel in glorious sunsets and gardens filled with flowers. One of the sights I love the most is the sight of my child, eyes closed, breathing shallow, curled up in blankets, dreaming her star-dusted dreams.

It is true that of all of our five senses, our *hearing* is the last to leave us if we are ill and dying. And for those of us fortunate enough not to be hearing-impaired, we take this gift so much for granted. We cannot imagine never to have heard the sounds of children laughing, church bells on a Sunday morning, good music. Of course, as I said earlier, there is a downside to most things if we look for it. Cars hooting impatiently in heavy traffic, a child's distressed crying, and that awful sound of the alarm clock in the morning.

One of my dogs, Karma, now well and happy in the spirit world, would sometimes make a sound that was so thrilling, so wonderful, his way of speaking to me. It was usually when his chew or bone or toy had lodged itself under the sofa, too far back for him to reach. He would crouch down, his nose pointing to the given object of his desire, his eyes lifted up to mine, and he would make the strangest noise. It wasn't a whine or a growl, more a warbling, trilling sound, in his throat. If I seemed not to take notice, the sound would grow louder, the warbling like a pea rattling through a wind tunnel. Sometimes, to my shame, I would

215

pretend indifference to his plight, for a while anyway, just so he would keep on speaking to me. This is one of the sounds in my life I have loved the most, and certainly one of the sounds I have paid particular attention to, becoming aware of my acutely attuned senses and emotions as I listened.

All the exercises in this chapter have been designed to enhance each of our five senses, and of course, the more you practice, the better the results. Spending at least one week for each exercise will give you the best and most effective results, but each person must work in the way that is good for them and that fits in with their daily routine. It all depends on what you want, how much you want it, and the reasons why you want it. As I wrote this last line, my memory was triggered and I was reminded of how much, what, and for what reasons I wanted. Way back at the beginning, when I first discovered the absolute reality of the spirit world, and the enormous part it would play in my life.

I would try anything. Put my fingers in my ears, cover my head with the blankets, grit my teeth, hold my breath. Nothing worked. The voices would still be there, whispering, whispering, soundless sound, noiseless noise, deafening, frightening, seeping though the soft skin of my young and terrified body. How I wished I couldn't hear. What irony then, when I couldn't hear well enough, my ears straining to pick up the slightest sound, the smallest movement.

I didn't want, I desperately didn't want. And then I wanted with an eagerness and passion I had never known before.

"Let me hear you," I would cry. "All of you, God, Christ, Grey Eagle, let me hear you. Teach me, teach me."

I was so frustrated, and wanted to improve my skills so much, wanted to be the best that I could be. Fame and fortune were not my incentive, nor did any possibility of such occur to me at all. I wanted to be the best that I could be for a variety of reasons, I suppose. I had finally found myself, discovering that I was not insane. That was a great feeling and I wanted more of it. Also, I had found something that I was good at, and I knew if I worked hard, I could even excel in my field. Having lacked confidence all my life, this knowledge was a revelation, and I knew it would only change my life for the better. I wanted to be the best that I could be, for my life to be the best that it could be. But most of all I felt that I had discovered the most incredible truth, and I wanted to share it. I wanted to share my knowledge with as many as would listen, to shout it from the rooftops, and I hoped that others would be as enlightened and excited as I was.

In the days of my beginnings, nearly twenty years ago, you must remember there was no such thing as the "New Age section" in bookstores. People who believed spoke of their faith in hushed whispers, although interestingly enough, once one person in a group voiced their beliefs, everyone got to talking. Most found the idea of communicating with the spirit world a fascinating topic. It was, however, only the supposed eccentrics, the fanatics or cultists who were apt to be seen entering a spiritualist church—indeed, that was the opinion of the majority.

I am not sure which of these terms—eccentric, fanatic, or cultist—anyone in the early days would have applied to me. Certainly in the small village in which I lived people had their opinions and their small jokes at my expense. "Go up there on a Friday night" (Friday night was class night), the rumor went, "and you can see them all dancing naked in the moonlight." Another joke, said with humor and a great amount of elbow nudging, if I was seen about in any public place, "Be careful, she'll put a curse on you." Of course, most people didn't believe such things, it was just a bit of fun!

It didn't stop me, though, it didn't dampen my ardor, my passion, for passion it indeed was, and still is. Every day I would strive for more. How could I hear or see more clearly? Why is it, I would ask myself, that sometimes I hear more clearly than at other times? These and a thousand more were my questions. Often I would stand in the middle of the living room and call out, dare the spirit world to show itself. "I'm ready," I would boldly announce. "Come on, what are you waiting for? Show yourselves, let me see you more clearly, hear you more clearly, feel you, touch you, taste and smell you. I want it more clearly. What are you waiting for?"

Imagine this scene. A scene that many of you, I'm sure, have played out for yourselves, perhaps with the same degree of passion and frustration that had bored its way into me. "What are you waiting for?" I would say, gazing heavenward, defiant, demanding, insisting on an answer I rarely got. Well, what were they waiting for? Waiting, possibly, with a certain amount of impatience, passion, amusement, and frustration.

"Why don't you hear me?" I would call, impatiently, passionately, not with any degree of amusement, but definitely frustrated.

But I was not sensitive enough, not attuned enough, to hear their answer.

"Why don't you listen harder?" would have been their reply, if only I had known how to listen, and "try to relax and just let it happen," would have been their advice, had I been able to tune into their thoughts. But I was young, headstrong. My five common senses were not in tune, in harmony, with my sixth sense. I was not "at home" to them and it was causing me some confusion. I had to build on them, to fine-tune each of my senses, to be more disciplined and mindful of what my body, mind, and spirit were telling me. The only way forward, I discovered, was to become more aware of my senses and to exercise them. They were flabby, like unused muscles, and I had to tone them up.

You will see as we go through this chapter, and as we work with each of the five senses, that I might suggest, for instance, that you visualize a rose, but you may prefer to use another kind of flower. I may suggest that you taste chocolate, when in fact you favor roast beef, or I may suggest that you listen to Mozart and your preference is Scott Joplin. It is fine to go with your preference, and to try whatever you feel will work best for you. Be in tune with what you feel, with what you sense. Be in tune with your own sensitivity, and learn to listen to and trust your own judgment. Let's try taking some small but important steps in enhancing our five senses.

EXERCISE I . . .
HEARING

An easy exercise to begin with, and all you have to do is find your favorite music, sit in an armchair, or find a comfortable place to lie down, and indulge yourself. Close your eyes, become aware of the music, *listen*. Is the music soft or loud, gentle or fierce? Listen in a way you have never listened before, and allow yourself to feel.

Do you feel excited or soothed? Does the music make you feel? Of course it does, so then try to become aware of how you feel. Relax, and let those feelings grow. Don't suppress, but rather allow your body and mind self-expression. Become part of the music you hear, sink into it, indulge. Chopin or Brahms, whatever you choose, just give yourself up to the music. Can you hear? Are you aware of the feelings your music inspires in you? Are you carried away by the music, by the sounds you hear, and if so, where does your music take you?

When you listen to the music, how many sounds do you hear?

As you strain to hear each sound, how acute does your hearing become, and how aware of yourself does the music make you?

As you listen, ask, or rather float with the idea of yesterday, or memories of the past. Does the music inspire thoughts of long ago, and maybe dreams of tomorrow and of the future?

How many memories are there, and where do they come from? How far back in your life does your music take you, and what dreams of the future are you inspired to dream?

Each day as you listen to your music, think about these questions and try to express your feelings. You don't have to be a great poet or literary genius. As long as the words you write and the way you write make sense to you, that's all that matters.

Music is a great beginning, but you need to use other sounds as well. When someone speaks to you, listen hard. Is his or her voice harsh to your ear, or soft? Gentle or sharp? How does the sound of his or her voice make you feel? How do you react, and if you are listening attentively, you will definitely be reacting.

When Jim and I went to our first dog-training session—meant more for us than the dogs, of course—our trainer, Fred Bradley, a genius and gentle miracle with animals, stressed the importance of tone of voice. "Dogs have a finely tuned sense, and it isn't just that they hear us, but what they understand from the tone we use," he told us. Jim has a gruff, almost abrupt tone, and Fred suggested that he needed to moderate his voice, it was too commanding, and the dogs received the signal, through his tone, that they were being chastised, even though they were not. My tone, on the other hand, Fred told me, was just the opposite. Too soft, too gentle, and not enough of a command.

Having listened to Jim, I already knew what Fred was saying, and when he suggested to Jim that he might want to train his voice to sound a little softer, a little gentler, I jokingly asked if he could practice on me, as I had often mistaken his abrupt tone as irritation or dismissal. My ultrasensitivity gave me the same impression the dogs had, that somehow I was being chastised. Sometimes I was right; often, though, I was mistaken. This sort of thing happens to most of us at one time or another, and I know that this is a problem that is only solved if we can learn to give others the benefit of the doubt, the benefit of believing that others come from a place of goodwill. As you listen to others, and giving them the benefit of believing that they come with a feeling of goodwill toward you, listen carefully, not just to what someone says, but to how they say it. Listen to their tone of voice and try to react in a nonjudgmental way. And when someone asks you, "Are you listening to me?," know that yes, you really are.

How does that make you feel? Does being more acutely aware of someone else's voice make you more aware of the tone of your own voice?

When you really listen to the sound of your own voice, are you aware of how much sense you talk? Ask yourself these questions.

How often do you laugh?

How often do you cry?

How often do you complain?

How often do you really listen to yourself?

How aware of your own sound are you?

The world is full of sounds, and it can be fun to try some of them out, to become more in tune with yourself and with the world around you. With practice, your ability to truly hear and really listen will become more acute, so acute in fact that some of you may become more attuned to the sounds of the universe and the spirit world. First, though, before we race too far ahead, why not try some down-to-earth sounds, like church bells, or birds singing. The sound of the sea. A clock ticking. Babies crying. The sound of the wind. Bees buzzing. Children laughing. The sound of rain, or running water. The rustling of leaves, and how about this, the sound of summer.

All of these sounds are the sounds of happiness, and you may find it beneficial to write down your thoughts and feelings, and don't be surprised at how acute your ability to hear has become. One sound that you must learn to become aware of, an all-important sound: *the sound of silence.*

When you have tried your exercise and begun to tone up your senses, to learn how to listen more intently, with more concentration, and also hopefully, with more ease, maybe some of you will want to try a next step.

Why not see if you can train your ears to listen to the sound and signs, to the music and the song of the universe? Who knows, you may hear the whispered voices of your loved ones in the spirit world as they call out to you.

But remember first, how can you expect to hear your "dead" mother, sister, husband, loved one, if you fail to hear your "living" family?

EXERCISE 2 . . .
SMELL

The kitchen might be the best place to begin this exercise, or you might prefer the bathroom with all its soapy smells, or maybe the garden. Wherever you choose to be, try first to locate a smell that you really enjoy. Fresh-baked bread or nice spicy smells. Talcum powder or toothpaste. Or the smell of roses or lilac.

As you train your nose, ask yourself how many smells you can find? A dozen? Two dozen? As you concentrate on each smell, how acute does your sense of smell become?

How many feelings are triggered when you use your sense of smell, and how aware of yourself does your awareness of these smells make you? Ask, how many memories are there, and where do they come from? How far back in your life does this exercise take you, what do the smells remind you of? Then ask:

How often am I aware of my sense of smell?

How often do I sense smell?

How often do I enjoy my ability to smell?

How often do I find my ability to smell distasteful?

How often do I smell myself?

Try to ask the same questions you asked as you worked with sound, with your hearing, and ask these same questions as you work with each of your five senses, as the principle is the same. Working on your sense of smell, a good question to ask is: How aware of your own smell are you? All of us have an individual smell, and it is easy for a parent to recognize the individual smells of her children, and a mother can often tell if her child is ill from a certain smell that she associates with sickness in that child.

Interestingly, Samantha could always tell when I had been crying. She would smell my skin and know I had been upset. Her sense of smell was obviously acute, and in tune with me and my emotions.

Animals use their sense of smell to smell us. We are animals, too, but because most of us do not live out in the wild, do not rely on our senses for survival, going to the supermarket is so much easier, we have not lost, but have certainly mislaid the acuteness of our senses. Let's try to see if we can discover them again.

Here are some more smells to try, as well as those you will already have thought of.

Salty sea air. Apple pie. Baby talc. Fresh-mown grass. Cooked cheese. Perfume. Roses. Biscuits, fresh-baked. Soap. Freesias. Strawberry jam. Hand cream.

All of these smells are good smells. Try them out, then, if you can, write down all of your thoughts and feelings, and be surprised at how acute your sense of smell has become.

And one smell that you must learn to become aware of, an all-important smell: *the smell of earth.*

• • •

In the early spring of 1998, I traveled to Italy, to Rome, one of the most architecturally amazing and beautiful cities in the world. I had been invited to be a guest on *The Maurizio Constanzo Show,* one of the most popular shows in the country.

This was not my first, but my third or fourth time in Rome. Nor was it my first appearance on the Constanzo show, and I was one of seven or so guests. Each guest had a particular subject, and each subject had to do with our five senses. I was the guest talking about our sixth sense.

We all sat onstage together, and I listened with varying degrees of interest as each person explained their reasons for being on the show. One was an aroma therapist, another a masseuse, a brain surgeon, a hypnotherapist, and a man who had something to do with pyramids. Then there was a lovely young actress, whose name I must confess I've forgotten, one other Italian celebrity, and a man whom I found the most fascinating of all. He was a doctor, a psychiatrist, and he worked in a very specialized field dealing with children, mainly, from what I could understand, children who were unable, for various reasons, to communicate in the usual way.

He told a story, a most moving and curious tale of a young boy, only four years old, who was one of his patients. The child seemed to him at first autistic, for he neither spoke in a language that anyone understood, nor did he seem to hear or respond in any way to anyone or anything, and he would avert his eyes if anyone tried to make contact. No one knew what to make of the boy, or how to help him, and he had been referred to this psychiatrist as a last hope.

The boy's mother visited every day, and as the psychiatrist got to know the child better, watching closely for any signs of awareness of his world, he began to notice a pattern. Although he never looked in his mother's direction when she entered the room, even so, the sounds he made seemed the same each time she visited. Then the psychiatrist noticed that in certain circumstances, the boy made particular noises. Each time a certain circumstance arose, the boy made the same response. The doctor realized that indeed the boy was responding to his environment, just not in a way that anyone else could understand. He did have a language, just not one that was known. It was his own, and his alone.

The doctor knew that if he could not learn to understand the boy, at least to understand his language, then the boy would be lost. He consulted his team, and it was decided that they would record the child's sounds, garbled and undecipherable, and try to decipher them.

Not of a technical mind, and speaking almost no Italian, I became somewhat lost in the details of the types of special equipment and techniques that were used, but simply put, if the tapes were played at a certain speed, and on a particular piece of machinery, it became possible to decipher much of what the boy said.

I was fascinated, and totally involved in the story, as in the strangest way I could relate to what the doctor was saying, and was truly in sympathy with the child. For often the sounds that come from the universe, from the spirit world, sound garbled and indecipherable, even to a trained ear, and it requires much patience and a mind willing enough to sift through the sounds again and again and yet again, sometimes a hundred times, before they become language, become communication that we can recognize.

The doctor continued his story, telling us how eventually the child became more sociable, more approachable. "Then," the doctor told, "one day I picked him up, and as he sat on my knee, he began to sniff at me. Climbing up, he sniffed my hair, my face, my skin and mouth. Moving down, he went to my neck, my hands, my chest. Like an animal, he was sniffing me out, recognizing me by my smell. As each new person came into the room and picked him up to talk to him, he would do the same. Never rejecting anyone, and obviously he was gaining knowledge of the person by their smell. Well," the doctor continued, "I have seen animals do this, but I have never before seen humans, a child. But his sense of smell must be very acute, and he had begun, in his way, to communicate with us."

I listened intently, fascinated with this story, thinking how very sensitive this little boy must be. How I wanted to know more, to become more involved. But it was not possible, except perhaps, through my prayers.

225

Toward the end of the show, my host asked my opinion of his other guests, of their talents and abilities. It was my chance to ask a burning question about the child I had become so interested in. "Doctor," I said, looking directly at the psychiatrist who was seated at the end of the stage, "Doctor, you told us you were able to decipher some of the sounds the boy made. Could you tell us some of what the child was trying to say?" The psychiatrist smiled a sad smile. "Yes," he said, "we were able to understand quite a lot. There are two phrases in particular that he repeats on a regular basis. One: 'There is the one who comes and goes.'" This, the doctor told us, the boy spoke when referring to his mother. The second phrase he spoke more often, and this one is self-referential. The child, four years old, speaks of himself, saying, "Here is the madman."

EXERCISE 3 . . .
TASTE

It is easy to understand how developing our hearing, sight, and even smell might enhance our ability to sense, to see, to hear, to communicate with those who are usually beyond our ordinary range, and I'm not just talking about those in the spirit world. I am also referring to our friends, relatives, colleagues, loved ones, and indeed anyone on this earth plane with whom we might wish to have a better understanding, better communication. But somehow, working to improve our sense of taste doesn't seem to fit into the pattern. How could developing the ability to taste, to increase the sensitivity of our taste buds help us? It seems, surely, a mere self-indulgence?

Well, first, let's be clear. There is nothing wrong with a little self-indulgence: in fact, one might view all of the exercises in this book as a program of guided self-indulgence. Years ago we were taught that it was wrong to want for ourselves. Many religions preached that it was a sin to be discontent, that we should accept our lot, our God-given lot in life. To want more was seen to be a sin of avarice and greed. Since the whole New Age movement began, some who have held themselves up as teachers have taught that the only thing that matters is that we know who we are. That we must step out on a journey of self-discovery, find ourselves.

In the first instance, the pendulum, way over to one side, meant that many people were subservient. Those who wanted more lived with feelings of guilt, and often condemned themselves for their discontent. In the second instance, the pendulum, for many, swung way over to the other side. Here was freedom, here was a way to become unsuppressed, to throw off the shackles of guilt and responsibility for others. Some used this New Age newfound freedom as an excuse for leaving husbands, wives, children, responsibilities, leaving devastation, pain, hurt, confusion, leaving these things in their wake. Running blindly forward in an effort to break free, trampling on the feelings of others in the process.

Excessive behavior of any form is unhealthy, and in the long run can only leave us confused. When we were taught not to want, not to question, we were taught by those who wanted to control us, who wanted us to be submissive ... to them. Then, when we were taught that it was good to question, right to want, some of us, in an effort to break control, wreaked havoc in the lives of those around us. The New Age fervor became the New Age fever. The pendulum swung too far.

I am not an advocate of the so-called New Age, but more an advocate of the "Old Age," the age of wisdom, of knowledge, timeless, forever and always, of the beginnings of time, and before time as we know it. I am an advocate of the pendulum steadily ticking in a central place, moving a little to the left, taking in, accepting, and learning from the past, moving a little to the right, looking forward to the future and what it might teach us. I believe that it is necessary to question, to want, to be selfish, to gain, but not at someone else's expense. Not if it means deliberately causing pain and hurt to someone else. Not if it means abandoning your responsibilities. It is so important that we learn to appreciate, to savor life, but not ever, ever, if it means ruining, without thought or compassion, the life of another human being.

Savoring life. How do we do that? How do we begin to learn? Strange as this may sound to some of you, if we can learn to appreciate, to delight in, to relish and enjoy the small things in life, then we can begin to understand and appreciate the larger and more complex issues. We are trying to raise our level of sensitivity to a point of discovery. Discovery of ourselves, of all we see around us, and of all that is there that we do not yet see.

One small problem with this next exercise is that it will be hard for those of you on a diet to stay on that diet. Of course, this could be your perfect excuse to eat, to savor, all those goodies you have been so good about not eating. Be self-indulgent. Every day chose some one special something to eat or drink. An especially nice or different something, for example:

Monday . . . chocolate

Tuesday . . . strawberries

Wednesday . . . pancakes.

You can try something new, or you can stick to the same special treat every day. Your choice, but you may get better results if you do vary.

This exercise also applies to drink, and you may feel that this is a good time to try the many varieties and different kinds of herbal or perfumed teas that are readily available nowadays.

See if you can become aware of your taste buds, not only with those things you have chosen to savor especially, but every time you eat or drink. Explore your taste buds. Explore and delight in your senses.

Ask yourself the same questions as before, and try to write down your answers. As you write, become aware of your feelings, your senses.

How many tastes did you discover? When you were eating and drinking, how acute was your sense of taste?

How many feelings were triggered when you were aware of your sense of taste?

In what way and how aware of yourself does tasting make you?

How many memories were there, and where did they come from?

How often are you aware of your sense of taste?

How often do you sense taste?

How often do you enjoy to taste?

How often is taste distasteful to you?

How often do you taste yourself?

Look back to the previous exercises and remind yourself of all the other questions you could also be asking, and remember *the* question.

How aware of your own taste are you?

Below is a list of tastes that we like. Some you may have tried and some you may not even have thought of. Try to taste as many things as you can.

Strawberries. Leek soup. Jasmine tea. Mint tea. Hot buttered toast. Fish 'n' chips, a very English dish. Smooth pâté. Lemon pie. Hot chocolate. Crusty bread. Trifle with cream. Milkshake.

Of all these tastes that you might learn to become aware of, an all-important taste is this: *the taste of life.*

• • •

The woman I saw was quite ordinary, as most of us are, and her two daughters were listening intently as I attempted to describe their mother. Truthfully, though, as is usual, that description could have fit a thousand women. Short, about five feet two inches, around one hundred and thirty-five pounds—or in my eyes, a little on the plump side—curly gray hair, short and wiry. No distinguishing marks or features that I could see. Even so, the two sisters were nodding, already believing that their mother was here. After all, who else could it be? They had come to me, hoping to form a link with their mother, and here she was. This was enough for them, but it was not enough for me. Not nearly enough for me. We had time, at least an hour, and in that time I hoped—no, I expected—that the woman I saw would speak to me, tell me a little about her life, her daughters, her family, life in the spirit world, and more. I wanted more. So I waited and I watched, tuning my senses, hoping to miss nothing.

"I am their mother," I heard her say quite clearly. I nodded, waiting, patient, knowing that this was just the beginning.

"I was sick for quite some time, my stomach you know. It was ever so painful, and there was nothing anyone could do." Smiling at her encouragingly, I repeated to her girls their mother's words, and as often happens in these circumstances, they began to cry.

Soothing them as best I could, I then turned my attention back to Ada, the mother, and asked, "What was it—cancer, ulcers, what?"

"These." Ada chuckled, and thrust forward what looked like a small, white, and somewhat crumpled paper bag. "They were my downfall, you know," she whispered conspiratorially. "It's what really finished me. Ate away at my intestines, that's what they did."

Not able to see what was in the bag, I asked Ada what "they" were. She chuckled again. "Hooked on them, I was, since I was a little girl. Used to buy five pounds a week, sometimes more. They rotted my teeth and they rotted my stomach, but I didn't care. I had to have 'em, just couldn't live without them." And she went on to describe how she always kept a bag by her bedside in case she woke in the night.

"But, Ada," I pleaded, "tell me what they are. I have no idea what it is you're talking about."

Ada looked back at me in surprise. "Well," she said, "surely you can smell them. People used to tell me I smelled of them all the time. And the taste of them...ooh, so good." And it was as she said this that my mouth watered up, my taste buds began to tingle, and the strongest taste filled my mouth. At the same time I was surrounded by the smell, the unmistakable smell and taste of mint.

Instantly Ada saw recognition dawn on my face, and gleefully now she said, "That's it, that's what you can tell my girls...it was the mints that killed me...and what do you think of that?"

I can still hear her laughter as I remember her words.

EXERCISE 4...
TOUCH

Instinctively we reach out, from birth, and are comforted by our mother's touch. Made to feel safe. And as we grow we are cosseted, cuddled, and we cuddle in return. The need to touch and be touched by others is innate in all of us, and maybe that is how we should begin this next exercise.

Find someone close by and put your arm around them.

Approach someone you know, maybe a colleague or shop assistant, and shake their hand.

Try stroking someone's hair, or even your own hair, and as you do this, ask some questions:

How do you feel?

How does touching make you feel?

For many of us, reaching out, touching, is hard, even with our loved ones, but especially with those we don't know too well. The idea of shaking hands or putting our arms around a stranger can be a most alien, even fearful, feeling. Yet there are those of us who will not think twice about throwing our arms around anybody, stranger or friend. Sometimes it's a cultural thing. The

Italians kiss, the Greeks hug, the Irish, a generally friendly race, will quickly become your bosom pal. The English, now—well, the English are known to be remote, standoffish, and cold; in fact English men have probably the poorest reputation as lovers. I think it's safe to say that the view of the outside world is that the English are about as passionate as a lump of coal.

I would agree that we seem to be a rather cold and unemotional race, but I have known the warmest hearts, the most caring and loving souls, and I have known Englishmen and -women to be passionate when it comes to their homes, their rights as human beings, and their families.

I began wondering what it is that makes neighbor different from neighbor, sister different from brother, son different from father, but I realized that this is a discussion too great and complex for the here and now, and is of no real consequence to us at this time.

What makes us different is not important. That we are different is exciting, a curiosity, and our differences make us the individuals we are. Our differences can also make us wary of others, uncomfortable with ourselves, and can be the source of our shyness or nervousness at the very idea of touching. Being different, feeling different from others can give us feelings of insecurity, inadequacy. "Why would someone want to hug me? Why would anyone want me to hug them?" Yet we are all different. Not one person's fingerprints are the same as another— nor anyone's feet, hands, or eyes, or ears. Similar maybe, but not the same. Our emotions, feelings, the way we sense, react, act ... similar maybe, but definitely not the same. And yet, in our humanness we are the same. We have the same needs of love, some more, some less, but all requiring, all needing love, comfort, caring, gentleness. We all have a need to know that someone cares. We all need to feel that touch of love.

So let us try to develop our sense of touch. Let us ask some more questions. Questions like ...

How many different textures are there to touch?

How acute can your sense of touch become?

How many feelings are triggered when you use your sense of touch?

How aware of yourself does your awareness of touch make you?

How many memories are there, and where do they come from?

How often are you aware of your sense of touch?

How often do you sense touch?

How often do you enjoy to touch?

How often do you find touch distasteful?

How often do you give yourself a gentle, loving, touch?

And, of course, you really should ask this question: How aware of your own touch are you? Is your skin rough or smooth? Does the skin feel different on different parts of your body?

Yes, of course it does. But how? Why? And how does it make you feel?

How does your touch feel to others? How do animals respond to your touch?

Are you a gardener? How do your plants respond to your touch?

When asking these questions try to be as expressive as you can be when writing down your answers, and try to be aware of your feelings.

When we look at the five senses and try to associate, to feel something about them, the one sense that is easiest to associate with is touch.

If someone asks, "Just feel this," then we automatically touch. So when you ask, "How do I feel?" not only are you asking, "What kind of texture is this?," but also, "What are my emotions, how do I feel inside, what things touch me, move me, stir my emotions?"

There are so many varieties of texture, soft, smooth, scratchy, rough, hard, etc.

Below is my list of different things to touch. Some you may have used, and there are some that you may not have thought of.

Soil. Child's hair. Carpet pile. Flower petals. Eyelashes. Smooth wood. Tree bark. An unshaven chin. Fabric. Grass. Water. Sticky buns.

All of these textures are good to touch.

Try writing down all of your thoughts and feelings, and be surprised at how acute your sense of touch has become.

And one touch that you should learn to become aware of, an all-important touch: *The touch of love.*

• • •

The touch of love. The giving and the receiving of love, expressed in so many ways. Yet the most beautiful is to be touched by love. To have that feeling of love welling up inside you, filling you, expanding and warming you. It is truly a feeling of being made whole. It is truly a feeling of power, an inner power, which tells you that nothing else matters, that you are of God, and indeed well loved.

When I was a girl I would wish so hard to be loved as my youngest sister was loved by my mother. We would be sitting on the floor playing, or at the table eating, asleep in bed, in a thousand places, and I would see my mother. She would come upon us and, as she passed, would reach out to give my sister a kiss, or stroke her hair, or tuck her into bed. Tickle the back of her neck with a gentle finger, that same finger she would use to prod and poke me in the harshest way. My mother showed her love of my sister in a thousand ways, and the way I noticed most and envied most was the way she touched her.

That was a great lesson for me. My mother may well have loved me, but I never knew it, for she never showed it. I learned. And the hardest lessons are often the best remembered. I learned. "If you don't show it, they don't know it!" It's a lesson I take to my students, to my clients and patients, a lesson I try hard to live every day, even though I fail every day. And it is a lesson I have brought to my child so that she knows she is well loved. "If you don't show it, they don't know it."

In the night I lay trembling, afraid to be touched. Saying my prayers, I would beg God to stop them from coming. He never seemed to hear my prayers. Little did I know, growing up, that those in the spirit world came to comfort me, to care for and to nurture me. To touch my pounding, terrified, aching heart with love.

• • •

As I watched, I saw him lean toward her and put his hand to her hair, his fingers gently lift some of the silky strands.

"Your husband is stroking your hair," I softly said, knowing this to be a tender, loving moment.

"Can she feel me," he asked, "can she feel my fingers in her hair?"

Looking to my client sadly I had to acknowledge that she could not, for even as her husband had asked his question, she was asking me to tell her where he was standing, and which side he was touching.

Grey Eagle squeezed my shoulder. The joy I felt in feeling the pressure of his fingers pushing into my flesh was indescribable. "How is it," I asked him, "that I can feel your touch, yet she cannot feel his?" A soft breeze wafted across my face as my guide blew me a kiss. "Maybe she cannot feel his touch because she does not believe she can. Perhaps she does not believe in herself enough, or in the power of the universe." Sadly, I nodded, understanding the truth of Grey Eagle's words, and I wondered in that moment if there was any way I could help people to be more aware of their loved ones in the spirit world. What could I do? The answer to that often-posed question is found in the pages of this book.

To a mother who has lost her child, I will often say, "I can see your son. As I speak with him, he has placed his arms around you and is holding you tight." Or to a father, I might say, "Your daughter is playing with your ears, or ruffling your hair with her fingertips." I see their faces, looking at me, believing yet disbelieving, for they are asking themselves, "How could this be?" Yet I can say to you all, for I know this to be true, that all of us, at one time or another in our lives, has felt the touch of our loved ones in the spirit world. And what Grey Eagle says is right. We don't believe in ourselves enough. We don't believe that we are capable of receiving such a gift. How many times must we dismiss the incredible, the unbelievable, put it down to imagination, before we can accept that the impossible is sometimes very possible? How many times will we refuse to see, to hear, to feel, taste, or smell that which we can taste, can smell, can feel, see, and hear? Only when we believe in ourselves, only then.

EXERCISE 5 . . .
SIGHT

Probably the first thing we do in the morning when we wake is to open our eyes. And what do we see? Through blurred and tired eyes, our senses still a little numb from sleep, we perhaps see very little. But as we become more awake, we become more aware.

Are the curtains drawn?
Is the room dark or light?
Is the sun shining or is it a gray day?
What do you see?
What do you feel?
How do you feel?
What do you sense?
What are the sights that lift you and make you feel good? What are the sights that distress or confuse you, that make you

feel sad or muddled? And how often have you caught sight of your reflection in a mirror and been surprised, pleased, or horrified at what you see?

I can remember once, quite a long time ago, as I had finished cleaning my teeth one morning, lifting my head, being startled by the reflection I saw in the mirror. Not mine but that of my sister, whom I look nothing like, or so I had thought. But perhaps I was wrong, and there were more similarities than I had realized. How did it make me feel? Surprised. Thought-provoked. Curious about myself and my perceptions.

And when you look? When you see? How does that make you feel?

And what do you feel?

And how aware of your feelings are you?

Wherever we go there are things to see. Ordinary and everyday things that we often take for granted. And then there are the more extraordinary sights. Sights that we don't ordinarily see.

Beautiful scenery when we go on holiday. Unusual foods in exotic countries. Trees and plants in a botanical garden. Luxury homes and expensive clothes. We might ask, where are we going to see these things?

Some of us may be fortunate enough to have those exotic foods, beautiful scenery, or luxury in view most of the time. But all of us can experience these sights either on the TV or in magazines. We can read, we can look at pictures, but how aware are we that we are using our sense of sight?

We have all taken sight for granted—that is, those of us who have good sight—and it is only as we get older, and our sight begins to fade a little, that we become more thoughtful and caring of what we see, and how we view things. In this exercise, as with the others in this chapter, we are going to try to see if we can lift our senses and our sensitivity, our awareness of our gift of sight, to a higher level of understanding.

Our five senses, our common senses are given to us as a gift from God. However, there are those of us who were born without sight, without hearing, or touch, smell, and taste. There are also those of us who through illness or accident have had one or more of our common senses taken away. When this happens, I believe that God compensates, gives us something extra, something more. He gives us His guidance and His inspiration. Just because the blind man has lost his sight does not mean he cannot see. In fact, many years ago, a client of mine, born blind, would have long conversations with me about all that she could see. Her physical eyes might be blank, but her mind's eye was extraordinarily active. She could see colors and people, hills and valleys. Sometimes she would describe a scene. A small, fast-running stream, a house, sitting high on a hill, surrounded by trees. At other times she would describe how people looked. Tall, short, craggy-faced, or smooth-featured. The way she saw was different from the way most of us see, but no one who knew her doubted that she was not blind. God compensates by giving us a more acute awareness of our other senses, by giving us a wild and unfettered imagination, definitely in aiding us to become more sensitive and creative.

A person who is deaf discovers a way of hearing that is often beyond the comprehension of those of us whose hearing is sound. Yet I am asking you to try to comprehend, for if you can, if you can catch just a glimpse of comprehension, then as you explore your senses you will gain so much more from your exercises.

Those of us who do not have all our five common senses can still do the exercises in this book, can understand, comprehend, just as much, if not more, than those of us who have our five senses intact. In fact, those lacking one or more of the five senses might do better than those of us who have them all. They have the advantage. Their sensitivity is already heightened. Can the blind really lead the sighted, who cannot see what the blind can see? Yes, I believe they can. So once again, what must we do? How can we learn? The answer is simple.

Each day ask your questions and then question your thoughts

and feelings. Become aware of yourself, and of all that you see around you. Try some of the questions below, and don't be afraid to ask your own questions, too. Questions like:

How many sights are there?

How acute can you allow your sense of sight to become?

How many feelings are triggered when you use your sense of sight?

How aware of yourself does your awareness of these sights make you?

How many memories are there, and where do they come from?

How often are you aware of your sense of sight?

How often do you sense sight?

How often do you see cruel sights?

How often do you catch sight of yourself?

And then other questions could be:

How aware of your own sight are you?

How clear is your sight?

How much can you really see?

What do you look like, and what do you see when you see yourself?

Here are a few more sights for you to use, to add to those you have already used:

Rainbow colors. A starlit sky. Rolling hills. Flowers growing. A full moon. A waterfall. Blue sky. Green grass. Paintings. Swans. Feathers. Washing blowing in the wind.

All of these sights are good sights.

Try writing down your thoughts and feelings, and be surprised at how acute your sense of sight has become.

Ask yourself, what do I see when I close my eyes? And one sight I feel you should really learn to become aware of, an all-important sight: *the sight of instinct.*

• • •

We have all had it, all known it. That little nudge, a feeling, a thought that seems to come from nowhere. A glimpse of something not quite tangible, a shadow that passes across our mind and an instant later is gone. A sight of instinct.

There are thousands of stories to tell, to illustrate what is meant by the sight of instinct, but the one I tell here is one that was told to me this very morning by Jim, before he left for the office.

"I was in the car and must have been daydreaming. The next I knew, I had a flash, something, I'm not really sure what, but it made me come to with a start, and at the same time I yanked the steering wheel to the right. Good thing I did, or I would have had a collision. I took a deep breath, a sigh of relief, then I was startled again, for I saw my mother's face, and she was smiling at me."

Jim's mother had passed to the spirit world several years before this incident, as I'm sure most of you had gathered.

We all have our angels. Jim would say his mother was his angel that day. I believe she was, and I believe she will be there with him in the future also, just as we will all have someone. But how good it would be if we could see our loved ones, catch that brief glimpse, see their face before we went to sleep. Many of us do, of course, but are unable to see it as anything other than in our imagination.

What was different for Jim that day? What was it that enabled him to see his mother so clearly at that moment? Some would say that his mother was the one determined that he should see her, that she in some way became powerful enough to force her image upon him. And to some small degree they would be right. But seeing or not seeing, hearing or not hearing, has more to do with how we are than how much energy the spirit world can muster.

We call out, "Why don't you show yourselves?" They call

back to us, "Why don't you look in the right way, for we are here, and waiting?"

Another story. It was about seven-thirty. The table was set and our guests were arriving for an informal dinner. There were eight of us in all, all friends, although Bill, Anabel's husband, had never been to the house before, and this was the first time I had spent any real social time with him.

The food was good, the conversation even better, as we went from subject to subject in a very lighthearted and fun way. Dessert was coconut cream pie, or ice cream, or both, and it was Jim who brought the conversation around to my work, when he insisted that everyone should have their chocolate ice cream in a dish so that I could "read" them later. I had done this very thing with Jim a few nights earlier, showing him how I was able to see certain things, and he had been so intrigued, though a little scared as to what his ice cream dish might reveal, that he wanted to share the experience with our friends.

Inwardly I groaned a little, for the last thing I wanted to do was to create the wrong image about my gift. However, my friend Nancy, who was sitting to my right, and totally involved and interested in the subject, was immediately excited. "Oooh, good," she said, nudging me with her elbow, "you can do me first. I'm dying to see what you can see." I laughed and nodded my agreement and took hold of her bowl, which she thrust at me, having eaten her ice cream in double-quick time.

The bowls were white china, and the remains of ice cream were very visible to everyone. To an insensitive eye, the patterns left by the dessert meant no more than a dirty dish to put in the dishwasher. However, to a more sensitive eye, certain pictures could be clearly seen. And to a trained eye—remembering that our vision is not just our physical sight—a more detailed story could emerge. Let me give you a few examples from that night. In my friend Nancy's bowl I saw a boy; not surprising, as I know she has two sons. Next to the boy I saw an airplane. These things I saw with my physical eyes. What I saw, felt, intuited next, was that the boy was looking forward, possibly planning a trip overseas, in the near future. Nancy confirmed that just a few days before, one of her sons had shown a very strong interest in going on a trip with his school, in the spring, to Spain. Definitely a plane trip. This information I did not know.

In another bowl I saw a man's face, a small goatee, and I also saw roses. It turned out that this friend, three times a week, went to a spa with a good friend of hers, a man with a small goatee, whose hobby was gardening. His proudest effort in this domain was his rose garden, his pride and joy. Again, I had known nothing of this until I looked into her bowl. When I looked into another friend's bowl, I saw a pen, and something resembling paper with writing on it. Using more than my physical sight, using my sensitivity, I was able to see that this symbolized a contract, which was ready for signing. I looked at my friend, who, having seen me work before, laughingly admitted that he was about to sign a very important contract that would, to a great degree, change his working life. "Just tell me if I should sign or not?" he playfully asked.

Around the table we went. It was fun for everyone, and fun for me, and it reminded me of how much there is that is pure energy, which we can use if we want to. The ice cream smears on the dishes were like the fingerprints of our world. Some small part of our mind, our thoughts and future, imprinted, printed out for us to see.

Then Anabel spoke up. "You didn't do Bill," she said, somewhat mischievously, knowing that her husband did not believe in my gift or in the ability of anyone to see further than that which is in front of our faces. The idea of someone able to communicate with the spirit world, the possibilities of someone able to use psychic vision, or psychic anything, these ideas were alien to him, and totally unacceptable. Anabel, undeterred, handed me Bill's dish, and he, shrugging and smiling, just let it happen. After all, it was just a game. A party trick, he thought.

I cannot remember too much of what I saw in Bill's dish, a bird, a . . . but then I was not looking into the bowl anymore. On either side of him I saw a man and a woman. Visitors from the spirit world whom, as I described them, Bill did not recognize. Then I saw a house set up on a hill, with splendid grounds, an estate. The house itself was more like a mansion, nothing I knew that Bill would own, and I felt that what I was seeing was more directly connected to Bill's work than to him on a more personal level, and I told him so. Describing the house in the most intricate detail, as my two visitors from the spirit world described it to me, I began with the outside and worked my way in. The interior was quite fascinating, unusual ceilings with heavy moldings, a curved staircase, an unusual room with lots of glass and water, maybe some kind of spring or spa. Back outside, I again described what I was seeing, then my concentration went once more inside, to the ceilings, which seemed to me to be somewhat of a problem area, and would cost more to renovate than would at first be thought.

Recounting all I was seeing and being told, as I was seeing and hearing it, I then heard Grey Eagle's voice. "There has been talk of Bill being offered a contract. It isn't final yet, and he is still awaiting the decision of the man who owns the house. Tell him it's his if he wants it, but tell him to make sure he quotes the right price, for if he goes too low he could lose money on the deal."

When I was done, in a calm and quiet way, Bill Hahn told us all about the house. Just as I had described, in the most exact detail, he had understood it all, and was indeed waiting to see if the contract was his. Bill and his partner own a painting-and-decorating company.

It was quite a bit later that our guests left, and although we had all had a good time, I did wonder why I had begun the ice

243

cream bowl readings, for it was very unusual for me to do such a thing. I came to the conclusion that there must be a good reason for it, and I smiled to myself a few days later, when, talking to Anabel, she told me how intrigued Bill had really been by what had happened.

"When you spoke to him that evening," she said, "Bill was in a state of shock, and was unable to really react. But as the shock wore off, he began thinking what it all meant. There was no way," she went on to say, "that you could possibly have known about that house and the contract. And Bill knows that. That's what has disturbed him the most. He's now having to rethink his beliefs. The whole experience has opened his eyes to possibilities he had never believed could exist."

"Maybe he has been a little enlightened," I replied, and smiled as I thought to myself that that was no bad thing.

"Reading" ice cream bowls seems to be as far-fetched and, some might think, ridiculous an idea as the concept of a gypsy "reading" tea leaves. Yet I believe there are many who have the knowledge, capability, and "sight," or, if you prefer, insight, to do just that. But how is it possible from a commonsense and down-to-earth point of view to even remotely conceive or begin to explain this kind of phenomenon? Easy. Very easy, in fact, as long as you understand the concept that all living things are energy. We are powerhouses, containers of the purest and most powerful energy. When we walk, we create energy flow. As we speak, we do the same. Every movement, even the blink of an eyelid creates energy flow. Even as the wind blows, even as it flows through trees and earth and sky, affecting everything it touches, even as it blows through our hair, or lifts high off the ground any litter we have left behind, even as it flows softly over our faces, and cools or stings us, this is how our energy is. Always with us, seen or unseen, felt or not felt, yet it is still there, affecting everything it touches. We cannot escape it, nor would we be, nor would we exist, without it. Our energy imprints itself on everything we do, say, or think. As we eat, as we eat our ice cream or as we drink our tea, our energy is flowing out of us, touching everything near to us, leaving its mark. When we have eaten our ice cream or drunk our tea, and we gaze into our bowl or cup, at the residue left behind, all we are doing, feeling, sensing, or seeing is our expended energy that is reflecting back on us. An imprint of our conscious, our subconscious, an imprint of our mind, our power.

All we are doing, feeling, sensing, or seeing is our expended energy reflected back on us. Did I say that? Is that all we are doing? How easy I make it sound, how simple and straightfor-ward. And I believe it is, if only we would make the time to take the baby steps, learn to tune into our senses, develop an awareness of and a keenness toward all that is around us, and "tune in" to who we really are.

Primitive man lived on his six senses, and yes, I did say six. His life depended on them. He was truly attuned to himself, his spirit, and the spirits of those around him, both the living and the unseen living, for even if he didn't or couldn't "see," one of his other senses told him what he needed to know. His life was uncluttered, no material distractions. No TV, no car, no won-derful and mechanical creations from our twentieth-century tech-nological age. He was reminded every day of his humanness, his frailty and his vulnerability, and he lived and acted accordingly. And we, who have lived so long in an age where science and technology joined together have created an impression that nature is secondary, we have allowed ourselves the luxury of believing that technology is the answer to all our needs.

If we have health problems, we tell ourselves that it's no prob-lem, not with all those miracle bypass operations, heart trans-plants, liver and kidney transplants. We tell ourselves that a cure for cancer, for AIDS, is just around the corner—and I believe it probably is—so, no problem. Except that when the problem oc-curs, and medicine and technology and science fail us, as they so often do, what do we have left? Our senses, our instincts, our very tools for survival are blunt, and of little use.

Here we are, at the very beginning of the twenty-first century, and who knows, but God, what this millennium will bring. All I know, all I believe is that if we sharpen our tools, help our children to sharpen their tools, then whatever our future, it can only be healthier, brighter, better, for our true sense of who and what we are, for our true sense of what humanity is, and what the universe can bring to us.

And who knows what we can bring to it.

Every parting gives a
Foretaste of death.
Every coming together again
A foretaste of the resurrection.

ARTHUR SCHOPENHAUER

CHAPTER 7

How Much Sense Does Our Sixth Sense Make?

As we near the end, the last chapter, and at the risk of being thought to have no words left of my own worthy of writing, let me again use another man's words, those of Francis Bacon, who said, "If a man will begin with certainties, he shall end in doubts; but if he will be content to begin with doubts, he shall end in certainties."

As I thought, in the beginning, to write this book, my mind was full of doubt. How would I be able to express what I needed to express, in a way which would be understood? Was I able to inspire, to encourage, and help you the reader to dare to own your own power? Having begun with doubt, and now almost at the end, my one certainty is that I am just one very little human being, striving to do the best I can, urging you, all of you who, like me, are very little human beings, to try and do the best you can. It's enough.

The theory of Jungian psychology is that we are born knowing our archetypal language, the language of symbols, a universal language. Primitive mental images that we inherited from our earliest ancestors. Mental images supposed to be present in the collective unconscious. When I first began working as a spirit communicator, almost twenty years ago, I knew nothing of Jung, nothing of his philosophies, and even now I know very little, yet my way of working consisted of the very things he talked of. I had discovered a language, or should I say I had discovered I could speak a language that through the years I had glimpsed but had not understood. Indeed, had not realized was a language, a form of speech, of communication, at all. And who could say if it was my own, or if others here on this earth plane would know, would recognize and understand it? So far I have yet to meet a human being who speaks or understands my archetypal pattern. Yet I know those who have their own, different from mine, but with similarities.

How did I know that the symbol X equals emotional trauma? How did I discover that to see the symbol in one place meant one kind of problem, seeing it in another place meant something different? How did I know? Simply, I don't know how I knew, I just did. My sixth sense made sense. A great deal of sense. I followed it, trusted it, and understood.

Everyone has a sixth sense. In fact every creature, every insect, everything that breathes has a natural-born sixth sense. You could argue the merits of such a statement, you could argue that plants and trees breathe, but don't have any sense at all. I would disagree. When I was home in England a few years ago, I was given a cactus plant, an Easter flowering cactus. It was a sickly thing and for two years did absolutely nothing. Although I was ignorant of its needs, too busy to pay it any attention except for the very occasional watering, the cactus didn't die. Looking back, I consider this in itself a miracle.

Then came the day of spring cleaning. A friend was helping, and with great zest we were entering every corner of every room in the house. I found myself holding the cactus, nothing more than a stick really, with a couple of sorry-looking leaves on it, and making a decision. Hating to throw out anything live, I also recognized my lack of respect for something living. "One more chance," I muttered, not sure if I meant the plant or me. Finding a larger pot, some potting compost, I set to work and pretty soon the cactus was transported to its new home. My friend laughed. "I think it's dead," she told me, "and besides, the pot's too big."

"We'll see," I replied, with good humor. "You never know, everything deserves a second chance." And so saying, I placed the cactus on the kitchen windowsill. Every day I talked to it, just as I had when I was repotting it, soothing and gentle, encouraging, and apologetic for my previous lack of care. Pretty soon the plant began to respond, to grow, and then to flower, sensing, I believe, the warmth and love it was being given. You may scoff, you may say that the act of replanting alone was responsible, but those of you who tend your plants and gardens in this way will fully understand and agree with me when I say that plants have ears and eyes, they know and respond to loving care. They sense.

Edward O. Wilson once said, "If insects were to vanish, the environment would collapse into chaos." He was right, of course, and when thinking of the world we live in, we should not underestimate their purpose, strength, energy, or sensitivity. If we were to be more mindful of our insect communities, we could learn so much about our own strengths, our own energies, and our own sensitivities. Small creatures working together, if nothing else, teach us about teamwork, the benefits of working together in harmonious societies.

Each of us is born with a sixth sense, and our sixth sense is about harmony. The ability to use our sixth sense is found in creating and harmonizing our energy.

Instinct shows itself best in trying and difficult situations. That is because we are more "on edge," more attentive and alert. These are the times when we react to our gut, our deepest and most sensitive feelings. Animals have the ability to sense or to intuit danger, and it is likely that the only animal species who is neglectful of that ability is the human being. It is also probable that the human being, though very much neglectful of this talent, is the only animal species capable of extending its mind power beyond the capabilities of basic animal instinct, although extensive experiments with dolphins may tell us something different.

The other evening as I climbed into bed, I asked for a dream vision. A vision that would guide me, steer me in the right direction. I asked to be shown a clear path. Not looking for one thing in particular, trusting that God, that the universe, and that my guide Grey Eagle would know more than I did what I was asking for and what I needed. Closing my eyes, calming and relaxing my spirit, in just the same way that I showed you in Chapter One, I waited. My breathing easy, body, mind, and spirit in total harmony, I waited. But I did not sleep, nor did I dream. Instead, thoughts of writing came into my head. Ideas half-formed now became formed, and instead of relaxing into sleep, I became wide-awake. Pretty soon I was up, making hot water, finding my glasses; I sat in my chair by the window, only night peeping in now, and for several hours my pen moved across the pages of my yellow, wide-ruled writing pad, and I became oblivious to all else but putting my thoughts to paper. It was five in the morning when I finally went back to bed. Still time for a vision, but my mind sought only sleep. No matter. This had happened before, many times. I knew that it was only a matter of time.

I didn't have to wait long, in fact it was only a couple of days later when I woke in the early morning hours, my dream vision still clear and fresh. I had been given a bird, a large brown bird, as a gift, from whom I had no idea. As I took the bird in my hands, it felt soft and warm, its feathers silky smooth, and I could hear its heart beat. I could also hear, in my head, a voice, repeating over and over, "It's a gift, a gift." Musing on this, I wondered if perhaps the bird was a dove, a symbol of peace, but even as the thought entered my head, another pushed it away. "The bird is hungry, and I have to find food for it." A cage appeared. Inside was birdseed, lots of it, and I placed the bird inside the cage to eat. Watching the bird hungrily pecking away at the seed, I thought, "This bird sure eats a lot, it's going to take a lot of feeding." The dream ends, and as I lay in my bed waiting for dawn light to appear, I begin the process of trying to figure out the message. Trusting Grey Eagle, trusting my sixth sense, I know there is a message, and although dream visions are often more clear in their purpose than this one seemed to be, I also understood that there was a purpose to this dream.

An hour or so ticked by before the gray light of December dawn appeared, and all I could come up with was that perhaps I was being told that it is not enough to talk about wanting peace in the world, a topic that is always prevalent as Christmas approaches and we are reminded of such things, but maybe it was being pointed out to me that peace needs feeding, the idea of peace and unity in the world needs feeding. This was a great thought, but I knew my interpretation of the dream was lacking. My sixth sense told me so.

During the December and January that followed, many events intervened that halted a process of thought that at one time I would never have allowed to be halted. Having asked for and been given a vision, I had always, in the past, thought it important enough throughout the following days and weeks, sometimes even months, to spend a few minutes each day in reflective contemplation of the message the dream was conveying. Even if I came up with no real answers, I could at the very least show my gratitude, acknowledge the power of the gift, and give thought to the lesson my teacher was trying to impart. It was only as I sat down to write of the experience that realization dawned, and the message became clear. Like most of us, I had allowed Christmas, visitors, shopping, a new year, and various other unimportant, in the larger scheme of things, life-consuming trivia to get in the way of my spiritual growth and progress. With a thousand and one things to do, meals to plan, to cook, others' needs to see to,

I had neglected the one food, the most important need, and was in danger of starvation.

The vision came back to me, and with some deep sadness I understood fully the meaning of it. I looked back over the last year or so, realizing what it was that I, and I alone, had allowed to happen, to happen to myself. It was easy to see, and in some ways easy to understand, although I knew that none of the excuses I might try out would be good enough. Neglect is the word that springs to mind, for I had been neglectful of my soul, my spirit.

In England it had been much more simple, as I had far more time to devote to my clients, my patients, and students. At some point during every working day, and each day was a working day, I would give time and thought to my healing organization, to my patients, and in doing so, was reminded of the precious gift I had been born with.

It is easy, when faced with the families and friends and patients who are dying, it is so easy to be mindful of God, of the spirit world and all that it means to us. Easy to remember how vulnerable we are as human beings, but also how powerful as spiritual beings we are. With my team around me, with my many friends who work with me in my native country, it was always easy to remain single-minded, dedicated to my work, to my own growth process. There was never an event, a dinner party, an outing, a celebration or occasion, a day, never a day, that excluded thoughts of the spirit or spiritual beings, and conversations with my guide.

Since I have come to America, my life has been vastly different. First, I lost my team, my entire workforce, some of whom I worked closely with every day for almost twenty years. I have had to make do with faxes and telephone calls, which makes keeping in touch with my team more difficult, and it has been hard on all of us. Coming to a strange land, leaving behind good friends, unable to find new ones, people who can truly understand who I am and the work that I do, has been the most difficult. Add to that the extra work, different, very different than before. Swapping hospital visits for TV studios, deep and important conversations with people who have lost a loved one, or with patients and their families who are facing death, with some reporter of a fancy magazine who only wants to know about the rich and famous clients I have. Climbing aboard yet another airplane, to tour yet another country, and oh yes, please don't misunderstand me. I know how important it is to spread the word beyond my own small corner of the world and I will do what must be done. Add to these things the small but important changes in my life as a human being, the stresses and strains of simply trying to make a new life, new involvements, new office, new people, new place to live, oh yes, I can find plenty of excuses for my neglect, but in my heart, I know that none of them is good enough. So many changes, so many more interruptions, so many more reasons not to find more time for my own spiritual sustenance. And yet of all the people I have ever known, I, above all, have so many more reasons to make sure that I feed my soul.

I look back to the vision, and as I do, I thank God for my guide, Grey Eagle, for his vision and insight, for his patience and love, that he should give me the gift of empowerment.

I am the brown bird, my soul soft and warm, my spirit silky smooth, my heartbeat, life itself . . . a gift, a gift.

"The bird is hungry, and I have to find food for it." I remember as I write, and the words resound in my head.

A cage appeared, and inside the cage was lots of birdseed, and the bird ate hungrily.

It is a simple message, but perhaps one of the most important in my life so far. I must put my soul, my spirit, always in a place where there is food, protection, and the possibility of growth.

"This bird sure eats a lot, it's going to take a lot of feeding." These are the last words before the dream ends, and I know how true they are, and I, more than most, should never have allowed anything to get in the way of remembering that.

Some of you may think that the easy solution to my problem,

the danger of neglecting my soul, would be for me to hotfoot it back to my own country, to my friends and colleagues there who have supported me all these years. Don't think I haven't thought of it, dreamed of it even, and on an occasion or three even been close to buying a one-way ticket back. But my responsibilities are greater now, more people worldwide are looking to me for inspiration, teaching, enlightenment. I am not my own person anymore, and perhaps I never have been, and that's okay, I'm happy with that. The truth, though, which came out of my dream vision, is that although I am not my own person, I am my own soul, I am responsible for, and must feed, my own soul. For when my soul is starved, I become empty and sad and powerless, and then I become not much to speak of at all. And in this, I am not very different than anyone else.

We all need to feed our soul, we all need to bring light to the spirit, we all need to be empowered, to be inspired, to find spiritual sustenance. By prayer and meditation, good thoughts and unselfish acts of kindness, we give food to the soul, and the heartbeat of the soul beats more strongly for it. But there are many other ways to feed the soul, to find strength, happiness, confidence, empowerment, and you will find some of those ways here as you read.

Acknowledging that you have a sixth sense is one of those ways. Learning to listen to it, to be in tune with, and to tune into it brings empowerment.

Our sixth sense. What is it, this feeling, this instinct we all have? Our sixth sense enables us to know. To know more than our five common senses tell us. It is a seemingly intangible thing, yet when we feel it, we know it.

We think about someone and a day later, out of the blue, they call. Or we call someone and the line is engaged, because they are calling us at the same time. We go shopping and, without thinking, turn into a street we've never been down before, only to see a friend we haven't seen for ages. "Oh, what a coincidence," we say, those of you who still believe in coincidences.

It is easier for us to reason with coincidence than with the idea that our sixth sense moved us to take an action, have a thought, told us some unconscious thing. It is easier for us to say, "Well, these things happen," to shrug our shoulders and move right along, without any thought as to why or how these things happen. Many people do not want to know the unknown, or to see that which is unseen. They are afraid, and understandably so. But hiding is not the answer, for hiding, closing our eyes and ears brings only confusion.

Our sixth sense. When we feel it, we know it for what it is. Like a wire, pulled tight, which runs through us, our sixth sense, taut, vibrating, makes a humming sound, inaudible mostly, except at those times when we make ourselves acutely sensitive and aware, and we do that by training our five common senses. We train our five common senses to the point of sensitivity where our sixth sense automatically kicks in, becomes a live wire, like a tuning fork. Now we are more able to hear, to sense or feel, to see or touch, and yes, even to smell, the humming of that live wire as it begins to tune in. Tuning, tuning, tuning, into our spirit, into our spirituality, connecting with our soul, reaching out into the world, out into the universe, then back to us. Tuning in, feeding us, feeding our soul, our hearts and minds. This is what our sixth sense does, naturally and easily, if we give it the right energy, the right encouragement.

Working our way through this book, we have found tools that can help us. Searching, discovering, tuning into our sixth sense, not only requires time and patience, we need tools to help us on our journey. Before we go further, however, let's go back and take a quick look at what we might have achieved so far.

In Chapter One we discovered the importance of self-discipline, how necessary it is in our spiritual growth process. Chapter Two gave us an awareness of energy, our own, and that which comes from God and the universe. Learning to look beneath the surface, working on our own self, with gentleness, was what Chapter Three helped to teach us. Chapter Four helped us take the shutters from our eyes, it encouraged us to dare to really see. In Chapter Five we learned about power, we learned that power is always in us, that we are, indeed, never powerless, unless we wish to be. And in Chapter Six we had fun and real discovery when we examined, used, and exercised our five common senses in a way we perhaps had not thought to do before.

Now we come to our sixth sense. We all have it, we all know it, and as I've already said, most of us don't use it. Why? Well, some of us genuinely aren't aware of it too often, we have become desensitized for one reason or another. Many of us, however, ignore, push away, even fight the idea of a sixth sense because we are afraid. Afraid of the unknown, the inexplicable, the strange, and what appears to an uneducated eye, the unexplainable.

There was a time when I was afraid, when I was fearful, and as these next stories show, fear breeds fear, then more fear, and more, until I became afraid even of my own shadow.

FEAR

Even though it was only four-thirty in the afternoon, it was dark. A November day, miserable and cold, and the girl, fourteen years old now, would have given anything to be able to go inside and get warm. Instead, she continued to walk, around and around the block, circling the house, praying that someone would come home, put the lights on, make a fire perhaps ... then she could go in.

Every night it was the same. She would dawdle home from

school hoping that one of her sisters was home before her. Many times someone would be there, but often she found herself walking around for an hour or more, rain or shine, until she saw a light in the window. It was only then that she felt safe enough to go in.

• • •

It was common practice for the older kids to try their very best to scare the pants off the younger kids, and this night was no exception. As they sat at dinner, about fifteen in all, all differing ages, boys and girls from six to sixteen, the older ones were intent on telling their stories.

"The green hand, dripping blood, crept slowly up the stairs, making its way into the bedroom where the little children lay. Slowly, slowly it crawled up onto the bed, and made its way to where the child's head rested on the pillow, its blood staining the sheets. Making no sound, the green hand flexed its fingers, its nails, grown long and gnarled with age, making long stroking movements as it reached the child's slender neck, pausing only for one delicious moment before wrapping its fingers around the slim, white throat and squeezing, squeezing tight. The child's eyelids fluttered open, once, twice, before the blood began to ooze through them, through the child's mouth, and nose . . . and only when the child had stopped breathing did the green hand move on. On to the next bedroom, to find the next small child asleep in bed, dripping blood along the way.

"Beware the green hand, beware the green hand. It might come for you tonight."

The little girl, only six years old, having listened to the stories, wide-eyed and terrified, now lay in her bed, afraid to go to sleep in case the green hand came for her. She could hear the other kids in the dormitory of the children's home, she could hear their breathing. But this gave her no comfort, for she knew all about visitors in the night, and the green hand could just be one more.

257

She lay very still, remembering every part of the story, as she would for many years to come. Her heart was pounding so loudly, so strong, seeming to shake her slender six-year-old body, and she was afraid, afraid that the green hand would come for her.

• • •

It was only a TV movie, and for goodness' sake, she was seventeen years old. It was time to know better, but she couldn't shake the fear. The doll, just an ordinary china doll, had come to life, had sat up on the bed before sliding off and making its way, its evil way, toward the bedroom of the master of the house, intent on scaring him, literally, to death. As it moved across the floor, the skirts of the doll made whispering sounds, but the sound that haunted the girl, the sound that would haunt her for many years, was the sound that came from the mouth of the china doll, with its painted face and long black hair..."Mama," it cried, in a voice that chilled, "Mama, Mama, Mama..."

• • •

Always when she was alone they would come. The faces. The voices. The strange, strange noises. And if she were in the house on her own, especially in winter, when the days were short and, with the coming of night, shadows appearing, threatening and menacing, all noise, all sounds and sights seemed exaggerated.

It had always been this way, and try as she might, the girl could never master her fear. It only grew and grew and grew. Until it seemed that all she was, and all she ever would be, was full of fear. Paralyzed by fear.

Living her life through treacherous cobwebbed corridors, narrow, dark, and twisting, blindly she took each tiny step. Stumbling, often falling, and always with the sound, that changing, wailing, weeping, voiceless, voicing, whispering, silent, comforting, terrifying sound. Never alone, never alone. Always someone there.

Seen yet not seen, heard yet not heard. How could she block it out? Oh God, if only she could block it out. And be alone.

• • •

Fear. A terrible, though sometimes necessary emotion.

I used to daydream. Believing that I must be adopted, if not snatched from the cradle by my wicked (step)parents. I would imagine the day, the glorious day, when my real parents would finally find me and take me home. Many of you, as you read this, will be laughing, or crying, as your own memories, similar to mine, surface, for it is not unusual for unhappy children to imagine such things. I was so sure, so very, very sure, that my parents were not my own. They just couldn't be.

How is it possible to be afraid of one's own mother and father? How can it be that from childhood into adulthood, and beyond, a child can fear the woman whose womb she came from, or the man whose seed created her? Fear that you won't please. Fear that you will. Fearing the sound of his voice, her voice. Wondering did you do right, or did you do wrong? Fearing, then knowing and fearing more, that you will never be good enough, no matter what you do. And if you can't be good enough for them, the parents who love you, then you will never be good enough for anyone. So now you fear the world, the world and all it brings. The fear grows, gets bigger, until there is just one thing you can do, and you had better do it well. Hide. Hide. Any way you can. Anyhow. Be quiet, wear a mask, stay in the shadows, keep a low profile, pretend to be somebody else.

Pretending to be someone else is not always a conscious act, rather it is a natural development of an inadequate being, and inadequate we must be. Why else would our parents not like us, or love us differently, gently?

It seems that I was born timid, and as a girl, from my teens to early twenties, I was painfully shy, nervous of everything and everyone, and impossible to get to know. I rarely spoke unless spoken to. Shyness was its own nightmare, bringing more reasons to fear, and yet at about age fourteen I discovered the stage. Drama was my favorite subject at school, and the drama department had everything. A stage, great lighting, makeup rooms, dressing rooms, a wonderful tutor whose name I have long since forgotten. We had costumes, an extensive wardrobe in fact, and a sound system that was the envy of the schools around. It was indeed a magical world, full of curiosities and intrigues, and when I stepped into this world, I could hide. I could make-believe I wasn't me. When I began to play a part I would live it day and night, as much as I could, whenever I could. In doing so, I could step out of Rosemary's life, of Rosemary's mind, of her emotions and feelings. I could even step out of her body, become a man, a boy, an old woman. One of the best parts I played was Rumpelstiltskin. I reveled in his cunning, his twisted face and gnarled dwarf body, so unlike my own and yet so similar. I felt empathy for him in his ugliness, believing myself to be ugly, crooked, flat-chested, and thin. There was no shyness onstage, for I became anyone but me, and that was heaven. The stage held no fear for me, for if I was hurt or lost a lover or died, it was all part of the plot. Walking offstage was when my fear began again.

We are born with certain instincts. Fear is one, and necessary, as we need to know when danger threatens. Throughout the book we deal with instinct, learn to acknowledge and listen to it, be guided by it. We must also understand that by heightening our senses, our instincts are controlled, heard correctly, heeded in a right way. Living, breathing, everyday fear, the kind I have been talking about, has nothing to do with the necessary instincts that tell us of danger, that instinct meant to help and protect us. The kind of fear I have been talking about is anything but constructive; rather it destroys any possibility of self-esteem and confidence. This is the kind of fear we must deal with. The fear of self. Being in touch with the world can be terrifying. The thought of being in touch with oneself can be more than terrifying, and being in touch with our spirit, our soul, well, that idea can be worse than terrifying. What might we find? How hard might the experience be? Who will we then see in the mirror, and who might we see standing around us? What of faith? And what of those of us who have so little of it?

This next story tells of a man forced to commit heinous crimes because he had no faith in himself. Feeling powerless, afraid to die, in his fear he murdered others. Which of us in a similar situation could honestly say we would have done differently? Thank God that most of us will never be so tested.

THE DEVIL HAS COME

He was not my patient. I was not his healer. And how I came to him is not important here, it only matters that I came.

Joseph lay in the hospital bed, not sick, not that anyone could tell anyway, physically in perfect health . . . and yet he was dying. Numerous tests, X rays, etc., had been carried out by the hospital staff, and they could find nothing wrong. But his wife had watched, as over the last twelve months or more, Joseph ate less and less, became tired and listless, complained of constant headaches. Eventually, now weighing less than half his normal body weight, no longer eating, yet still no signs of any cause for his physical sickness, he was taken into hospital.

This was my first and only visit, and I found Joseph lying in bed, his fingers nervously plucking at the bedcover, his head moving from side to side as he mumbled away to himself in a language I didn't understand.

As I positioned myself on the edge of the bed I realized that not only was he mumbling, he was also crying, very softly. I

261

reached out and gently took his hand. His head jerked around as he realized someone was there, and I instantly recognized the look in his eyes, as only someone who had experienced that same emotion could . . . it was terror I saw, sheer and absolute terror. And I knew, too, in that moment, how important it was for Joseph's well-being that I discover the source of his terror so that I might lessen it, or, God willing, rid him of it altogether.

I began by giving him my name, and by explaining that his wife had asked me to visit as I was a healer, and perhaps I could help. Without a word he violently shook his head and began again to cry. It was obvious to me that here was a very troubled spirit, and instinct, my sixth sense, told me that the fact that he was dying was only part, if not the result, of a much greater issue.

I tried again, squeezing Joseph's hand as I did so. "When I was a little girl," I began, "I was afraid of the dark, I was afraid of so many things. In fact, until just a few years ago I was almost afraid of living." Although Joseph's sobs had become less, he was still crying and had shown no sign that he was listening to me. "I think my faith in God is what really saved me." I continued, behaving as if I had his full attention. "Knowing that God loved me, and that He wouldn't let anything really terrible happen to me, was what helped me overcome my fear."

At this, Joseph's sobbing became louder again, but for the first time he spoke to me. "God doesn't love me," he whispered vehemently. "I know that God has abandoned me." And as he said this he became almost totally distraught, and almost screaming now, he sat up, crying, "And the devil has come, the devil has come, the devil has come to take me."

My sense of smell acute, the smell of his terrible fear poured out from him and broke my heart, and reaching across, I put my arms around him and pulled him close to me. For an instant he resisted, afraid to trust, to let go, then he came to me, sobbing uncontrollably, and begged, "Help me, oh please help me, please don't let the devil take me, help me, help me, please."

It took a while, and I rocked him in my arms like a baby, until eventually Joseph was calm enough for me to suggest that he talk to me, tell me what was troubling him so greatly. Gently I pushed him away from me, reaching behind him as I did so, to prop up his pillows so that he could sit up comfortably. I knew that this would take some time, and so I poured him a glass of water, urging him to drink a little, which he did, before I said, "Joseph, why don't you tell your story from the beginning. I'm a good listener, and although I can't promise, I might be able to help."

Nodding, gulping, holding on tightly to my hand, he said, "It began almost from the beginning of the war. I was just a young man then, seventeen years old, when Hitler invaded my country. All the boys, including me, were conscripted into the army, even though most of us did not want to go. Eventually I was forced into the S.S. There was no other choice, except to join the Jews in the camps, or be shot. We did as we were told, afraid to do otherwise."

Every now and then, as Joseph continued his story, he would break down and begin to cry again, but his need to talk was great, and he pressed on.

"Toward the end of the war some of us escaped the German armies, crossing whichever border we could. I was captured, and eventually taken to England. I met and married my wife and stayed here. For over forty years I have lived in your country," he said, "but the nightmares have never stopped, and I knew that one day I would be severely punished for my crimes."

I urged him on, asking him to tell me what it was he had done that he felt was so terrible. At first he refused, saying that he had never spoken of his sins, of his time in Hitler's army, to another soul, not even to his wife. She, he said, believed that he was a good man, and so did his children. "But God knows," he cried, "God knows that I am evil, and He has turned his back on me . . . and the devil has come in His place."

I waited until he had quieted a little, then asked him again. "Tell me, Joseph, tell me what happened. I'm not here to judge you, only to listen," and somehow, whether it was the tone of my voice, my healing prayers, or simply Joseph's dire desperation that did it, the floodgates finally opened, and for the first time in more than fifty years, he was bringing it out into the open.

"The burnings were the worst," he cried, "but they made us do it, we had no choice. They would have turned on us, and I was just a boy, helpless, powerless, and afraid to die." He then described how the soldiers, he among them, would go into the camps. "We would pile the prisoners into trucks, and drive them out onto the edge of the woods, where they were made to stand in groups of a dozen or more. It was always the same. The officers and many of the soldiers would jeer at the prisoners, make sport of them, and the prisoners would huddle together like frightened rabbits. I am sure," he said, choking on his words, "that they always knew they were going to die. It was in their eyes. In my nightmares, I always see their eyes."

Throughout his story Joseph would stop, then begin again as his tears subsided, relieved to finally be telling someone, for until now he had been afraid to utter a word of this to another living soul, not to his wife, not to his priest.

"Sometimes we would fetch two or three at a time, make them stand in the clearing, and shoot them in the head, while the others looked on. But it was quicker and more efficient, that's what the officers said, to use the flamethrowers. The smell would follow me for days. In my dreams I smell that terrible smell of roasting flesh. And I hear their screams, and see them writhing in terrible agony. I had to do it," he sobbed, "I had to fire the guns, or they would have killed me. Oh God, how I wish now that they had killed me."

I listened in pain to his story, hearing many more horrifying details than those I am recounting here, as once he had started, it seemed difficult for him to stop. It was easy, as he was talking, to visualize the brutal and terrible deaths of the prisoners he was describing, easy to feel pity for them in their ordeal. But as I looked at Joseph, I felt more pity, more compassion, for he had lived for more than fifty years in terror of retribution, and his ordeal was not over yet. Now his eyes grew wide with apprehension, his voice trembled even more, and now with greater fear... "He's come," said Joseph, "I can feel him close to me. For years I have been fighting him, but he is too strong, and God won't help. He is inside my head, inside my body, destroying me, he's come for me now and I can't stop him. The devil has come to take me to hell."

Joseph's voice rose high on this, and he broke down in tears, begging me for help. Somehow I calmed him, soothed him, then I began to talk.

"I believe that God is a good God, a loving and forgiving God, Joseph, and He is able to see into your heart. He sees your pain, and I believe He sees your torment. I do not believe that God turns His back on any of us, nor do I believe that He has turned His back on you. God knows when we are truly repentant, and will not condemn us for our mortal sins, or mortal weaknesses. Rather, He will, I believe, understand, and have compassion for us in our fragile and confusing mortal state." I went on, feeling more as a priest might, giving the last rites, hoping that what I was saying was right, seeking God's guidance and inspiration in the words I spoke. Looking to Grey Eagle, who had been with me from the beginning, hearing him tell me to go on, I said, "Joseph, God is a loving and forgiving God, and will, if in your heart you are truly repentant, forgive you the sins you have committed on this earth."

Joseph squeezed my hand. "What about the devil?" he whispered again. "The devil has come."

"No," I said firmly, believing my words, knowing them to be true. "We are all sons and daughters of God. None of us is cast aside if we need God's love." I reached out and touched Joseph's face, and quietly said, "Joseph, God has sent me here to you. He is in my hands as I touch you. God is in my heart as I give my heart to you, and God is in the love that I share with you. Have no more fear, Joseph, for God is with us now. He hears your prayers, you are His son, and He loves you. And where God is, and where God loves, the devil cannot enter. Now go to sleep, have no more fear. God will keep you safe."

Joseph, already lying back on the pillows, closed his eyes. The tension of the last several hours, if not years, had finally left him. I stayed with him until he fell asleep, and I can hear his words to me now, as he repeated them over and over, while tears of relief streamed down his face. Softly, so very softly, as he fell to sleep, he repeated over and over again, "Thank you, oh, thank you, God bless you, God bless you, God bless you."

Early the next morning Joseph died. The wonderful, most joyful thing, was that he died without fear. He died at peace. Of this I'm sure.

• • •

Here then, is the story of Joseph, a man who in anyone's eyes has committed heinous acts of terror and destruction, now in terror of his own destruction. Here, too, is the story of a healer, a gentle soul, who, born after the Second World War, has never known or been personally touched, and therefore, personally affected, by such cruel and hideous crimes as those perpetrated in wars. A healer, not understanding, yet forgiving anyway, and convinced that God, too, will forgive. Would I be so forgiving, so understanding, so compassionate, if one of those whom Joseph blasted with his flamethrower had been one of my own, father, mother, child, husband, or friend? I like to think, of course, as I strive to be more spiritually minded, that though it might have been hard for me to sit on Joseph's bed, to give him healing, hold his hand, and comfort him, though it may have been hard, it would still have been possible for me to rise above my own grief, my own anger and resentment, and my own terrible night-mares, to recognize another human being's terror. "Please, God," I earnestly pray, "never put me to the test."

• • •

"Terror is the widening of perspective and perception," writes Stephen King, and he should know. As the author of so many terrifying thrillers, he probably has a greater perception of the world, maybe even the universe, than most of us and is able to perceive more easily than most the depth and breadth to which terror can take us. Such dark and fathomless depths.

Degrees of fear range from simple anxious concern to dread, horror, trepidation, terror! The opening of our eyes to the un-known and unknowable forces that surround us, even as they are of the earth, are of the universe.

For those of us, then, who may be nervous or fearful of ex-ploring our sixth sense, and all it might mean, for those of us who remember those frightening childhood memories of dark nights and strange noises and ghoulish stories, here is our first tool. An exercise that will help you to feel comfortable and pro-tected and in control.

EXERCISE 1 . . .
YOUR INNER SANCTUARY, YOUR SECRET PLACE

The bubble. Everyone should have one. Everyone could use one. And it's easy to own one.

This is a great exercise, and one you can do by yourself or with a group, which is always fun to do. You will find it easier if you have been following along with the exercises in the previous six chapters: however, for those of you who have skipped some, I would urge you to try this anyway, as it is perhaps one of the most useful tools to have on a day-to-day basis.

The bubble. To be used in times of stress, anxiety, nervousness, for the purpose of relaxation, to give you a sense of safety, protection, it enhances a feeling of harmony within the mind, body, and spirit. So let's begin.

Just as you did in Chapter One, find a place to be relaxed, comfortable, making sure that your surroundings are good and that you will be undisturbed. Close your eyes, breathe in deeply yet gently, allowing your breath to become slow and even, in tune with your mind and body. Begin to relax every inch of your body as you prepare for a simple meditation. Remember, don't float off, don't forget that you are in control at all times, and keep in mind the purpose of the exercise.

When you feel fully relaxed and in tune with yourself, take a slow and controlled next step. Visualize your bubble, out in front of you, large, round, or oval, floating gently, hardly moving. Breathe gently, easily, watch the bubble as it takes on life and form.

Remember how in Chapter Two you learned about energy. Your bubble is full of energy, soft, gentle healing energy. Visualize its colors as it sparkles blue, green, the rainbow colors. Be positive, as you learned in Chapter Three, know that your bubble is there for you, to heal, to protect, to keep you safe and warm.

Look to the colors again. Refresh your memory about what each color means, as you discovered in Chapter Four. Decide what colors your bubble should be, and make it so. You own the power. Visualize it.

As your bubble dances lightly before you, put into practice the knowledge you gained in Chapter Five. Feel your spirit, feel the needs of your spirit, remember the power of the mind. The bubble is yours. Slowly, but with gentle determination, visualize yourself stepping into your bubble, your inner sanctuary, your secret place.

Relax, breathe deeply, easily, and become aware of your feelings. You are inside your bubble. No one else can enter it unless you choose to invite them in. The colors of your bubble surround you, sending rays of healing energy.

What do you hear?

What do you see?

What do you smell?

What do you taste?

What do you feel?

What do you sense?

Using all of your senses, as you did in Chapter Six, explore your sensations as you sit inside the bubble. Have fun. Be calm. Soak up the peace and tranquillity of your safe place. Everything inside the bubble is positive and good, peaceful and protecting, especially for you, and the more you practice the better it gets. You can take just a moment or two, or you can take an hour or more. The results will become self-evident as you yourself become more calm, more tolerant, less inhibited, more powerful.

Everyone needs a secret place, a place to hide away, to recover from the day, to renew strength. The Native Americans would send out their youngsters to seek out their own secret place. A place where they could renew their spirit. Unfortunately, in the world in which we live, this fast-track, fast-paced competitive world, very few of us are able to go out and seek their sanctuary. This exercise shows that all you have to do is reach out with your mind, your energy, your power, and your secret place of healing will appear before you. Your bubble can be your place to renew your spirit. To be "at home."

• • •

"The only way to understand your spirit is to work on it. The more you work on it, the bigger it gets." This quote is taken from the 1997 movie *The Education of Little Tree*. I was at home, lying on the sofa, in front of a log fire, only half listening, but hearing these words I sat up, searched out paper and pen, and wrote them down. Thinking on it, I believe it seems both strange and at the same time perfectly natural to hear such ancient wisdom, normally spoken around a campfire, at a peace gathering, a church or holy place, coming instead out of an old but still trusty TV set. And though I heard the words in this not especially spiritual place, yet still the words were full of power, as all wise words seem to be. I smiled, and am smiling still, as once again I write them down, hoping that they will urge you on, inspire you to go forward as they inspired me.

EXERCISE 2 . . .
SEEKING OUR POWER SYMBOL

"The only way to understand your spirit is to work on it. The more you work on it, the bigger it gets."

So, taking those words literally, as we must, let us move forward, to try to connect with, to become aware of, our sixth sense, our universal connection. We need more tools. We need something that reminds us of our power, something that we can hold on to and use to give us courage, just as a soldier would use his sword, or a preacher his Bible. In ancient times and in all ancient cultures, totems, amulets, and lucky charms were an accepted and integral part of daily life. Something to use, to hold on to, a sign of faith, of acceptance of the unknowable.

Native Americans believed that every thought, every object, every living thing had a purpose. Not one breath of energy was too small to be ignored. They used their totems or amulets as a way of tuning into the Great White Spirit, in just the same way as Christians might hold a Bible in their hands when they pray.

A Bible, a holy book of words, is no more or less important to those who consider them holy than the American Indian's totem, which he or she also believes is holy, has spiritual meaning.

An object or even a thought pattern that to them is holy was always treated with the greatest respect.

A cross, to a Christian, is a symbol of power, spiritual power. To the believer, a Bible or Koran is not only the divinely inspired word of God or Allah, but by many, the book itself is used as a symbol of that belief, a symbol of spiritual power.

To some, water, moving, flowing water, is a symbol of power, is seen to reflect some universal force. To others, a small stone, or a mountain, a bird in flight, a feather, a flower, a pyramid, so many things can be seen as symbols of power. A rabbit's foot, lucky pennies.

The reason we might need a power symbol, or at least find one useful, varies with the individual. Why does one need to hold a cross in one's hand, or wear one on a chain around the neck? Why do some people carry "lucky pennies," or a rabbit's foot, a feather in their pocket, or a special stone? When I was a girl, I used to collect bus tickets with the number 7 on them. For me the number 7 was a symbol of power. Why did I need to collect bus tickets with the number 7 on them? The answer is simple. These things inspire us, strengthen us, help us feel more powerful.

How we use a power symbol is something for each individual to determine. In the quest toward self-discovery and spiritual awareness, a power symbol can be a very useful tool, to be used constructively in aiding the journey. To help toward attunement with our own self, and of all around, our power symbol encourages us to reach out, and to reach up, toward the light and toward enlightenment. It does not give us power, it simply empowers us, reminds us of the power we already own.

So a power symbol can be a very useful and exciting tool, and I thought it might be fun to discover our individual power symbols in the way the ancients did. To embark upon a vision quest.

The ancients, the Grandfathers, as Native Americans call their ancestors, would often encourage their young men in the art of vision making and would send them out to find a secret or special place in which to seek a vision. Any problem they had, any matter that needed clarifying, any situation that required communication with the inner self or with God or the spirit world was made by embarking upon a vision quest. This custom was, and still is with some, not just special to many Native American Indian tribes, but something we know to have been practiced by many ancient cultures around the world.

Before embarking upon a vision quest to seek out your power symbol, it is important to understand that a power symbol is something that is recognized by the individual as being special to him. A vision quest is only one way of discovering a power symbol. Many people instinctively know their power symbol without having to seek it out in any way. It just comes to them, presents itself, and that which we call the sixth sense instantly recognizes it. As a child the number 7 was incredibly important to me. I had no idea or reason why this was so, until my daughter Samantha was born. My only child, my miracle, born on April 7, 1970. This was my truth made known to me.

Here is another truth, taken from *Hanta Yo*, by Ruth Beebee Hill: "The grandfathers say that truth flows in gently. They say that spiritual growth happens slowly. Nothing a person will recognize until a change comes through one of his senses, usually the sense of feeling. Afterwards, different senses will tell him something."

When you experimented with your common senses, did they tell you something?

• • •

Embarking upon a vision quest: Begin as you did when seeking out your bubble, and create a state of total relaxation and calm; feeling a true sense of inner peace and tranquillity, breathe in through your solar plexus. Visualizing a mass of energy around you, draw this energy into you, and allow yourself to acknowledge your awareness of the sensations of energy coursing its way through your body. Breathe in again through the chakra that seats itself around the area of your solar plexus, relax, and gently, slowly, begin the vision quest.

As you learned to do in Chapter Four, with eyes closed and your mind alert, visualize your own energy field. Reach out with that part of your mind that desires knowledge and learning, and visualize your energy. Remember, your aura is a rainbow of color, moving, dancing, full of life, indicating life, indicating power, and as you remember, breathe deeply yet gently and become calm.

You are seeking a vision, a quest of great importance, searching for a symbol, a symbol of great energy, of great power, which you will be able to use all through your life and in any circumstance.

In Chapter Five we created energy using the power of positive thinking. Remembering that, using the power of your thoughts, create a mental picture of yourself as succeeding in your vision quest, and know that your power symbol will come to you. Whatever it is—an object, a thought, a person, animal, bird, or insect—when you see it, trust your sixth sense to know it and to own it. Don't be concerned if you draw a blank, and never think that you must be that one person who does not have a power symbol. We all have one, every one of us who needs or wants one, so be patient, keep trying until you succeed. Reach out and into your energy field, and test your knowing senses, stretch your mind, keep your goal always in view, you are seeking your power symbol, you have embarked upon a vision quest, so go forward on your journey, be patient, work on your spirit until you see clearly that which you seek. As you search, try asking these questions.

Where is my power symbol?

What form does it take?

Do I recognize it?

Have I seen or been aware of it before?

Your "knowing" sixth sense will recognize and accept the right picture immediately; it sees it, and your heart will be touched by a truth, knowing that you have found your power symbol.

Your vision quest may take you no more than a few minutes, or it may take days or weeks. Learn to trust in your sixth sense and accept your power symbol only when it feels right. Once discovered, your power symbol will be a true reminder that you own your power. Using mind energy, you will be able to recall and to create a mental picture of this symbol at any time of the day or night, no matter where you are or what situation you find yourself in. However, I often encourage my students to draw their power symbol on a large piece of cardboard and to place it where they can see it every day, as this is a good way to get used to it, to the feel of it, to the sight of it, and to the sense of it.

Using a power symbol gives you confidence, it gives you courage, and will give you a sense of determination, a sense of being, of being you.

I was in California, waiting to go on the set of the *Leeza* show. Although I am never nervous about appearing on TV shows, there are times when I have serious concerns, and this was one of those times. The what-ifs had begun to pop into my head as I was waiting, for I knew that many of the guests appearing on the show with me, and also many people in the audience, had enormously great expectations of me. There are always the what-ifs, but usually I accept that I can do only the best that I can do, and no one can expect more, not even me. If it works, then it's wonderful; if it doesn't, don't be disappointed, God knows what we need better than we do.

Today, though, the show was about murder victims. The other guests and many in the audience were the parents of those murder victims. I have always said, as a mother myself, that the worst kind of loss must be the loss of a child. To have your child die before you die must be the most terrible thing to live with. But the knowledge that your child died at someone else's hands has to be unbearably painful in the extreme.

Now the time had come. They were all out there waiting for me to produce the miracle of communicating with their children, trusting it would happen. I trusted, too. I trusted in the right process, that God and Grey Eagle would be right by my side, helping me in my work. But what if? People's emotions were high, powerful energies were in play. What if I could not ease a mother's pain a little? What if a father needed more than I could give? What if, in their eagerness and desire to communicate, these young people who were murdered so brutally, what if they stumbled, became tongue-tied, emotional, and unable to express themselves clearly? I so wanted to help them. To do a good job, and so, through my concern, the what-ifs began to pile up. Lost in thought, I didn't notice it at first, and Grey Eagle had to prompt me to look. I heard his voice, and turned to where the sound was coming from. I saw a feather. Not just any feather, but the largest, straightest feather I have ever seen. It was standing, as if balanced, upright, and right before my eyes. Immediately I felt better, stronger, more sure of myself and my gift. The what-ifs faded from my mind, and I stood and stretched and made ready to step out onto the stage and into my world, my reality. To do my best. Only my best.

I had not asked for it, nor had I consciously looked for it, yet in my need it had presented itself to me. My reminder that I own the power. My power symbol, the feather.

• • •

A friend and patient of mine had just been diagnosed with a serious cancer. You can imagine her state of mind. Depressed, scared, confused, she went off for a walk one day by herself. She had been very close to her grandmother, who had died several years earlier, and had often, especially in times of stress or anxiety, felt her presence, and would sometimes talk to her, sure that grandmother could hear and was listening.

Crying a little, angry at God, calling out to her grandmother for help, my friend continued on her walk, until she came to a resting place, where she sat for a while, her head in her hands, wondering what she should do. "Grandmother, Grandmother, if only you were here. I know you would help me, I know you would." She sighed, tears trickling down her cheeks. Then she noticed, from the corner of her eye, something glittering in the sunshine. Bending forward, she examined the ground before her, and spied the newest, brightest penny she had ever seen. "Oh," she gasped out loud, "a penny, a lucky penny." And as she spoke, she felt the presence of her grandmother. Picking up the penny, she held it tightly in her hands. It was a sign, she knew it was.

Months passed. Harrowing, scary months of treatment. Then surgery, then more treatment. But the amazing thing was that as she approached each new stage, more frightening than the last, a penny would turn up. Sometimes she would find them on the ground at her feet, or sitting in a coffee shop there would be a penny found on the table. At the movies she would find a penny on the seat, in the waiting room at the hospital. Pretty soon she had a pocketful of pennies. Pretty soon all she had to do was think about the pennies to feel good. It became a joke in the family and everyone began looking for them. Lucky pennies. Pennies from heaven. And long after her recovery from cancer, my friend still has her pennies. Her penny is her power symbol. She carries it with her, in her mind, wherever she goes. It reminds her of how powerful she is, owning the power.

• • •

Having found your power symbol, it is easy to keep the image of it in your mind, easy to conjure it up whenever you feel the need. Lacking confidence when going for a new job, stressing out over the kids, problem solving, needing inspiration in a difficult situation, or simply tuning into your sixth sense, or to your spiritual nature, which is really one and the same thing, bring to mind your power symbol. Visualize it, hold it, touch it, feel its power, your power. I can guarantee, if you do it right, you will feel instantly empowered, able to cope with anything, and totally in tune with your spirit.

Just like the Scarecrow, the Tin Man, and the Lion, in that wonderful old classic *The Wizard of Oz*, the Scarecrow needed a brain, the Tin Man a heart, and the Lion courage. Each was told that the Wizard had magically given them their heart's desire, and each was given a symbol—a diploma, a heart, and a badge of courage. We all know that the moral of the story was that the Scarecrow didn't really need a piece of paper saying he had a brain. He was already clever, but his diploma helped confirm it. It empowered him. The Tin Man already had a heart, was loving, gentle, and kind, but he lacked confidence and his symbol encouraged him to be more of who he already was, and he felt empowered. Of course, the Lion, my favorite, was already brave, had proved himself to be so, but his medal of bravery, pinned to his chest, empowered him and gave him the courage to dare to be what he wanted to be. This, of course, is a simple story, a child's fairy tale, but the theory applies. You are already who you want to be. Your power symbol will merely empower you to dare to show it.

• • •

Earlier in the chapter I used a quote that tells us that if we want to know our spirit then we must work on it. Just as we did with our five common senses, we must exercise our sixth sense, tune it more finely, use it more often. Only then will it grow.

We have discovered a great tool in our power symbol, which will help us in our task, and our task is exactly this. To attune to our own spirit, our own soul. To be more in tune with others, to connect with others around us. To attune to the energy of our world, to the spirit world, to the universe, and to God. To own ourselves. To own our power.

In visualizing and using our bubble, and also by finding and using our power symbol, we are exercising our sixth sense. But we should go further and see if we can recall the feelings we had on that first moment of recognition of our power symbol, and ask the questions:

What did I see?

What did I feel?

How did I feel?

Visualize your power symbol again, and use it to remind yourself of the initial sensations and feelings you had. Repeat the exercise and ask:

What do I see?

What do I feel?

How do I feel?

It may help to write down your thoughts and feelings, and try being as expressive as you can be. Every day ask these questions and any others you might think to ask, and as you do so, try to be aware of your feelings.

From the beginning, from childhood, we have a "knowing," a sixth sense that within most of us lies dormant, waiting for us to recognize it. We know without knowing that we know. Let's explore, ask ourselves questions. Let's ask . . .

What do I "know"?

In what way do I "know"?

How does this "knowing" show itself?

How many times have I "sensed" something more, something "different," too difficult to define, and have shrugged these "feelings" to one side?

And what have I "felt"?

How have I "felt"?

How aware am I and in what way have I been aware?

Everywhere we go there are things that we have a "knowing" of. We meet someone and our instincts, our "knowing" tells us, gives us a good feeling or a bad feeling. We encounter many situations where our instincts, our "knowing" tells us, gives us positive or negative vibrations, so here are more suggested questions:

How aware of my vibrations am I?

How aware of the vibrations around me am I?

How do these vibrations show themselves to me?

How strong are they?

How strong do I feel they can become?

All animals have an acute sixth sense, wild creatures especially. The more we use it, the more acute that sense becomes.

How can I perceive this sixth sense in others?

How can I perceive this sixth sense in animals?

How acute is my own sixth sense?

How many feelings are triggered when I use my sixth sense?

How aware of my own self does my awareness of my "knowing" make me?

How many memories are there, and where do they come from?

We use our sixth sense more than we realize. You "know" you are going to like someone or not at a first meeting, although it is possible to change your mind. This happened to me many years ago. I was still married, my daughter was just two years old, and we had moved to a new neighborhood, more than two hundred miles from home. The new house was only partially finished when I met her, my new next-door neighbor, and I had an instant distrust of her, which was unusual for me, as normally I like to take my time in getting to know people and make up my mind slowly about friendships.

There was nothing obvious about her to dislike. She was extremely friendly, offering to make us tea, saying that we shouldn't hesitate to ask if we needed help. She wasn't beautiful or ugly or anything other than quite ordinary. But my wire was taut from the moment I saw her, before she even spoke. I did not understand, but I did not trust her one bit.

Three months later we finally moved into the house. It was a gray December day, just two weeks before Christmas, and my husband and I, and Samantha, were very excited. Many neighbors came to welcome us, including Ann, the woman next door, and it seemed to us, my husband and me, that we had made the right decision to move.

Spring came, then summer, and it was a busy time for me, as I had new gardens to design and plant. I loved every minute of it. Samantha was happy, her playmate, Joanne, was practically the same age, and they played together every day, without fail. This, of course, meant seeing Joanne's mother on a regular daily basis, and pretty soon we became good friends. Yes, you're ahead of me, I hope, your sixth sense working, you know that I'm going to tell you that Samantha's friend's mother, Ann, was the neighbor I had so mistrusted. I told myself I had made a mistake, judged too quickly. That not only was I wrong about not liking her, I was now willing to call her my very best friend.

It is not necessary to go into the whole story. The reason I have told this much is to illustrate how easy it is, even for someone like me, to ignore our knowing, to brush aside what our sixth sense tells us is right. I know that there are exceptions to all rules, but in the main, when we refuse to listen to our instincts, we do so at a heavy cost.

My very best friend Ann had been carrying on a long-standing affair with my husband. They cheated on me and my child, on her husband and three children, and eventually they cheated on each other.

It was odd, when I look back, to remember that I felt more hurt and betrayed by her than I did my husband. In the end, though, I have no one to blame but myself. I should have listened.

Many people's sixth sense kicks in when they are in a sleep state. Precognitive dreams are very common and will often tell us of some future event. A wedding, a birth, a death, a win on the horses. Our knowing sense, connecting with the universe, with some external energy, will gather in knowledge that plays out as a dream.

Your back is to the door. It opens. You know who is there without even having to turn around. The telephone rings. You know instantly who it is. A letter arrives. As soon as you see it, you know who it's from, and realize you have known it was coming for days. You have a bad feeling, can't shake it off, knowing something is wrong, and the next day bad news arrives.

How many times do we think to ourselves or say to ourselves, "I knew that was going to happen"? How many times? Enough times, I think, to know that it's about time we took notice and did something more practical. So what other questions should we ask?

How often are you aware of your sense of knowing?

How often do you sense knowing?

How often do you enjoy your sense of knowing?

How often do you feel sad in your knowing?

How often do you feel you know yourself?

How aware of your own knowing are you?

How clear is it?

How much do you really "instinctively" know?

How much and how often do you try to sense and know?

What instincts do you have?

How often do you use them?

Are you in tune with nature?

Are you in tune with those around you?

Are you in tune with yourself?

As you ask these questions, remember your power symbol, use it to help you with your questions, know that you own your power. Be constructive and make your power symbol work for you. Find out each day, and for the rest of your life, how much you can really know, if you want to.

Here is a list of the things that I know. That I know to the very depth of my heart and soul, and I know them through all of my six senses.

I know love.

I know light.
I know being.
I know loving.
I know other beings.
I know joy.
I know kindness.
I know life.
I know hope.
I know gentleness.
I know after life.
I know *power*.
I know my own *power*.

These things I "know" with that part of me, that sixth sense, that instinct born to me, which I have worked at, developed, as I have learned to gain attunement, with myself, with God, and with the energy of the universe.

Keep working at it. Find yourself. Know your spirit. Learn to be still and to listen to the heartbeat of your soul.

When you are truly still within, and really in tune with your sixth sense, here are more questions you can ask yourself.

Can you hear the sun rise?

Or the sun set?

Can you hear the sound of grass growing?

Can you hear the roots of a tree spreading?

Can you hear the moon swinging in the sky?

• • •

I was giving a seminar in New York. A full day, spent with wonderful people, all of whom had pretty much the same interests as I had. They had come to learn. What, then, could I teach them? We began with the questions "Is your glass half-full or half-empty?" and "How can we get our glass full to the point of overflowing?" Of course, sitting in on a spiritual seminar, you may feel that your glass is indeed overflowing. After all, the atmosphere is right, your mood is perfect for positive and constructive thinking, so yes, most of us said our glass was already overflowing. But what would our response be a week from now, maybe after a tough few days of "real life"? Could we be so enthusiastic? For most of us, probably not. We might waiver between half-full and full, some of us might feel so down that no matter how we felt a week ago, and no matter how much progress we had made in our spiritual existence, looking at our glass in the cold light of day, we might see it as perhaps even less than half-empty. In moments like this it is good to remind ourselves of the good things we know.

• • •

The soul, the soul, the soul.

It speaks to us. It tells us things. It shows us who we are. It lies with us, and sleeps with us, and breathes the air we breathe. So close to us, a part of us, the whole of us, we touch it every day. And it is us, and we are it, and changing come what may. The soul, the soul, the soul.

So close, it seems not a separate thing. We hear it speak, and confuse the sound with our human sound, our physical voice. We recognize its thoughts, yet again, we cannot separate from our human thought mechanisms. We feel it breathe, but so in tune is it with our physical body, and so wrapped up in our physical way of life are we, that we mistake its breath for the breath of our lungs. Separate, apart from the physical body, yet joined tightly together until that moment of parting that we call death, the soul's heart beats loud and strong. Yet unlike its voice, its thoughts, its breath, the soul's heartbeat has a rhythm that is so often not in sync with the physical heartbeat. The physical heart rate is affected by so many things, is easily damaged, traumatized, sometimes sluggish, often racing faster than it should. The heartbeat of the soul is a steady, trusting, patient, knowing, uncomplicated, uncompromising, and indestructible thing. Unless we wish it otherwise, in which case, it and we become nothing. Steady, for it trusts God's almighty process. Trusting, as it patiently awaits the realization of that process. Patient, in all its knowing. Knowing, for its learning process is uncomplicated. Uncomplicated, for it does not compromise the truth. Uncompromising, understanding its indestructibility. Indestructible because it is uncompromising, uncomplicated, knowing, patient, trusting, and steady. We began at the beginning, went around, and then back again. In a circle you might say. If we remember the second law of the universe, it speaks of the circle of light, unbroken. If we look at the sixth law of the universe, we are reminded that each soul has choice, and by its very existence has exercised that choice. Can, if it chooses, become nonexistent, but only by "its" choice. No one else's. Reminding ourselves of the rules of the universe, cited in *Proud Spirit*, rule four clearly says that we should give gentleness to our own heart, which I take to mean not just our physical heart, which we have for only a short span of time, but more, to the heart of our soul, which we so neglect. And the fourth universal truth tells us quite clearly that we must somehow acquire leadership of our own soul. So how, in what way, can we do this? How can we proceed to know our soul more, to know our soul better, to assume leadership, to own our soul, and to own our own power?

First, we must recognize that our soul has life, is life, and gives us life. That its life is trusting and patient, knowing and uncomplicated, uncompromising and indestructible, and steady, steady in its heartbeat, steady in its sound.

If we take a flower bulb in the palm of our hand, only the most experienced of us, the most knowledgeable gardener, would be able to say what type of bulb it is. The layperson, Mr. or Mrs. Average and nonexpert, might be able to pronounce it a flower bulb, but no more than that. And also, the layperson would not be able to say whether the bulb was healthy and capable in the right conditions to flower or not.

If we take our soul in the palm of our hand, most of us would recognize it for what it is, for we are born with a knowing sense that tells us of such things, but without experience, we would know not much more than that.

I am an apprentice gardener, and am being taught by the best and most patient of teachers. Although I have had many years of experience and know a great deal about the workings of the spirit, the soul, I know, too, my limitations, my limited understanding, and I know that it is essential, if I want to get it right, to take my time, go slowly, and not try to hurry a process I cannot hurry. If we want to learn more about the soul, then experience tells me that first we must learn to hear it. First, we must learn to hear the heartbeat of the soul, for only then will we hear its voice and understand what it says to us. Only then will we hear its thoughts and benefit from its knowing. And only then will we hear its breath, and feel its life force. Our life force.

EXERCISE 3 . . .
LISTENING TO THE HEARTBEAT OF THE SOUL

It should not be surprising to you, after reading and perhaps trying the exercises in the book, that we almost always begin in the same way. Relaxation, visualization, producing a positive thought process, use of the right kind of energy for the required outcome, which means using certain patterns of color. So, beginning the process, prepare yourself in just the same way you did when finding your bubble, and when seeking your power symbol. Your state of mind and body should be relaxed, open, powerful, and positively constructive.

Seated comfortably, hands on your knees, palms placed upward in a receiving position, you should have a feeling of peace and tranquillity flowing gently, uninhibited, all through you. Your question, as you begin, should be, "What is my purpose?" The answer: "I am looking for my soul, that I might hear its heartbeat."

"I am looking for my soul, that I might hear its heartbeat."

Not knowing what form the soul takes, not able to conceive its shape or texture, in order to seek it out we must give it form, shape, and texture. A form that in our limited human vision we can conceive. We envision the soul as a child, a baby, a pure and simple entity that is lying within you. Visualize a perfect being, untouched by all but that uncorrupted God force. Seek out the child, which lies waiting for you to find it. The child that is you.

Some of you may be tempted to run away from this exercise. Tempted perhaps to run from painful memories of your abused childhood. Others of you might feel too weakened by the terrible memories of a lost child, too hurt, too reminded of a situation in which you feel you were held powerless. This happened in one of my seminars to a young woman who had recently had a miscarriage, lost the child she so desperately wanted. She ran before I could stop her. She ran before I could hold her and help her to heal, to help her discover her soul, her power. We seek the child within, the essence of our being, our soul, yet we must understand that this is not an easy process, nor did I promise that it would be. The journey is a tough one, our labor hard, yet the rewards are great.

If you are tempted to run, don't. Use those tools you have been given. Find your power symbol and be empowered by it. Please don't be afraid. You own your power. Let this knowledge lead you to the owning and the leadership of your soul.

Visualize the child, the baby, the unborn waiting to be recognized, waiting to be reborn by your gentle touch. Reach out your arms and gather the child to you, with all the so-far-unleashed love and compassion that you have within you.

Now wait a while. Get used to the sight, the touch, the feel of this pure spirit. Don't breathe, don't move, don't make one motion more than is absolutely necessary. Be perfectly still, and wait.

Continue to repeat this exercise as many times as it takes for you to get to the moment of contentment, peace, and fulfillment at the sight of your child within. You may accomplish this at the first try, or it may take weeks, months, or even longer, depending upon how often and how much you are willing to persevere. Don't panic because it doesn't seem to be working. Go back through the book. Repeat some of the exercises you feel might be helpful to you. You'll know which ones to choose. Don't rush or try to hurry the process. You have spent a lifetime without knowing your soul, you can afford to be patient and to wait a little longer.

So now you have brought yourself to the point where, with loving-kindness and incredible gentleness, you are holding your soul child in your arms. You know her, you know him; he/she is you. Listen carefully now, not to your sound, not to your thoughts, your breath, your heartbeat. Listen carefully now to the sound of your soul child, to the sound of its heart, beating loud and strong. This is the sound of the heartbeat of your soul. Let that sound sink into your mind, your body. Learn its rhythm, discover its music, find its pattern. Here is the magic you have been waiting for. Don't misuse or ignore or neglect it again. You own it. You are responsible for it, just as you are now responsible for yourself.

Here is something I once wrote to myself, for myself, and perhaps, without knowing, I wrote it for you, too: "If you could see my spirit, the light, the energy, which comes from my soul, you would not want to damage or harm me, either physically, emotionally, or spiritually. Rather, you would want to nurture, honor, protect, treasure, and cherish me for all the days of your life."

Nurture, honor, protect, treasure, and cherish for all the days

287

of your or my life. If I could see my soul...Perhaps through our efforts in trying to understand the universal process, we have come a little closer to both seeing and also understanding our soul.

Every time you doubt your own power, or your own ability in any given situation, visualize your power symbol. Keep the image of your power symbol, hold it in your mind's eye. Feel the surge of power that it can bring, the power that is within you, that is within us all. Use your power as a determining energy. Discover the potential that your power brings and explore the depths of it. Its roots are within you, you are that power.

Within this power comes "knowing." Once recognized, having accepted its presence within you, you will come to understand that you own your power, and its "will" is your "will."

" 'Will' I achieve?" you will ask yourself.

The answer should be "Yes, for I will it to be so."

• • •

Attunement is to recognize your "knowing self." Your knowing self is already in tune with God, with spirit, with the universe. So when you ask your knowing self, can I hear the sun rise, can I hear the sun set, the sound of the grass growing, or the roots of a tree spreading, and when you ask, can I also hear the moon as it swings in the sky, these will be your answers:

Yes...I can hear the sun rise.

Yes...and the sun set.

Yes...I can hear the sound of grass growing.

Yes...I can hear the roots of the tree spreading.

Yes...I can hear the moon swinging in the sky.

All of these things, and more, you will begin to hear, to feel, to taste, smell, and see. More and more, your sixth sense, your knowing sense, will tell you something.

NO ONE CAME BACK TO TELL US

Who knows what happens when we die? Who knows what heaven or hell is like? After all, no one every came back to tell us, did they?

Many years ago, before my work began, when I heard people say this, I would remind them of Christ. "Well, Christ came back," I would say, and "Well, yes, but that was way before our time," or, "Well, that only counts if you believe in Christ; and it's not as if we can ask him questions, is it?" were the replies.

So here, as we draw to a close, I thought it fitting that I tell the following three stories, all true, which illustrate the fact of life continuing after death. A fact I no longer feel I have to prove, a fact that for me just is. They illustrate, too, how clearly "at home" I am to the spirit world, and what a magical and wonderful thing that can be.

ITALY

Sadness, sickness, anticipation, hope, and of course apprehension. These are just a few of the emotions that face me every day as I go about my work, as I look into the eyes and hearts of those who seek me out, wishing, praying that I might help them. Today was no exception: in fact, the emotions of my small audience were indeed perhaps more intense, more needing, as this was a group who had lost their children, and it may seem to those of you who have read my many other stories that I do rather put myself into these difficult situations quite often. You would be correct; I do. This time I was in Italy, Rome to be exact, in a large comfortable apartment, owned by a couple who were artists, and there were paintings of all sizes and styles on every inch of every wall in the place, even the bathroom, where I was tempted to stay much longer than I needed to, as some of the pictures were fascinating to look at.

Not able to speak much Italian, I had brought along with me my publisher, and the group had provided a translator. But as I walked through the door and saw the thirty or so people waiting there, I clearly understood the language that was loudly spoken, the silent language of grief and pain.

I began, as always, by explaining that I could only do my best, that I was not God, and did not have the power or the authority to determine how things would go. All there present nodded their understanding, accepting my words, still hoping, still anxious, still praying that I would succeed in connecting with their children. For one or two, I did not succeed, not because their children were not there, but because I am a human being, with only so much energy and only so much time to give, and we simply ran out of time. But for the majority, I did succeed, and there were many wonderful and emotional reunions, as sons and daughters gave real evidence of their survival after death. Fast and furious they came, excited, sometimes stumbling over their words, some young, small children, many in their twenties and thirties, and the noise and clamor from the spirit world was wonderful to my ears.

One of the most forthcoming, more forceful and determined, was the son of the couple whose apartment I was staying in, and he proudly showed me a painting of himself that was hanging on the wall behind me, before he told me how he died. Sensitive, loving, and gentle, he was eager to talk to his family, and gave them many loving messages and reassurances that he was not only alive and well, but that he had a fulfilled and happy life, that he often visited, and desperately wanted his loved ones to be reassured by that.

It was, for me, a normal setting, with grieving parents, and stories, all different, yet all too familiar to my ears, and though I have heard these stories a million times and more, still each one touches my heart as I feel the pain of all concerned.

Yet there was a story to come, so terrible, so shocking and disgraceful, that had I not heard it with my own ears, I would have found it difficult to believe.

She was a teenager, beautiful, bright, happy, with a wonderful future ahead of her. Her headaches began while she was in college, and at first everyone assumed they were due to extra study and stress, but eventually, having gone through numerous tests, she was diagnosed as having a malignant brain tumor, and was given only a short time to live.

Her mother sat before me as I spoke with her child, described her, described her illness, and gave her wonderful and inspiring messages from her precious daughter. There were tears aplenty, as no one listening had a dry eye, and there were tears from those in the spirit world, and from the child, the teenager, as she described to me her mother's pain and anguish.

I listened quietly, and heard her urgent plea. "She has to understand, it was my time, that this was meant to be, and that nothing she could have done would have prevented it."

I had heard this said so many times, and as I repeated the girl's words to her mother, I thought how amazing and yet confusing God's plan can be. I reached out to the mother to try to comfort her when I heard the girl's voice again, directed straight at me, and looking to where she stood, behind her mother, I saw her shake her head at me in utter frustration. I hadn't understood, I had missed something, and smiling, hoping the child would have patience with me, I asked her to explain a little more.

"They were wrong," she said. "Tell my mother, they were wrong. Frauds, frauds, frauds. They caused more pain than they will ever know, but they don't care, they were all frauds, all frauds,

291

just frauds." Her tears fell on her mother's hair as she leaned forward to hold her tight, and as I repeated what I had heard, the mother moaned and cried in understanding.

It took a while to calm everyone down, the room was electric with emotion, and it seemed that most there understood the child's message, and knew the story I am about to tell.

On hearing that her child was terminally ill, with only months to live, and being a good Catholic, the mother turned to the church, and to the priests she had been taught all her life to trust. She presumed that her way to God was through the priesthood, and so she sought out priests of great reputation and had great faith in their abilities. Traveling the length and breadth of the country, she sought healing and a miracle for her child. Many of the priests she spoke with were honest, telling her that it was up to God, but that they would pray for a miracle healing, for the tumor to disappear. Some of the priests, however, were not honest, and indeed criminal in their behavior, asking for money in exchange for prayer, instilling fear in the mother by telling her that her child could be healed only through them.

In her desperation, the mother had made a pledge of ten million lira to the healing sanctuary of Padre Pio, the legendary priest of healing, whose work with the sick is well known, even after his death.

Going from priest to priest, this desperate mother said, the ugliest of these stories were the ones where she was promised, for a fee, that her daughter would be "on the list." The list, apparently, is God's list of those to receive a miracle. One priest even said to the mother, "Don't give the ten million lira to Padre Pio, give it to me, and I'll make sure your daughter goes to the top of the list."

Although I am sure that most priests, ministers, men of God, representatives of their particular religions, are men of good faith, honest and honorable, we know that there are cheats and charlatans in all walks of life, people who are willing and eager to take advantage of any situation. But this is not a story about one priest, but about many, and I was assured by the group, all grieving parents, mostly Catholic, that this was not only common, but an accepted practice. To bribe, to promise, to hold ransom, the fate of a young girl's life. And this is not just a story about a beautiful young girl's tragic death, but about the pain and suffering, and mostly the betrayal of both the child and the mother, by certain representatives of the church.

I asked the group, "Who did you tell this to?" They cast their eyes down for a moment in embarrassed silence, then told me it was impossible for them to stop what was going on. I asked the mother, whose anger and frustration was so raw, "Why didn't you complain, write to the pope, write to a magazine, something, anything?" Her answer: "The church is too powerful, and no one would believe me, no one."

I looked from the mother to her child, standing so straight, so vibrant and alive, and I knew their story was true, and I knew that if it was true for them, then it had been true for others in the past, and it would be true for others in the future. Unless someone could do something about it. Unless I would do something about it.

It is truly not my intention to disparage the Catholic Church (or any other religious order), its beliefs and ways, only to condemn those in a position of authority and power who abuse that authority and trust that are put in them.

It is my intention, however, here and now, to ask the pope, the archbishops, the priests, the rabbis and ministers, and all those of good faith, and of God, no matter what church you represent, "What do you intend to do to safeguard your flock, to keep them from harm, to ensure that in their frail and vulnerable state, they are not abused?" What, I am asking, in all humility, and with good grace, and painful heart, "What do you intend to do?"

For my part, I will attempt to educate those of you who are unsure. Please do not think me too bold or self-important, only caring and concerned. A priest, a minister, a rabbi, or vicar, a man of God, whatever cloth he wears, no matter how high up in the hierarchy of his particular church or faith, is still only a man. Mortal, and as such not able to make good on any promise of a miracle or cure, no matter how close his ear is to God, and no matter how much his pocket or the church's pockets are filled. Miracles cannot be bought, are given only from God, and no other. Not even a pope or bishop or archbishop or king can change or alter or argue this truth...a miracle is not for sale, but given only with God's good grace.

I am only one small voice, witness to the persons who have been betrayed, and refusing to stand by and say nothing, for fear of the wrath of men who may feel their position in life is more important that mine. I challenge those men and women. Educate your flock, weed out your betrayers, and put your house in order.

ABDUCTED

I needed to be open, sensitive, to hear and see this child's story. For all who heard it, there can be few who refused to allow their sensitive side to shut down.

This is one of the worst but best examples of someone coming back to tell us that life goes on. This story is an extremely delicate and somewhat difficult one to tell, so I have decided to write it just as it happened. I hope you will stay with me as the story unfolds.

She was just four and a half years old and we will call her Emily. I was giving a lecture, and had onstage with me several parents and siblings of children who had died. I was talking with Emily's mother and father, who were standing with their arms around each other, hanging on to my every word. Emily was with us, too, and I was recounting all I heard and saw, for as Emily was describing what had happened, she had taken me to the scene and so I was witness to her fate.

Emily had been abducted. There were two of them, a man and a woman. They had simply snatched Emily as she was playing in the garden at the front of her house, one bright sunny afternoon. Her mother had gone into the kitchen only moments earlier to get them both a drink. When she came out, glasses in her hands, her baby was gone. Emily's mother never saw her child alive again.

She was roughly bundled and taken into an apartment building, and there she was pushed into a small closet and told she would stay there until she stopped crying. It was dark and cold and Emily was very frightened. Eventually she curled up in a tight ball in one corner of the cupboard, put her thumb in her mouth, and slept. Several hours passed, then brutally and cruelly the closet door was yanked open, the child, still sleeping her terrified sleep, was pulled out, the woman's mean and vicious fingers sinking into the child's arm, and Emily's torture began.

I will not recount here, nor did I recount to Emily's parents, the vile and inhumane acts that these two dark souls performed, in their desire to satisfy their own corrupt and ungodly needs. To them, Emily was their plaything. The more she cried, the more she whimpered, the more afraid she was, the better for them, and this heinous game they played.

So I recounted only that Emily cried. "They hurt me, Mommy. Mommy, help me. Help me, Mommy, help me." And this she said, again and again. I heard her, sometimes in a whisper, sometimes in a scream, as she called to her mommy and daddy for help.

Still watching, listening quietly as Emily continued to tell me her story, continuing to see and hear, helpless to stop that which had already taken place, ready to do all that I could, now that I was able to help. What did Emily want me to do? What could I do to help her now? "Tell my mommy and daddy my story," and as I looked to Grey Eagle, needing all my strength to be able to stand and be witness to this wicked, wicked crime, he nodded, telling me that Emily's parents had a need inside of them, a great need to know, to know once and for all, the truth of what had happened to their child.

I looked back to Emily, back to the scene before my eyes, saw the child, bound hands and feet, bruised and beaten, no strength left in her, limp and spent. I heard her whimper, "Mommy, Daddy," saw her head fall back, and then the scene was gone.

Clearly now I saw my audience, many weeping quietly, as were Emily's parents, still standing with me on the stage. There, too, was little Emily, looking well and happy, but still not finished with her story.

"They have nightmares every night, and every waking hour is dark and sad. All they can think about is what those people did to me, how they hurt and tortured me. I want them to know I was hurt and in pain, but it was not nearly as bad as they imagine it was, really it wasn't, see..." and this child, this precious angel who had spoken these words in such a grown-up way, now pointed, back in time, so that I could again witness and tell of the way she had passed.

She had been untied and was now lying very still, half propped up, on the bed. A rope hung loosely around her neck, ready to be tightened, but Emily was beyond struggling, she was more than half-dead anyway. A small, almost imperceptible movement, her eyelids fluttered, then opened. Slowly she moved her head. She appeared to be listening... then this fragile child smiled. It was a smile to take your breath away, for with that smile came peace, and I could see it on her face. Then I heard it. At first it was faint, I wasn't sure, and then I smiled, too. The sound grew louder, and with the sound I saw the light, and then I saw her angels. "Emily, Emily," they called, "you can come back now, you can come home to us, the worst is gone, and we will keep you safe."

Emily sat up straight on the bed, the little four-year-old now bathed in light, surrounded by beings of light. She laughed, and reached out her arms to them, happy to be going home.

· · ·

Who knows what happens when we die? Who knows what heaven or hell is like? This is how I began this chapter, and I have told a couple of stories to illustrate just who does know, and how clear the information is that we can receive from the spirit world. Emily came back to tell her parents and also to tell any of us who cared to listen. It was easy to understand why Emily's family would want to know, for as Emily explained to us, the reality of what happened to her, no matter how painful, is far less than the constant nightmare of the imagination. But why should the rest of us want to know? Do we care to know? And if so, how can we use this knowledge in our quest for self-discovery, spiritual discovery.

During the telling of Emily's story, I mentioned the two dark souls who murdered her. As I read through the story and came to that part, I wondered and asked Grey Eagle, as I had asked before, are there souls born to this earth who are already dark, or is it life, and their life experience that make them dark? As always, there is, of course, no black-and-white answer. A simple yes or no will not suffice, for the answer is more complex. But for now I can tell you that for all of the billions of souls who have been born to this earth, so few are born dark and remain dark through their earth life. The comparison might be to a flea on top of Mount Everest. Most souls are born light, born beautiful. Not without problems, and certainly with a need to learn and to grow in a way that is dependent on their souls' need, but bright and healthy and strong, having made the choice to be born, then the soul begins to be.

297

What kind of world is it, this world that we have chosen? What kind of terrible and wonderful, confused and disgusting and beautiful place is this world we call earth? It is ours, and we, and our forebears, have made it as it is, and so we can make it as we would want it to be, for our children and our grandchildren, and God willing, their grandchildren.

I think back, to the pain of the child whose story I just told, to her parents and their suffering. In these times, no matter how much I may know some of the truths of the universe, it seems almost wholly unacceptable to believe that these souls, prior to their birth here, actually chose to suffer so much, did indeed decide that such pain was necessary for their growth. Yet I trust my teacher Grey Eagle. I trust his teachings, marvel in his wisdom, and believe him, even as he talks to me now as I write, when he tells me that another's pain can be a lesson for us all. That as we listen, with all of our senses in tune, with our hearts open, and hear of the pain of others, then our hearts will open more. Our senses and our sensitivities become more finely attuned, our emotions flow even as a river flows, and as all rivers do, eventually we will reach an ocean, a great tidal sea of emotions that comes from all, and from the universe of which we are a part.

Bringing ourselves closer to nature, closer to the nature and order of the universe, to God, but most especially to our own spirit, is an incredible achievement. Fine-tuning ourselves can be so enlightening and transforming, and also great fun. We become who we want to be, not who we suppose we should be, or what others want us to be. And we dare. We dare to live, really live, not just to exist. We don't have to wait until we have died, passed on to the spirit world, before our eyes are opened to the truth. The steps we have taken to uncover our power have given us clear vision. We know our soul.

DEATH IS NOT A PUNISHMENT

It has always been a mystery to me, and perhaps to many others, too, how God can weave so many threads at the same time, and, no matter how much chaos there seems to be in the world, how each living creature has its place in God's rich tapestry. Accidents ... there aren't any, coincidences ... there's no such thing, and all things occur as and when they are meant to occur. If we accept this as fact, and I do, then, of course, it is so easy not only to thank God for the good things in life, but also to blame him for all that is bad or catastrophic. Those of us who have lost someone close will, a thousand times and more, ask God the question why? Why did you take her, why couldn't he have lived longer, what did they do wrong? In a world where science and technology make us feel we own the world and can conquer most problems, we view death as a punishment, a failure to succeed, a flaw to be corrected. The cry—why did it have to happen to him, to them?—is the cry of the desperate, the confused, the angry and hurting human beings who have been forced to accept the fact that no man can control or change that which God has put in place.

There is a saying, that as we humans beings make our plans for the future, the gods look down on us and laugh. I don't believe that God laughs at us, but as we plot and plan for the future, presuming that the years before us will be lived on this earth, I think that from time to time God may well smile a small, wry smile.

Death is not a punishment. But when we hear of terrible tragedies, it surely feels as if it is, and for those of us who live our lives without our loved ones around us, it certainly seems that

God is a cruel and punishing deity. Mass murders, genocide, the annihilation of races, it is so easy to blame God, to ask accusingly, why did He let these things happen? So much easier than our taking responsibility for the way we have allowed ourselves to become. And yet still God weaves His tapestry, each tiny thread, a life, a thought, a pulse of energy, stitched gently and with love, our best interests in mind.

Over the years, from time to time, I have given this a great deal of thought, this mystery of life, of God and the universe. I have questioned God's motives, tried to reason and understand the intricate and amazing workings of His plan, but as yet I am still trying to figure it out. Each time I think I'm coming close to some small understanding, something happens that makes me aware of my own limited human concepts, and at the same time makes me realize how much more power I own than I previously believed I had.

One of the most incredible experiences I had, which is a great example of what I'm trying to say, happened when I visited Marin County, California, a visit organized by the Jewish Community Center of Marin. It helped me to see that not only is death not a punishment, but that life on this earth, so often painful and hard, is also not a punishment, merely an experience, one we chose to have, and one which can extend the understanding of our souls.

The event was held in the community center, a large hall with a stage and small tables and chairs, which gave the appearance of a nightclub. On each table there were candles, each table seating six to eight people, and there were about three hundred people in all. Maybe it was the seating, or perhaps it was the candles burning, giving the room a soft warm glow, or it could have been the stage setting, two comfortable armchairs, an unobtrusive microphone, flowers, and, of course, candles on the small table placed between the two chairs, but as I walked out to face my audience, I knew that something special and wonderful could happen that night.

My audience was warm and welcoming, and listened attentively for the first forty-five minutes as I was interviewed by a lovely young woman with a gentle voice and a keen interest in my subject. Then came the time I love the most. The time when my audience can participate with me in asking questions of the spirit world, a time when, if we are fortunate, we can hear directly from those in the spirit world wishing to give us their messages, to communicate with us. As I reached out into the audience, many hands went up, questions were asked, and before we knew it, the process had begun.

Question after question, communication after communication, as one by one people came through from the spirit world to speak with their loved ones. Wonderful, gratifying, emotional, and joyful, all these feelings and more, as I stood between the two worlds and became the conduit, the messenger.

It was when my cup was full to overflowing, when I felt it could get no better than this, that God showed me a glimpse, an understanding of something more, and I felt, and saw, and experienced the wonder beyond all that is wonderful.

"I would like to know how my father is?" The question, like so many other questions, came from a lady sitting close to the front of the stage.

Her voice was the trigger, her energy, her vibration, reaching out, even though she was unaware of it, and hearing her voice, connecting with her vibrations, her loved ones in the spirit world drew close around her.

"I can see two men, standing together by your left shoulder," I replied, and even as I was saying this to her, I had begun my own questions to the man I knew to be her father.

First, he introduced himself, then, pointing to the other man, quietly told me that they were brothers, and that they had passed to the spirit world together.

"An accident?" I heard myself asking, my voice silent to my earthly audience, but loud and clear to my audience in spirit.

The father, smiling, knowing his story was complex, said, "Let us show you." And watching, narrating, Grey Eagle close by my side, I stepped into a world, an experience that had existed before I was born.

I was in Germany, during the Second World War, in a concentration camp, in fact, although I am not sure which one.

I was a voyeur only, seeing but not touching, smelling but not quite tasting, all my six senses in tune, alert and aware.

There could have been thousands, but my attention was on a small group, perhaps several dozen, a hundred or two, the number was hard to tell. Thin and bent, cold and naked, they stood in lines before several small tables, behind which stood white-coated or uniformed men and soldiers. It was hard to believe that so many human beings could look like just so many bags of bones, but bags of bones was all they seemed, until or if you dare look closer, to see their eyes, the shape of their mouths, drawn into gaping holes with no sound coming out at all.

Who were they, these men, these bones, these walking, stumbling bones, which bore little resemblance to the human race? It was hard to remember that they were all God's children, and yet I knew they were.

Walking, stumbling bags of bones, with minds, and thoughts, emotions . . . souls.

Scanning the group, I wondered what was happening, but quickly understood they were undergoing some sort of examination. As each in turn approached the tables, they were given a cursory check, then ordered to stand in one of two lines, left and right.

I watched the two brothers, staying close, one behind the other as they came up to the tables, watched as they were both ordered to stand in the line on the left. For a fleeting moment I saw relief in their eyes as they realized that they had not been separated, but it was only a momentary thing, to be replaced very quickly by fear and apprehension of what was to come.

Hours passed, and the process of dividing the prisoners into groups was long and exhausting. Bags of bones held up bags of bones, men supported men, fearing that anyone who fell was a dead man.

As I tell the story, I can still taste the smell of fear, of hopelessness, of great and terrible human despair, that emanated from that place of indescribable horror. Yet still I watched, and still I narrated, as I became more and more a part of what seemed to be a godforsaken place.

A godforsaken place? A place where there is no God presence? If I were truly to believe that, then I, too, would be godforsaken, for to believe that a place exists in this world, or in the universe, where God is not would be a contradiction of all I believe to be true. But if God was here, then I could see no sign of Him, no sight or sense or feeling of his presence, no presence other than the presence of the most mighty evil. And so as I watched I asked the question, of my guide, of my angels, of God himself, and of no one in particular, "Where is God, and why is He letting this happen?"

No answer came, no phrase or sentence designed to ease my discomfort, calm my confusion, and remembering my role, a conduit, a messenger only, I brushed aside my questions, I would ask them later, and continued in my work.

It was hard to tell which of the lines held the most men, as they stood so closely, huddled together, more from fear than from the cold, but as the exercise came to an end, and the group on the right was sent back to the place they had come from, I sensed a difference in attitude. The group being sent back was obviously relieved, though as yet I had no understanding of why. My eyes followed them as they moved to a pathetic bundle of rags heaped in the dirt, and I watched as they dressed. It was only as they began to talk softly among themselves that I realized what a deathly silence had reigned before.

The group on the left, where the two brothers stood close

together, was still silent. The fear I had seen earlier had, if anything, grown worse, and the sound of that silent fear was deafening.

"Move," I heard them yell, "move, move," said the men in uniform, God's children, every one of them, surely, for are we not all sons and daughters of God? And the shuffling lines of bags of bones began to move forward, hundreds of souls, all God's children, each being with its own heartbeat, its own thoughts, living its own fear. And the fear became terror, and the sound grew until it became a terrifying scream, more terrible in its silence.

Completely caught up in what was happening, at the same time somehow detached, my mind calling out to God for the things I knew I could not change, calmly accepting that I could not change them, I watched as the shuffling lines of bags of bones were pushed and beaten into the ovens.

"Human beings, they are human beings," my mind sobbed. "In God's name, someone help them." But my silent scream was swallowed up in the terrifying sound now coming from the mouths of those soon-to-be dead men.

The two brothers had somehow managed to stay together, and as I watched, now also inside the chamber, apart, but seeing and feeling everything, I saw them as they clung to each other, pressed close together, among hundreds of bodies, it seemed, squashed like sardines in a can, unable to move. I heard them speak, their voices soft, teary, full of emotion, but without hope. "I love you," said one, and the other replied, his voice echoing in the darkness of the chamber, echoing the voices of the many who stood with them, "I am afraid, so afraid."

Although it seemed an eternity, it took only moments for the coughing and choking sounds to end. None fell as they were dying, each propped up by the bodies of the others. Only silence fell, only silence in the black horror of the chamber. Until something, a feeling, a sound ... and the chamber began to fill with light. Slowly at first, as the blackness turned gray, and the gray became pale, and I watched and narrated as the miracle unfolded.

I watched as they rose from the dead, hundreds of men, and women, and children, leaving behind them their bags of bones, as the light poured in, and they were warmed by the love of God. And the space that was the chamber was there no more, and instead was the place we call heaven. I saw angels, their wings filled the sky. I saw people come forward from the spirit world to greet their loved ones, and the sounds I heard were joyous and happy sounds.

Grey Eagle touched my shoulder, and turning to where he pointed, I saw the two brothers, not skin and bone, but whole and well and happy, surrounded by their loved ones who had gone before. There was much chatter and excitement, each soul greeting the other.

"Each one of us wept for joy," I heard the father say, wanting to send this message to his daughter, and now we were back to the present, to the now, as I faced my audience once again, and looked to the woman who had asked how her father was.

The candles still burned on the tables, my audience, emotional, enrapt, listening to every word. The hall, the stage, the flowers, all just as it had been when I had begun. No sound or sight or any indication of the horror of the camps I had just visited, so I turned to the father, to his brother, to look for the scars, for the pain and the suffering of their lives. They smiled, knowing my thoughts, understanding my humanness, my naïveté.

"Life is not a punishment," they said, "just part of God's rich tapestry. The suffering we endure on earth is, in the greater scheme, only momentary, a blink of an eye, yet it teaches us, it makes us strong. And the knowledge of our suffering can teach and make strong those we have left behind on earth.

"Death is not a punishment," they said, the father reaching out to stroke his daughter's hair, "only part of the pattern of life, a coming home, a resting place, before we continue our journey on."

I left the hall that night with a feeling of peace, so strong, I had never felt before, thanking God for the gift of pain.

• • •

It must have been two years or more ago. I was at the movies with friends. We had gone to see *Schindler's List,* one of the most moving and compelling films I have ever seen. I was so affected, in fact, that during the scene in the concentration camp where all the children are taken out in truckloads, their mothers watching, terrified, unable to do anything, I almost had to leave, as I felt the sobs rising up in my throat. As the movie ended, the theater was silent, no one spoke as the credits went up, and for a while no one moved. It was during this silence that I thought of the terrible, terrible atrocities that have gone on in our world, and as these thoughts went around in my head, I heard a voice, not of my guide, yet he was part if it, but the voice was somehow more . . . "Do something, do something," it demanded of me. Confused, knowing that somehow the demand was related to the Holocaust, to the evil of the world, but confused as to what I could do, I stood helpless. Again, and even more demanding now, the voice came again, "Do something, do something." But what was I supposed to do? The theater, still dark, hid my tears, my confusion, my smallness. Yet unrelenting, and for the third and final time I heard the voice, "Do something, do something, do something," as it followed me, my head bowed, out of the cinema and into the night.

I have been puzzled. I have not known what to do until this moment, as my pen has scribed the page, and my stories have been told. One small voice, with a hope to rock the world, to dare, with gentleness, to change the world.

Know evil, yet do not become part of it.

Know goodness, and live it.

Know God, and even in the times when He seems to have forsaken you, be joyful in the knowledge that you are His child, and that He will lead you home.

These are the words of Grey Eagle, my most wise and precious friend. These, too, I believe, if we could hear Him, are the words of God.

POSTSCRIPT

Each of the seven chapters that make up this book have been carefully constructed in such a way as to be most beneficial in helping you to reach a more complete understanding of your self, not only in a physical and material sense but most of all in a spiritual sense. In reaching a state of self-awareness, you will begin to know your power. Your intuitive nature will grow, your sensitivity will be unleashed, your world will open up. You will become a person people will like to be around, and you will be more sensitive to others and to their needs. Life will become more enjoyable, and as you learn to use your power, your life will become more and more fulfilled. The path you walk is rich with many treasures, as yet unseen. Unleashing your power gives you the sight, and the insight, to recognize these treasures, and to know your higher self.

Your sense of self will grow, as will your self-esteem, your confidence. You will become more creative, more self-assured, and will know your strength. These are just a few of the benefits of owning our power.

• • •

Most of the chapters contain at least one exercise, and although separate and individual, the exercises are combined and designed as a sequence, so that eventually a pattern is formed. Self-discipline is the key to self-discovery, and self-discipline will be the key to success.

It is important to remember that it is only when all the exercises have been completed that a full realization of what we might achieve and what this can mean to your life will take place.

It is also important to read each chapter through very carefully before beginning any of the exercises.

Being eager to learn can often make us impatient, but patience is the essence of true learning. Without it we can so easily miss the small details, simple thoughts and simple acts, wherein lie simple truths and wisdom.

Enjoy your growth.

Delight in your learning.

Be proud that you tried.

Own your power.

TO CONTACT
ROSEMARY ALTEA

If you are interested in writing to Rosemary, send your letter to the following address:

Rosemary Altea
P.O. Box 1151
Manchester, VT 05254

Please make sure to print your name, address, and fax number clearly. Please enclose $3.00 cash to cover the cost of a reply. Thank you.

You can also reach Rosemary via E-mail: www.raltea@vermontcl.com or visit her website: www.rosemaryaltea.com.

Rosemary's other works are:

The Eagle and the Rose, Warner Books
Proud Spirit, Eagle Brook/William Morrow
Give the Gift of Healing, Eagle Brook/William Morrow

For more information about signed, special editions ask your local bookseller or write to:

Joann Davis
HarperCollins Publishers
10 East 53rd Street
New York, N.Y. 10019